Jordan Peterson

Critical Responses

In Preparation

Sam Harris: Critical Responses

Jordan Peterson

Critical Responses

EDITED BY

SANDRA WOIEN

OPEN UNIVERSE
Chicago

Volume 1 in the series, Critical Responses®, edited by Sandra Woien

To find out more about Open Universe and Carus Books, visit our website at www.carusbooks.com.

Printed and bound in the United States of America. Printed on acid-free paper.

Cover photo of Jordan Peterson: © 2018 by Gage Skidmore

Jordan Peterson: Critical Responses

ISBN: 978-1-63770-012-9

This book is also available as an e-book (978-1-63770-013-6).

Library of Congress Control Number 2021941768

To Saoirse,
my unparalleled delight

Contents

Contents

Acknowledgments

This book simply wouldn't have come to fruition if it weren't for David Ramsay Steele. He deserves my deepest appreciation. He came up with the idea of this book, and his expertise guided me well from start to finish. Much appreciation also goes to Shawn Klein. He not only put me in touch with David, but was also a judicious mentor and sounding board throughout the process. I also thank Ron Dart whose breadth of knowledge astounds me and who is always willing to share it. And of course, I thank all the contributors for sharing their ideas, working with me, and helping to make this book possible. Last, but definitely not least, I want to thank my husband, Joe, for piquing my interest in Peterson in the first place.

Why Jordan Peterson Matters

MICHAEL SHELLENBERGER

In 2018 Jordan Peterson became a global celebrity almost overnight. The proximate cause was an argument over feminism he had with a British television host, which went viral. Shortly after, he was interviewed by podcaster Joe Rogan; that interview has since been viewed fourteen million times. And soon after that Peterson's self-help book, *12 Rules for Life*, became a global best-seller, turning him into "the most influential intellectual alive," according to *The New York Times*.

But the deeper cause was the need in Western culture for a spiritual leader. In 2021, a reporter asked Peterson if he thought he was a "new religious phenomenon."

"Not *new*," said Peterson.

The reporter pressed. "But are you a prophet?"

"No," Peterson said. "I see myself as a psychologist. And I'm a professor. And I'm doing it on a larger stage. That's what I'm doing. I don't see myself as a religious leader."

It is fair to ask whether the answer to that question matters. Peterson's two self-help books, *12 Rules for Life* and *Beyond Order*, do not seem to depend on any faith tradition. Neither do his research, his teachings, or his psychotherapeutic work, all of which have garnered respectful treatment from experts and lay people alike, even those who disagree with Peterson's conservative politics.

But from another perspective, they depend very much upon Peterson's faith. The decline of traditional religion, and the emergence of new "secular religions," particularly progressive or "woke" politics, are the forces against which Peterson is reacting. Tellingly, Peterson has published an online video series where he interprets Bible stories, and suggests they offer a way for people to orient themselves, spiritually and psychologically, in a confusing world. And when I spoke to Peterson in early October, 2021, he told me that his next book would be titled, *Wrestling with God.*

"Are you a Christian?" a journalist asked Peterson in 2017, to which he responded, "I suppose the most straightforward answer to that is 'Yes.'" But when he was asked whether he believes in God Peterson said, "I think the proper response to that is 'No,' but I'm afraid He might exist."

Religion still matters to politics. Whereas people on the political right tend to adhere more closely to traditional religions and moralities, whether Christianity, Judaism, or Hinduism, people on the political Left tend to be more secular, atheist, or agnostic. Perhaps not coincidentally, research suggests that progressives are more existentially anxious, neurotic, and unhappy than conservatives. Some researchers attribute higher levels of anxiety among progressives to lower levels of religiosity.

Over the last two hundred years, as science has grown in power and influence in Western industrial societies, traditional religions have declined. In the late nineteenth century Friedrich Nietzsche predicted that rising disbelief in God, and in life after death, would result in new moralities and religions. The reason, he predicted, was that such atheism would create a spiritual and moral vacuum. If people stopped believing that they would be punished for their bad behavior, what would stop sin from running rampant?

Another problem was the anxiety disbelief in God and the afterlife would create. One of the long-recognized benefits of religion is that it helps people to cope with their fear of death. If we follow a certain code of conduct, or morality, religions around the globe say, we can transcend death, and live on in a new world, whether heaven or a future world through reincarnation.

The two great political religions of the twentieth century that emerged into the religious vacuum were Fascism and

Communism. Where Christians believe that the kingdom of God is in heaven, communists believed the kingdom of Communism was in the future. And where Christians had believed in the ultimate Authority of God, Fascists believed in the Authority of the state as the manifestation of the spirit of the nation or race.

As these two great ideologies lost legitimacy and power in the twentieth century they split and changed into different moralities and ideologies. Today, the dominant secular religion is on the radical Left and is referred to as "Woke" ideology. Woke ideology has a simplistic morality. It categorizes certain groups as "victims"—racial minorities, women, the mentally ill, criminals, etc.—and demands they be given special privileges and rights.

Like other religions, Wokism, or victimology, promotes supernatural ideas. These include the beliefs that discrimination explains most if not all forms of inequality; that people can freely choose their biological sex but not their race; and that climate change threatens humankind with apocalypse. The scientific evidence does not support these claims, and yet they persist and have even grown stronger in recent years.

After the *Telegraph* reporter asked Peterson whether he considered himself a prophet, the psychologist had to think about it for a bit. He had, after all, implied that he *did* see himself as a religious phenomenon, just not a new one.

"Do you worry that you could become a pseudo religious figure for some people?" asked *The Telegraph* reporter.

"No," said Peterson. "I don't want it and my development of the individual is the best protection against it. I'm not asking people to follow. They need to figure it out for themselves. Each person is different."

But Peterson's response was so tentative I found myself wondering whether he himself believed it. Does he really think the self-help movement, and more rules for life, can serve as a sufficient counterweight to the morality and supernaturalism of Wokism? I am skeptical, and suspect Peterson is, too, which may be why he is wrestling with God, and why the rest of us, from hostile British journalists to the contributors to this volume, are wrestling with Peterson.

Arguing about Jordan Peterson

I first heard of Jordan Peterson in 2018. Around that time, his stance on the use of gender-neutral pronouns, coupled with the publication of his second book, *12 Rules for Life*, propelled him into public consciousness. Riding this wave of success, he launched an international book tour, filling up auditoriums around the world and delivering live lectures to hundreds of thousands of people.

Encouraged and accompanied by my husband, I attended one of these lectures. I was intrigued to say the least. I simply couldn't believe how this formerly obscure professor from the University of Toronto got on stage and talked extemporaneously about one of his rules for almost ninety minutes while keeping the audience captivated the whole time—I could have heard a pin drop. His popularity and success reveal that Peterson's ideas are potent and provocative. No wonder he has been labeled by the *New York Times* as "the most influential public intellectual in the Western world."

Peterson's addressing of such perennial topics as myth and meaning fuels his appeal, and his authentic and articulate approach also helps. It bestows on him an integrity not often witnessed nowadays. His pithy exhortations range from "Do not do things that you hate" to "Tell the truth—or at least, don't lie." Such moral platitudes come across as hollow when they are not backed up with action. But for Peterson who is part of the pragmatic tradition, actions speak louder than words. A man of his word, he became famous, in part, by saying what he believed to be true, even when such opinions are outside the current zeitgeist of postmodernism and political correctness. Peterson says what he means and means what he says. For that, he has garnered much attention, and the reactions he and his ideas generate range from blind adulation to vitriolic criticism.

The contributors to this volume avoid such extremes. Yet, they fall within different ranges on this spectrum. They have diverse points of view and philosophical assumptions. They often disagree with each other on many topics and they disagree on their overall evaluations of Jordan Peterson. Critical yet charitable, the writers explore a wide range of Peterson's ideas ranging from his use of stories to his philosophical assumptions about truth and goodness. While these essays all use Peterson's ideas as their springboard, more notably, they expand on his ideas. As a whole, this volume contains original thoughts and makes new connections to other notable thinkers, such as Aristotle, Marcus Aurelius, Karl Marx, Carl Jung, and Sam Harris. It covers ideas such as truth, goodness, and meaning to get to the heart of what humans truly find important. As such, it transcends the worldliness of politics and its petty tribalism.

Peterson, despite being subject to a multitude of mischaracterizations, politically identifies as a classical liberal. As such, he follows in the footsteps of giants who shaped Western civilization such as John Locke, John Stuart Mill, and Thomas Jefferson, for it was from Locke, an Englishman, that Jefferson found inspiration to pen the famous words "Life, Liberty, and the pursuit of Happiness." The tradition of classical liberalism has staunchly defended liberty in all its forms, and we see Peterson doing just that—defending the sovereignty of the individual and individual liberties such as freedom of speech. At this point, it is too soon to tell whether Peterson will go down in history like some of his like-minded predecessors, but for those who want to explore and engage with Peterson's ideas, in an open, curious, and thoughtful manner, this volume allows for the formulation of different opinions about Peterson's ideas, their influence, and thereby their ultimate longevity.

SANDRA WOIEN

Part I

The Culture Warrior

[1]
Jordan Peterson, Secular Priest

ALEX BROCKLEHURST

L ooking for a role model for twenty-first century human being? Perhaps you might consider Jordan Peterson. As a public intellectual, his independence of thought and unconventional courage in confronting contemporary challenges, offers prospect of guiding us away from any looming cliff edge. In the early twenty-twenties, fundamental questions about the nature of what it is to be human assail us, and it seems to me that this anthropological imperative is what makes Peterson so interesting. Attempting a wide-ranging understanding of his noteworthy contributions, therefore seems highly worthwhile.

When in *12 Rules for Life* Peterson says "Set your house in order before you criticize the world" we hear sage advice! Some may discern echoes of Confucius or the I Ching: *"Sincere commitment to higher things travels outward in powerful waves . . ."* Perhaps many immediately picture him rebuking loud-mouthed adolescents! Still others might recall him riffing on "Clean up your room" in an influential Joe Rogan podcast.

Incognito Christian?

Despite Peterson's evident fondness for Christian thinkers such as Tolstoy, Dostoevsky, and Solzhenitsyn, he does not *appear* to be a Christian. But this may simply be a classification issue. In fact, not being a 'professing believer' may not be the big deal we might imagine. Why? Because once we set up doctrinal and ritual 'correctness' as a hallmark of legitimacy, other avenues get closed off. The idea that following prescriptions of any sort could be a route to 'living faith' seems almost absurd.

And it isn't as if this has not been examined in popular culture. The central motif of the 1999 movie, *Stigmata,* involved an atheistic woman, Frankie Paige, receiving the wounds of Christ—an *impossibility* for orthodoxy and bone of contention within the movie. Suffice to say at this point that once truth statements and their corresponding ritualized confessions are jettisoned as *the* 'measure' of faith, Peterson's contributions might help us excavate a much deeper construal of the 'Christian' story.

Hero Myths Everywhere!

Primeval human experiences are archived in the collective human unconscious, according to Jung. His protégé Erich Neumann, explored this further and Peterson followed suit. Archaic stories are therefore considered to provide the backdrop to each *living* human drama. Think, for example, of Luke Skywalker as a modern expression of an ancient hero myth. Everyone has become comprised of these archetypal structures. Moreover, human beings wrestle with huge questions. When therefore, Peterson highlights Jacob wrestling an angel (Genesis 32:22–32), does this not apply equally to Jesus Christ in Gethsemane or Skywalker confronted with Darth Vader being his father?

Might Peterson seeing contemporary human struggle in this primitive story and others, such as the Old Testament story of Job, not sync with his drive for answers that really work? Was it, therefore, primarily clinical and 'objective' *research* that led him to instate the hero journey as *pivotal* to human meaning-making? Or did Peterson's own *narrative struggle* lead him to select this explanatory scheme? Even were Peterson openly to disavow Christ, his attention to Christian thinkers and Old Testament texts would remain striking. From a confessional standpoint, Peterson and C.S. Lewis, for example, might be considered 'miles apart'. Yet "Set your house in order before you criticize the world" (which is not an especially *original* insight), certainly exhibits an approach to *virtue* consistent with Lewis in *The Screwtape Letters: Letters from a Senior to a Junior Devil*:

> Do what you will, there is going to be some benevolence, as well as some malice, in your patient's soul. The great thing is to direct the malice to his immediate neighbours whom he meets every day and to thrust his benevolence out to the circumference, to people he does not know . . . Think of your man as a series of concentric circles, his will being the innermost . . . It is only in so far as they reach the will and are there embodied as habits that virtues are really fatal to us. (p. 37)

Unquestionably, as therapist, storyteller, and problem solver, Jordan Peterson has deployed all his tools and knowledge to help light the path of budding heroes. Could it therefore be that without becoming a confessing Christian, he has grafted a *Judeo-Christian framework of applied virtues and wisdom* onto the underlying, universal hero scheme—simply reading Christ as a particularly prominent and graphic expression of the archetype? Notwithstanding Peterson's character-ization of Lewis as a Christian apologist and himself as having an 'outside', psychology-based focus, the Christian imprint of vice and virtue upon Peterson's thought appears unmistakable.

Of course, we *usually* see a Christian confession first, followed by an ordering of the life in line with Christian prescriptions. There is no reason, however, why this cannot work in reverse. The evidence, since Peterson's personal crisis and return to public life, is certainly in line with such a trajectory. In any case, the hero archetype seems no less suitable a foundation for experiential Christian faith than mental agreement with doctrines and rituals.

Phenomenological Peterson

The insights Peterson wishes to convey to his audience involve 'inner hero awakening' (constituting a gestalt shift). Additionally, in a Gad Saad interview he provides a phe-nomenological schema for his twenty-four rules. The totality of reality involves both objective *and* subjective facets. He thinks

> . . . the phenomenological world has a structure and it's good versus evil, as a narrative structure. It's good versus evil, against a background of order and chaos. (2021, 26:36).

'Storied worlds' therefore are key to Peterson's sense-making. Insofar as individuals lack 'hero awakening' they will chronically mismanage order and chaos, leading to moral deficits. Yet once awakened, subjective and objective domains must be *harmonized* continually. Specific journeys contain *universal* themes, yet they also encounter *situational* challenges. So your story is both my story and *not* my story. Still, every story conforms to Peterson's aforementioned narrative structure—a structure prominent within the movie *Stigmata,* which configures it in both a novel and illuminating way.

Stigmata: The Death of Dogma

Peterson's great emphasis on archetypes suggests an approach to the four major characters of the 1999 movie *Stigmata*, as archetypal:

Cardinal Daniel Houseman represents the *corrupt leader/ institution.*

Father Andrew Kiernan (priest *and* scientist) represents the *authentic 'conflicted' mediator.*

Atheistic stigmatic Frankie Paige represents the *rebel/outsider.*

Murdered iconoclast, Father Paulo Alameida represents the *true voice of God.*

In a key scene, Paige appears to receive wounds to the wrists while bathing. This after her mother purchased the departed Alameida's Rosary from a Brazilian market stall, as a gift. After Paige receives the Rosary it becomes a trinket of contagious magic, connecting her with the departed Alameida. Thereafter, Frankie Paige is periodically wounded at differing body sites.

Houseman orders Kiernan to investigate a 'possession event' after her dramatic public scourging on a tube train. Kiernan quickly terminates this investigation, because Paige admits she doesn't *believe* in God. According to dogma, that such a person *"should exhibit the wounds of Christ is a self-contradiction."* After Paige's third wounding (crown of thorns) Kiernan re-engages, thus beginning a triangulation between himself, Houseman and Paige, revolving around a sacred text. 'Possessions' occur, that unveil suppressed text fragments, culminating in a shocking scene, where 'possessed' Paige challenges Kiernan about his rejection of her romantic advances, based on *purity doctrines*. Finally, it transpires that she is merely Alameida's messenger and Kiernan has to save her from Houseman's murder attempt. The closing scene portrays Frankie as the resurrected Saint Francis of Assisi.

So the pivotal story arc sees a tradition turned upside down. A cardinal became obsessed that a document would destroy the institutional tradition (equated with true faith). Kiernan (organic chemist as well as priest) demonstrates identity conflict between his old life as a scientist and later role as priest. Clearly, he has one hand clasping institutional orthodoxy and the other reaching into the modern world with its uncertainties and extremes. This scientist versus man of faith struggle bears striking resemblance to Peterson's Enlightenment versus depth psychology dilemma. The movie clearly accords with our earlier observation about Peterson perhaps offering a model of Christian virtue *without identifying as a believer* (paralleling Paige the atheist who 'becomes' Saint Francis at the climax).

This reinforces the message that neither beliefs, nor elected position; not sacred trinkets and traditions, determine fitness for office. Instead, deep-seated *human* qualities are vital and these revolve around *integrity.* Human struggle cannot sidestep the grey areas of lived experience, simply by adherence to prescribed 'holy' principles, as if living in a vacuum. The requisite integrity is portrayed as *necessitating personal struggle* and it attracts persecution for Kiernan from Houseman. In the same way, Peterson embraces the Kiernan archetype of authentic, conflicted mediator.

A Secular Priest?

Simplistic views of the priest might reduce to 'religious leader'. A priest is, however, best pictured as God and humankind's go-between. Thus, Peterson might be designated 'secular priest', as he discharges related teaching and pastoral functions, not ceremonial ones. Such functions are crucial in respect of identity and validation needs of followers, engendering belonging. We see in Peterson's pastoral concern for younger men core functions implied by the title 'Father' which indicate protection as well as challenge. These fit Peterson, akin to a priest facilitating the connection of the earthly domain to the heavenly domain. A specific language and practice develop, around a 'disciple-hero' story that involves a fresh, productive path opening up—*the follower's* hero quest.

Public Intellectual Peterson

Public intellectuals fulfil very important societal functions. Noam Chomsky was perhaps the last truly towering one prior to Peterson. His role was born before the Internet age, which makes his prominence the more striking. A deliberate and concrete communicator, Chomsky is quite the opposite to fast thinking and talking Peterson. While Chomsky positioned himself on the political left, Peterson has been categorized within the political right (something he contests).

Public intellectuals like Chomsky and Peterson (despite marked differences), function as defenders of the public good. They operate as proxies for the masses who must trust sources because their busy lives dictate their time pre-ferences. They address wide-ranging issues threatening society, at both the individual (micro) and structural (macro) levels. Chomsky has remained implacably against nation state tyranny, especially as constant critic and researcher of US foreign policy abuses.

In the mid-2010s, he became more vocal in his attacks specifically on the Republican party. In doing so he appears to have neglected the impact of Democratic party shifts upon the prevailing political climate. Chomsky remaining glued to his anti-Republican focus may have created a vacancy for Peterson! This despite public intellectuals not being elected, yet invariably arising because a counterbalance is required to the political zeitgeist (compare Trump's meteoric ascent, as non-politician in an exclusively career politician culture).

Becoming a Public Intellectual

Alan Lightman of MIT has offered two helpful descriptions of the public intellectual from Ralph Waldo Emerson and Edward Said. Emerson considered the intellectual to be the world's eye—evaluating, generating, and communicating worthy ideas as an integrated man. Said considered the intellectual to be constantly balancing private and public. Passionate ideals drive the quest, but that quest must be *significant for society*. Here we might make an important distinction between the public intellectual (tackling structural problems) and the self-help guru (addressing individual adaptations in the world). Coming out against mandated gender-neutral pronouns, in a way reminiscent of Chomsky's attacks on US foreign policy, Jordan Peterson entered the spotlight in October 2016:

> I'm against the use of legislation to determine what words myself and other people are required to utter.

This man was never going to applaud the creeping cancel culture! Small wonder that the heated Toronto campus debate and subsequent Canadian Broadcasting Corporation exchanges, brought about a sustained opposition to identity politics. As social policy critic, at this juncture Peterson, like Chomsky, positioned himself implacably *against the status quo*.

Yet in the five years since his media opening gambit (if indeed that is what it was) much has changed for Peterson in both his personal life and his professional focus. That should be taken as significant. We must examine all such changes when it comes to a public intellectual, so as to ensure they are still operating in line with the trust accorded to them. Such does not foreshadow a negative appraisal of Peterson. Yet it does necessitate our *continuing to monitor* his pragmatic decision-making (and its impacts) with respect to the public arena.

In this vein, Peterson's two latest best-selling books on 'rules' (notice he does not use *principles*) for successful living, deserve attention. This is because they reflect a potentially significant shift—from attending to problematic *structures* such as the state toward equipping *individual* adaptive resilience. Indeed, despite unpacking his pithy aphorisms at length with critical insights, this no longer quite feels like the punchy and uncompromising, *anti-Establishment* posturing that launched him into the limelight.

Critiquing Social Policy or Building Culture?

However, an important distinction is sometimes made in the marketplace of ideas between *public intellectuals* (often traditional academics) as critics of emerging policies and trends and *thought leaders* (powerful communicators and influencers) as change brokers offering novel ideas, more in the mold of the aphorism attributed to Buckminster Fuller: *"You never change things by fighting the existing reality. To change something, build a new model that makes the existing model obsolete."*

Overreach, Blunder, or Belligerence?

Are Peterson's changes symptomatic of a move from challenging the status quo to upholding it? Alternatively, has he changed basic approach to maximize influence? Or have his priorities just altered over time? Well, developmental psychology tells us that few people operate at the level of principles, preferring instead to follow prescriptions. So now Peterson producing mass-market *rules* for living might raise a few eyebrows! If making radical concessions to observed human nature, it would seem difficult for him simultaneously to offer any sort of vision grounded in the highest possible ideals—giving the best chance of human flourishing.

Moreover, Peterson merges being *similar* into being *identical,* upon noticing overlapping themes and historical connections across schools of thought. Specifically, we see his fusion of extreme social constructionism, the Frankfurt School, postmodernism, nihilism, and Cultural Marxism. He treats these *separate movements* as a *unified force* underpinned by relativism. But even if these highlighted commonalities have validity, he obliterates important distinctions. This is peculiar for somebody telling us to eschew identity politics and abandon ideology, elaborating:

The ideologue begins by selecting a few abstractions in whose low-resolution representations hide large, undifferentiated chunks of the world . . .

Let us refrain from attack here however, since ideological juggernauts almost *demand* ideological responses to meet their forcefulness head-on. Moreover, a noble vision arguably merits critique, refinement, and building upon, not demolition due to egregious errors.

The Morphing Peterson?

In a more generous vein, could it be that Peterson has reverted so far into the micro-level of analysis ('remedying' macro-level impacts through individual prescriptions for living) that, just as Chomsky, he has made significant concessions to the zeitgeist? Has his role therefore simply been *morphing* away from his public intellectual breakthrough (in slow, incremental drifts) via thought leader and finally toward *secular priest?* Doubtless Peterson *could* be portrayed as now *showing people how to fit into hierarchies successfully by following rules.* But this may be a cynical reading.

It seems much less plausible that Peterson has 'sold out' than that the direction of travel has changed somewhat, or even fundamentally. Could such be attributed to epiphany? Peterson's subliminal inclinations may well point in that direction and an eruption from a favored domain should not be considered a surprise. It does appear axiomatic that heroes on their journeys usually believe they are headed in a specific direction (this conscious focus being equated with 'the quest'), while in reality that direction morphs and the conscious relationship to it transforms over time. To me this is precisely what Peterson has undergone, arguably catalyzed by his own crisis.

Singular Truth versus Multiple Stories

So what exactly is Peterson's relevance to us? Sitting within a tradition he both strongly exemplifies and problematizes, he's attempting to address society-wide problems. In certain respects, though, he remains *part of* the problem. In an effort to untangle this let us return to *Stigmata* as a frame.

In one church scene a statue, remarked upon by Paige, depicts crucifixion through the hands, not the wrists. Thinking this literal, she considers her wrist wounds to mean she *cannot be exhibiting stigmata*. Kiernan however clarifies that scientific approaches have uncovered the reality that people *were* crucified through the wrists, not the hands. The statues are not 'wrong' therefore, they are merely icons or representations (visual stories) of what happened. There is no need to take them literally.

Ironically, in aiming for some *holy grail* of singular truth, *dogmatic thinking* will shut down multiple, alternative avenues to truth. This is precisely the 'postmodern' observation Peterson has failed to take seriously enough. Hence, he is obligated to give scientific truths superior valency than storied truths—something which philosopher of science (specialist) Paul Feyerabend (akin to Kiernan in the statue clarification) does not do. Science, he notes:

> offers not one story, it offers many; the stories clash and their relation to a story-independent 'reality' is as problematic as the relation of the Homeric epics to an alleged 'Homeric World'. (2001, p. 27)

The notion therefore that discovering truth (essentially via scientific method) should constitute the *touchstone of legitimate discourse* is fatally flawed. And at this point we see Peterson's attempt at wearing two hats come under pressure. As scientist (Enlightenment man) he deploys rigorous testing methods, whereas with his 'archetypes and heroes' hat on, he seems satisfied with Neumann's volume of research as 'proof' of hero myth universality—which is *solely* speculative. Regarding his Jungian hat, the refutation method of any rigorous philosophy of science is *nowhere* in evidence.

The four archetypal characters of *Stigmata*, in contrast, highlight *differing avenues* of exploring human journeys into truth—with the movie problematizing 'confessional orthodoxy' (irreducible and required core beliefs) in its claiming *sole* legitimacy. We see the trinity of voices of Kiernan,

Paige, and Alameida together 'defeating' the monolithic authority of the bureaucratic and prescriptive Houseman orthodoxy.

We can see both Peterson's dilemma and solution here. Such orthodoxies are pervasive and understandably he wishes to sit within the credibility/validation of the legitimizing narrative. Yet he still seeks to assert truth claims *outside* that domain. Perhaps therefore Peterson's identification with Old Testament characters *is* subliminal. He may not be professing Christian faith, but in selecting such characters, rather than from, say, the *Iliad*, he *is* making some sort of correlation with Judeo-Christian salvation history. Jordan Peterson endured a severe crisis over many months, since when he has *repeatedly* disclosed intense personal turmoil. He comments upon the experiences in several moving recovery interviews in the first quarter of 2021. Perhaps he has undergone a metaphorical crucifixion. Certainly, reaching some sort of limit, he appears more inclined to balance reason with experience these days, on his own hero journey.

Knowledge versus Life

Returning to this question of the essence of Christian faith, and Peterson's relation to it, we must travel further. Nietzsche ventured beyond the pale:

> Christianity has taken the side of everything weak, base, ill-constituted, it has made an ideal out of opposition to the preservative instincts of strong life; it has depraved the reason even of the intellectually strongest natures by teaching men to feel the supreme values of intellectuality as sinful, as misleading, as temptations. (1990, p. 129)

Nietzsche considers gnosis (knowledge) *sacramental* (life-giving), whereas Christianity considers it *heretical* (death-bringing). Indeed, religious and quasi-religious narratives, invariably cherish some utopian ideal of 'perfected' life. In Genesis the definitive choice represented by *two* trees is "knowledge *or* life?" In reality this is a false binary because once inhabiting an *open-ended* and *ever-evolving* story we can have knowledge *and* life. Right and wrong can therefore be placed on a practical ease/difficulty spectrum rather than a simple moral/legal one. Moreover, Peterson considers it a mistake to predicate identity upon group characteristics, such as with identity politics. Consequently, associations made by belief systems make little impression upon him, as compared with *substantive* expressions of human being, which reflects his core existentialist bent.

For me Peterson has grafted the *suffering and redemption motif* running through the Bible onto Neumann's hero archetype. The Jesus of the Gospels defined himself in terms of such. The Christ archetype was thereby incarnated. Peterson's scheme is therefore much more conducive to an understanding wherein what defines Christian 'identity' is *solely* actualization of the suffering/virtuous inner hero. It is both activated and maintained via continual alignment with the requirements of the archetype. This is about as far from requiring a necessary belief system as we can get!

Having survived his trials Jordan Peterson continues as courageous exemplar of flourishing twenty-first century humanity. He has often shown himself humble enough to say 'I don't know'. Perhaps that is his most telling contribution in leading us away from the cliff edge . . .

Bibliography

Bite-sized Philosophy. 2017. Jordan Peterson: Why Postmodernists Reject Logic and Evidence. <www.youtube.com/watch?v=CTBOU77czpY&t=139s>.

CBC News. 2016. Heated Debate on Gender Pronouns and Free Speech in Toronto. <https://www.youtube.com/watch?v=SiijS_9hPkM>.

Feyerabend, Paul K. 2001. *Conquest of Abundance: A Tale of Abstraction versus the Richness of Being.* Chicago: University of Chicago Press.

JRE Clips. 2017. Jordan Peterson on Cleaning Your Room. *The Joe Rogan Experience.* <https://www.youtube.com/watch?v=Z8_gUmt0k8o>.

Lewis, Clive S. 1989. *The Screwtape Letters: Letters from a Senior to a Junior Devil.* Glasgow: Collins.

Lightman, Alan. 2007. *The Role of the Public Intellectual.* <https://web.mit.edu/comm-forum/legacy/papers/lightman.html>.

Marks, Jonathan 2017. *We Don't Need No Stinking Thought Leaders.* <www.insidehighered.com/views/2017/07/11/why-academics-should-strive-be-public-intellectuals-not-thought-leaders-essay>.

Neumann, Erich 2014. *The Origins and History of Consciousness.* Princeton: Princeton University Press.

Nietzsche, Friedrich. 1990. *Twilight of the Idols / The Anti-Christ.* London: Penguin.

Peterson, Jordan B. 2018. *12 Rules for Life: An Antidote to Chaos.* Toronto: Random House Canada.

———. 2021. *Beyond Order: 12 More Rules for Life.* Toronto: Random House Canada.

Saad, Gad. 2021. My Chat with Jordan Peterson. YouTube video, 2:05:40. <https://www.youtube.com/watch?v=9KF2cwcADtU>.

Wainwright, Rupert, director. 1999. *Stigmata.* California: Metro-Goldwyn-Mayer.

Walker, Brian B. 2011. *The I Ching or Book of Changes.* London: Piatkus.

[2]
Confronting the New Puritans

RON DART

The cover photo of Jordan Peterson on the book I edited, *Myth and Meaning in Jordan Peterson: A Christian Perspective* (2020), reveals not much more than half of his face. There was an obvious purpose and goal in such a cover. No doubt much about Peterson is revealed in his many publications, lectures, guest appearances and interviews—much is also concealed and hidden to those who only insist on clear, distinct and absolute interpretations of Peterson and much else in the culture wars.

There are, when studying politics, two approaches and obvious overlaps between them. There is politics as formal politics: voting, parties, institutions, representatives in various levels of government, comparative politics, international relations and ways of reflecting on statist and non-statist actors on the stage of political thought and life. Many who study politics linger on this specific area of public life and much media attention is focused on it. There is, though, the equally important realm of cultural politics in which many of the hot-button issues within culture are, often, sadly so, debated and civility is the first victim of such heated clashes.

Jordan Peterson's primary activities are in the realm of cultural politics and his position is, predictably so, misread by both "progressives" on the left and "reactionaries" on the right. The responses to Peterson, at an initial and poorly thought-out level, tend to be a demonizing of him from the more Orthodox progressive liberal tradition to a welcome embrace and genuflection by various types of reactionary conservatives. This belies the fact that Peterson is a liberal of a more classical type who does not fit easily into a procrustean bed. There is a liberal politics of diverse perspectives and pluralism that, Hamlet-like, tends to paralyze a certain type of liberal from being committed to anything other than perspectives—this is the opposite end of the liberal spectrum from ideological progressives in which a reductionistic read of history and contemporary events is the shibboleth for social justice activism. But, to show this, a short detour into various misreads of Peterson from 2016 forward is necessary.

I have consciously chosen as the title of this essay, "Confronting the New Puritans," as a metaphor. Peterson is, obviously, not engaging, for the most part, literal English Calvinists of a more extreme stripe and variety. But, at the core of puritanism, in aspects of the early Anglo-American ethos, was the notion that both church and state had so compromised and corrupted the true faith that the pure ones (puritans) had to separate themselves from the betrayers of the genuine faith. Such puritans were convinced, in thought, word, and deed, their interpretation was the purest and truest one and those who opposed or questioned such a pure, clean, and clear read of the truth had to be opposed or weeded out (witch hunts and types of cancel culture very much the order of the day). Needless to say, many on the progressive left and reactionary right rarely doubt the purity of their interpretations of the hot-button issues in the culture wars, hence, in many ways, are just secularized puritans.

Peterson had been doing the academic, counseling and professorial role in the 1990s, but well into the twenty-first century, a turn to comparative mythology, psychology, multiple published papers and the lecture circuit became his focus. The publication of his initial tome, *Maps of Meaning* (1999), signaled an obvious attempt to thread together a more scientific way of knowing (with its focus on reason, hard facts, and objectivity) with a greater respect for the humanities (and the role of myth, subjectivity and imagination). Such a complex book was the child of much research, synthesis, and deeper digging. The academic debates about the book were typical for the cloistered virtues of the university, but no obvious offense was taken. 2016 birthed, in many ways, Peterson as a prominent public actor on the stage of the culture wars against an ethos of political correctness. Peterson's opposition to Bill C-16 on personal pronouns and the forced use of them smoked him out of the comfortable environs of the academy into the streets of heated and confrontational debates.

On its publication in January 2018, Peterson's *12 Rules for Life* became an instant best seller, and the public interview in 2018 (if it can be called that) by Cathy Newman made it abundantly clear that baiting and caricaturing had replaced thoughtful and respectful dialogue on troubling cultural issues. The Munk Debate in Toronto (May 18th, 2018) pitted Michael Eric Dyson and Michelle Goldberg against Stephen Fry and Jordan Peterson, and yet further elevated Peterson to a higher stature. The "progressives" continued their assaults on Peterson and many on the "right" viewed him as their champion of sorts. There is no doubt Peterson had become a lightning rod thinker and activist who created intense reactions; his turn contra cultural Marxism, postmodernism, and critical race theory obviously taking him to different places than the herd mentality of a form of liberal orthodoxy. The recent depiction of Peterson as "Red Skull" in the much-followed Marvel Captain America comic series is yet the latest in a series of simplistic and mindless rejections of him that, ironically enough, creates yet more affection for him by those on the cultural right opposed to the silencing of critical thinking and free speech. So, is Peterson a reactionary conservative or a classical liberal who holds high the rights of the individual to think critically and speak freely about various types of herdism of the right or left?

We do know that Peterson did an undergraduate degree in political science, and we also know he has, again and again, dared to question forms of groupthink of the Nazi-fascist right and Marxist-communist left. The content of the left and right on these macro ideologies often obscures the fact that both clans share a commitment to absolute certainty (Eric Voegelin calls 'gnosis') in their interpretation of the troubling issues of the time. It is this combination of certainty and groupthink that Peterson regularly questions. Needless to say, reactionary conservatism and trendy liberalism are but updated versions of intellectual tribalism that negate the rights of the individual to ask critical questions about the dominant clan they belong to.

It is in this sense that Peterson is very much a classical liberal, but there is more to his classical liberalism than has been mentioned. I think it can be legitimately suggested that Peterson was not at his best in the 2019 dialogue with Slavoj Žižek, "Happiness: Capitalism Versus Marxism," Žižek with a deeper knowledge of Marx, Marxism, and variations of communism than Peterson. Žižek, I might add, would, like Peterson, have solid criticisms of the left but he is more nuanced than Peterson and not as likely to wave the flag of capitalism in the way Peterson leans into (in a thoughtful manner).

Classical Liberalism and Alberta

The province of Alberta is, perhaps, Canada's most right of center province, and Peterson spent his most formative years north of Edmonton, the province's capital. The classical liberalism of Alberta is best embodied in the tract of a former Premier of Alberta, E.C. Manning, *Political Realignment: A Challenge to Thoughtful Canadians* (1967). The essence of the manifesto is that the ideology of liberty and individuality must be protected and held high, the state should be kept at a wary distance, and market competition will bring out the best in all and create a bumper crop economy. The fact that E.C. Manning's son, Preston Manning, did significant research for the booklet tells its own graphic tale. Preston Manning, in the 1990s, created both the Reformed and Alliance Parties that wiped out the Progressive Conservative Party in Canada in the early years of the twenty-first century. The present Conservative Party of Canada has, in the last twenty years, reflected, in most ways, the entrepreneurial vision and ethos of *Political Realignment*. This is the broader cultural ethos that Peterson would have imbibed while growing into his teens, but there was also, at such a season of his journey, a leftward turn.

Peterson grew up in Fairview, Alberta, a small town five hours north of Edmonton. Peterson's mother was the librarian at the local Fairview College, but equally significant for this phase of his life, Sandy Notley was the librarian at Peterson's high school. Sandy Notley was the wife of Grant

Notley, leader at the time of the leftist-leaning New Democratic Party in Alberta. Peterson, as an emerging teen,
became quite involved in the activism and political vision of
the New Democratic Party in the 1970s. Notley became the
leader of the provincial party in 1968 and won a seat in
Alberta's legislative assembly in 1971, and by the mid-1970s
Peterson was a committed true believer of the emerging
leadership of the New Left in Alberta, George Orwell's *The
Road to Wigan Pier* (1937) a sacred text of sorts for him.

I have spent time at Wigan Pier. When Orwell was writing about Wigan and similar northern towns, they suffered
under some of the worst conditions of the British post-World
War I slump. Such a tract of sorts, when read from a certain
perspective, reinforced a decided turn to the social democratic left. Peterson certainly found such a manifesto of much
support in his leftward turn. But, Orwell's description and
diagnosis of living conditions in the poorest parts of the
North of England (and his prognosis of the ways and means
of overcoming the dire plight of many in the area) was but
one version of social democracy, more extreme leftward turns
were being dramatically enforced in the USSR.

It was these more extreme versions of the left that, in
time, would turn the young Peterson both away from the left
and activist politics. It was this herd mentality of the left
(and right) and the sheer evil and brutality of both tendencies that nudged Peterson to explore and examine the deeper
recesses of human nature and the human condition. It was
such questioning that took him into the direction of myth
and a probing of the dark and destructive aspects of the
human psyche, hence his turn to doctoral work in psychology.
I might add that the deeper Albertan tradition of John Locke
and Adam Smith, as articulated and politically lived forth in
the Manning father-son duo and dynamic, is very much part
of Peterson's version and vision of how to bring into being
the just and good society, the state always of secondary significance, society, family, individuals and community of a
greater priority.

There was, obviously, a significant chasm between
Orwell's 1937 classic of sorts of the left and the more extreme
outworking of Marxist thought in the USSR under Stalin at
the same time. But, Peterson did tend to conflate the two

versions of leftist thought, social democracy as a political vision to embody in Alberta and Canada at opposite ends, in many ways, of variations of democratic socialism and communism. It is this lack of nuance that, in some ways, inspired a vigorous critique of Peterson's political vision in *Myth and Mayhem: A Leftist Critique of Jordan Peterson* (2020) and his rather poor showing in his public debate in Toronto with Slavoj Žižek in 2019. Žižek wrote the Introduction to *Myth and Mayhem.*

Peterson does tend, in many ways, to highlight, often, the worst aspects of the political left while giving a nod to the right (though acknowledging some of its faults and failures). It is in this sense that he very much reflects his Albertan roots and heritage. It is also somewhat interesting that Grant and Sandy Notley's daughter, Rachel Notley (who Peterson would have known in his early years when in Fairview), was the Premier of Alberta (New Democratic Party) from 2015 to 2019 and has been leader of the opposition since 2019. The reason Rachel Notley took the throne for a few years was a deep division and fragmentation in the political right that brought Notley to power.

But, underlying Peterson's turn to cultural politics was his fear, as mentioned above, that when a certain type of ideology comes to dominate, critical thinking is censured and a mindless herdism wins the day. The more classical liberal tradition of the role of the individual to think critically about hot-button issues that tend to divide and fragment people into cloistered virtues was a lesson learned by Peterson in his twenties and thirties, Solzhenitsyn's depiction of the Soviet Gulag a lesson Peterson did not miss. Yet, there was also Japanese nationalism, the Nazi-fascist ethos and the rightward tribal nationalism that was equally appalling to Peterson (content different, underlying tendency of groupthink the same).

Cultural Politics

When Peterson approaches the controversial ethos of cultural politics, he comes with two dominant concerns: a serious questioning of groupthink and the essential role of the thoughtful individual, thinking in a critical manner, and deconstructing both reductionistic ideas and the true believers of such ideas (on both the progressive left and the reactionary right). Peterson tends to be noted for confronting the progressive left for the simple reason that this form of thinking tends to dominate significant aspects of the academy, media, culture and political life of the center, center-left. It is this ideological power elite (and its acolytes, disciples and evangelists) that Peterson engages to the predictable anger and reactionary tendencies of such a clan. Needless to say, this family compact often lacks the ability to be self-critical while being other critical. It is not very liberal of a liberal not to critique liberalism but many liberals simply do not engage in this basic human activity—Peterson does and this enrages those who are convinced they have the answers to most of the dilemmas of the human condition.

Peterson is also committed to deeper dives into the human soul, mind, and imagination, hence his ongoing interest in comparative mythology (West, East, and elsewhere) and serious probes into the insights of Jung, Nietzsche, Kierkegaard, Dostoevsky, and many others who have dared to face into the complex and shadow side of the human condition and human nature. We are more than Cartesian *cogito ergo sum*, and it is this more and its darker reality and consequences within states, nations, groups, families and individuals that legitimately interests the ever inquiring and curious mind of Peterson. Many simply want clichés and formulaic answers to life's troubling questions and challenges, but Peterson, at his best, is wary of going too far down such a rabbit hole.

This does not mean, though, that he is a relativist—a serious study of comparative myths opposes such an indulgent pose and posture. There are pointers, hints, and standards that myth reveals and summons forth, but such a summoning does not fit easily into simplistic categories. This is why Peterson has locked horns with the too certain cultural Marxists, progressive liberals, and different strands and approaches of the postmodernists (whether of the more simplistic "power" epistemology or "perspectives" clans). The deeper and historic, perennial and timeless understanding of myths has done much to shape Peterson's vision of the good, true, and responsible life. The fact few know the classical myths of the past and many are raised on the myths served up by Walt Disney means Peterson (following the accommodationist approach to learning) works with what popular culture knows but, in time, he walks the curious and interested into the ancient myths and their contemporary meaning. Most of Peterson's lectures and books, again and again, return to myths as a more instructive way of growing into wisdom and insight. Needless to say, there are many scholars in the academy who question Peterson's interpretations of various myths, but such is the predicable academic and historic intellectual communities (ever clashing over how texts are to be interpreted and applied). If Peterson had only remained within the safe and comfortable confines of the university, he would have had detractors but never the ire he has faced by entering the fray with the progressive activists.

The fact that Peterson has engaged multiple hot button issues in the culture wars such as Black Lives Matter, Woke, Gender, Identity, LGBTQI, Social Justice Warriors (SJW), Blacks, Indigenous, Peoples of Color (BIPOC) and the inevitable equality-hierarchy issue often obscures his deeper turn to the underlying principles that often predetermine how and why we make decisions. The fact that Peterson, like many others who question those who surf the wave of trendy issues that inhabit a "cancel culture" ethos, speak much about the low level of cultural engagement and basic civility.

The controversial reception by the left and right to *12 Rules for Life: An Antidote to Chaos* and the more recent *Beyond Order: 12 More Rules for Life* means the actual content of the text often gets bogged down in silly interpretations (usually read in a reactionary and literalist manner) of the various metaphors that point to deeper principles of our life journey. *12 Rules for Life,* as its subtitle indicates, highlights the need for the ordering of life and desires for those whose inner and outer journey is erratic and indulgent and who live with the consequences of such chaos. Needless to say, antidotes are needed for those who indulge a wide variety of appetites and desires and live with the reality of doing so. The need to educate and order desires and choices is a necessary although not sufficient step on the maturing journey. But, as *Beyond Order* rightly notes, order is only an initial means needed by which longings, desires, and thirsts are ordered to overcome chaos so that a more meaningful and sufficient vision of liberty can be birthed.

There is no doubt that Peterson is questioning an immature *notion* of liberty but not opposed to the *ideal* of liberty. The question becomes more about the conditions and order needed for legitimate and mature liberty, hence the order-liberty tension, order being a form and structure through which substantive notions of meaningful and authentic liberty can be actualized. When the order-liberty tension is divided, order slips into various forms of legalism, authoritarianism, or totalitarianism, and liberty becomes reactionary and panders to various types of libertarianism and anarchy. Both the left and right, for different reasons, break the needed tension between order-liberty, the content issues being but the symptoms of such immature thinking and activism. It is, therefore, essential when reading Peterson to step beyond the hot-button issues he is often engaged in and probe to the principles that animate and do much to shape and inform his thinking; the equality-hierarchy tension, as mentioned above, yet another tension more than worth the noting.

Peterson, for example, would not oppose equality of opportunity, given the diverse types of equality of condition, but asserts that taking the additional step towards equality of outcome creates all sorts of problems. Does this mean hierarchy is the answer? There is good hierarchy (both that of merit and more importantly of character) but there is problematic hierarchy just as the distinction must be made between free speech and true speech. Those who attempt to dismiss Peterson often distort his more nuanced thinking at the level of principles and often those who defend him commit the same blunders and gaffes. It's always easier to simplify than to engage in subtler analysis of both ideas and more complex people.

I have mentioned in my other chapter in this book how Peterson approaches the *Bible*—unlike crude secularists, he sees perennial truths in the *Bible* but unlike Biblical literalists, he does not interpret the text in a literal manner—myth is more his golden key to unlocking the meaning of the text for personal insight and transformation. The secularists and Biblicists in the culture wars both have a one-dimensional and reductionistic approach to the *Bible*, their cyclopean way of interpreting the texts concealing the deeper meaning and significance of the text. This means that in the culture wars Peterson tends to offend both the secular puritans and the Biblical puritans, both assuming they are the pure interpreters of reality.

There is no doubt that in the culture wars Christianity has taken a perpetual beating by the liberal left. Because of this, those who defend Christianity are often seen, ipso facto, as being on the right; however, such a simplistic analysis creates a problematic progressive-conservative way of thinking—and binaries are not usually helpful when issues are complex. But Peterson, like most minimally thoughtful people, cannot be easily forced into such a procrustean bed. Those who do their culture wars thinking like rams in rutting season rarely understand how to do such surgical cultural operations in a subtle and nuanced manner—Peterson, to his credit, is much nimbler than those who either demonize him or genuflect at his feet. While there are many portals to enter the ethos and traditions of the culture wars, Peterson has, in many ways, done his controversial and oft confrontational best to awaken those who have been taken in by various types of wokism.

Transcending Puritanism

Peterson deftly eludes those who attempt, in a Manichean manner, to bury him in a procrustean bed of a right of center ideology in the culture wars. There are those on the decided right who uncritically laud Peterson such as Jim Proser in *Savage Messiah: How Dr. Jordan Peterson Is Saving Western Civilization*, with a foreword by Dennis Prager (2019). If Proser-Prager did too much of the Peterson fawning, then the publication from the left contra Peterson, *Myth and Mayhem: A Leftist Critique of Peterson* tends to misread Peterson's Canadian social-democratic ethos and the tensions between Alberta and Ottawa in forming a tension between right and left in Canada that Peterson, to some degree lives, moves and has his being within. The fact that Peterson was somewhat bested in his public debate by Slavoj Žižek (Žižek having a much deeper understanding of leftist theory and practice given his context) meant, in some ways, that it was quite fitting that Žižek would write the forward to *Myth and Mayhem*. It is more than accurate to suggest that Peterson finds himself somewhere between Proser-Prager and Žižek in the cultural and economic politics dialogue. But, sadly so, most prefer simplistic right-left categories as a way of interpreting and understanding the culture wars,

Peterson is beholden to neither tribe although his more attentive and docile audience tends to emerge from the right of center spectrum. So, in conclusion, it is probably fair to suggest that Peterson does oppose the trendy liberal establishment and his supporters tend to be on the right, but Peterson would, for the most part, be most at home in the soft right rather than the far or extreme right versions of reactionary conservatism, his brand of conservatism rooted more in the classical liberal way.

Although Peterson has an undergraduate degree in Political Science, his deeper turn to psychology means his overarching interest is in the deeper motives and myths that shape and impact how individuals make sense of their all too human journey in families, friendships, communities and the appeal yet limitations of formal and cultural politics, groupthink always a seductive temptation to be wary of and thoughtfully resist—such is the role of critical thinking that is so foundational to the best of Peterson's classical liberalism.

References

Burgis, Ben, Conrad Hamilton, Matthew McManus, and Marion Trejo. 2020. *Myth and Mayhem: A Leftist Critique of Jordan Peterson*. Portland: Zero.

Dart, Ron, ed. 2020. *Myth and Meaning in Jordan Peterson: A Christian Perspective*. Bellingham: Lexham.

Manning, E.C. 1967. *Political Realignment: A Challenge to Thoughtful Canadians*. Toronto: McClelland and Stewart.

Orwell, George. 1937. *The Road to Wigan Pier*. London: Gollancz.

Peterson, Jordan B. 1999. *Maps of Meaning: The Architecture of Belief*. New York: Routledge.

———. 2018. *12 Rules for Life: An Antidote to Chaos.* Toronto: Random House Canada.

———. 2021. *Beyond Order: 12 More Rules for Life.* Toronto: Random House Canada.

Proser, Jim. 2020. *Savage Messiah: How Dr. Jordan Peterson Is Saving Western Civilization.* New York: St. Martin's Press.

Voegelin, Eric. 1968. *Science, Politics, and Gnosticism: Two Essays.* Washington: Regnery.

[3]
What Jordan Peterson Should Have Said about Marxism

DAVID GORDON AND YING TANG

Jordan Peterson argues that the horrors of Soviet Russia under Lenin and Stalin should teach us that Marxism cannot work. The mass murders depicted in *The Gulag Archipelago* were no accident. A flawed ideology inevitably doomed Marxism. This ideology wrongly taught that people are motivated primarily by the desire for material goods. Marxists ignore the fact that human beings need meaning in their lives.

Further, even on its own chosen ground of economics, Marxism fails. It ignores the fact that human society is inevitably hierarchical, holding out the unrealistic hope of social and political equality. Acceptance of hierarchy does not condemn the poor to bad lives, though the role of suffering in a meaningful life should not be underrated. Market economies of the type now prevalent in the world have made unprecedented progress in ending poverty. We should reject "postmodern neo-Marxism," which threatens these achievements and instead be guided in our lives by the truths of psychology and the symbolic messages contained in myths.

That is Peterson's take.

Peterson is evidently right about the atrocities committed by Communist regimes in the twentieth century. *The Black Book of Communism*, a postmortem of Communist atrocities compiled by European and American academics, concluded that the human cost of genocides, extrajudicial executions, deportations, and artificial famines stood at over ninety-four million.

To put that number in perspective we can compare it with well-known historical atrocities. Between 1825 and 1917, the Tsarist regime in Russia carried out 6,321 political executions, whereas *in two months* of official Red Terror in the fall of 1918, Bolshevism notched up some 15,000 dead critics of the regime (Tupy 2017). Estimates vary for the death toll of the notorious Spanish Inquisition, 1478–1834, the highest being around five thousand.

For context, the twentieth century saw other mass killings by non-Communist regimes, the worst case being the atrocities of German National Socialism. However, the corpse count of regimes calling themselves Marxist far exceeds all others, in the history of the world, and National Socialism owed something to the Soviet example. We should also note that there are traditions of Marxist opposition to the deeds of "Bolshevism" and then "Stalinism," arguing on various grounds that the Soviet case does not comply with Marxist principles of socialist revolution.

Marxism Mischaracterized

Although we generally agree with Peterson's negative verdict on Marxism, we cannot accept many of the specific arguments he deploys. Peterson mischaracterizes Marxism in several ways, so that Marxists could actually take heart from his misunderstandings of their doctrines. Aside from specific errors, a few of which we shall mention in passing, Peterson tends to lump together different forms of Marxism. Marxism is almost as divided into competing sects and movements as Christianity. Just as it would be unfair to look at some specific episode in Christian history, say the appalling atrocities of the Franco regime in the period 1939–1945, and assume this to be the responsibility of Jesus or St. Paul, so it is unconvincing to look at the loathsome deeds of Josef Stalin and attribute them directly to the writings of Karl Marx.

To understand Christianity, we have to begin with the *New Testament* and then look at how Christianity was modified in various historical circumstances. To understand Marxism, we have to begin with the ideas of Marx and his close collaborator Engels, and then look at Marxism's evolution.

One striking difference between the version of Marxism which once had such a huge influence on the world and the kind of Marxism you most often hear voiced by today's leftists in the US is that the earlier Marxism was preoccupied with economics and with the abolition of the market economy. 'Cultural Marxism' is so called precisely because it is not primarily concerned with the economy. It is Cultural Marxism that Peterson has in mind when he speaks of "Neo-Marxism"—he occasionally refers directly to Horkheimer and the Frankfurt School.

Marxism Old and New

We can call the earlier Marxism 'classical Marxism'. Classical Marxism is encapsulated in Frederick Engels's pamphlet, *Socialism, Utopian and Scientific* (1880), which was seen by Marxists as an up-to-date summary of their views, replacing the historically relevant but now practically obsolete *Manifesto of the Communist Party* (1848).

Marxists from the 1880s to the 1930s (both classical Marxists and Bolsheviks) made a clear and coherent case that capitalism, while it had accomplished wonders of increasing output in the past, had now reached its limits. These Marxists considered that capitalism was now restricting output, so that socialism, defined as the abolition of private ownership of the means of production and its replacement with a centrally planned economy, would see an enormous increase in output and real incomes. They identified slumps as 'crises of overproduction'—meaning that the capitalist system was unable to cope with the inherent tendency of technology ('the forces of production') to expand production.

Hardly anyone argues like this anymore. If you listen to today's Marxists or other socialists in the US, they usually do not talk about increasing output by instituting central planning. This older Marxist concept is completely alien to the way these new Marxists typically talk. They are more likely to discourse about restricting technology and economic growth in order to protect the environment or in order to benefit some minority racial group.

Today's Marxists put all the emphasis on race and gender, not class. They don't place much stock in the working class— their contempt for the working class is often thinly disguised.

They argue for various government measures on the grounds that these will help poor people, especially blacks and other minorities. The conviction that socialism, or any kind of economic change, can unleash a tremendous superabundance of wealth for everyone has simply evaporated.

All the same, it's impossible to understand today's Marxism without understanding classical Marxism.

Classical Marxism

Marx both advocated and confidently predicted communism, a system without money and without a state. Money would be phased out immediately, and could be phased out because of the increased output that communism would engender. Marx envisioned that immediately after the abolition of capitalism, people in communism would continue to work for material compensation, but would be paid in labor-vouchers instead of money. Then output would increase, because of the superior efficiency of communism, so that eventually, in a higher phase of communism, people could take freely, without payment or rationing, from the common store. Labor-voucher communism would be succeeded by free-access communism and work would become detached from any individual material reward (*Critique of the Gotha Programme*). The state would wither away because there would be no need for it: there would no longer be economic classes pitted against one another.

In the last years of Marx's life, Marxists made a deliberate decision to employ the word 'socialism' instead of 'communism'. They did this because in continental European countries there were large and growing 'socialist' parties, founded in whole or in part by non-Marxists, and Marxists were becoming the intellectual leaders of all these parties. The word 'social-democracy' was widely used as synonymous with 'socialism'.

Towards the end of the nineteenth century, European Marxists, led by the theoretician Karl Kautsky, sometimes derided as 'the Pope of Marxism', gave up the idea of labor-voucher socialism, deciding that labor-vouchers would have no advantages, and some disadvantages, in the distribution of consumer goods. Money would therefore be retained in the earliest stage of socialism: people would continue to receive money wages. But in the organization of production, all Marxists still held that money prices would have no conceivable use. Industry would be run without any calculation of price or profit. The Marxists spoke of this as 'production for use', meaning that the people planning production would not think about what could be sold; they would simply think about what people 'needed'. The things to be produced and the ways to produce these things would all be determined by "a single vast plan" (Engels) without the use of prices or any notion of economic value. Planning of production would involve only physical quantities of goods and hours of labor, not prices.

In 1920 Ludwig von Mises published his famous article, "Economic Calculation in the Socialist Commonwealth," in which he made the bold claim that a socialist economy was impossible and would always remain impossible. What Mises meant was that there cannot exist a modern industrial economy yielding high levels of output, without a functioning system of market prices, and these market prices cannot be confined to consumer goods but must extend to factors of production ('means of production'). Market prices are vital, because they communicate precise and speedy information about the comparative scarcities of production goods such as raw materials, buildings, vehicles, and machines, and the shifting patterns of demand for consumer goods.

Following Mises's article there was a sporadic, prolonged debate around the world on the issue of 'economic calculation', involving economists and political writers of diverse ideological persuasions. The course of that debate has been analyzed by David Ramsay Steele in *From Marx to Mises*. The general conclusion is that non-market socialism, as envisaged by classical Marxism, is not practically feasible in any industrial or post-industrial economy.

Bigger and Bigger

A key proposition of Marxist theory was that, under capitalism, the size of business enterprises would increase indefinitely (not just in absolute numbers, but also in proportion to the total economy), tending to the limit that all of industry would be controlled by one enormous firm (*Capital*, Volume I, pp. 587–88). This theory, the 'centralization of capital', was vital to classical Marxism, both because it predicted a spontaneous movement in the direction of central planning, and therefore predicted that collectivism must inevitably replace capitalism, but also because it relieved Marxists of any need to worry about how socialist central planning would work. It was believed that capitalism itself was automatically solving that problem, which was seen as trivial and purely administrative.

Marx assumes that when a big firm and a small firm compete, the big firm will beat the small firm (Volume I, p. 586). Small firms either go out of business or are absorbed into bigger firms. We now know much more than Marx or anyone else knew at that time about the determinants of the size of firms. In a pioneering paper of 1937, Ronald Coase showed that a firm will co-ordinate production within a single organization when the cost of doing so is below the transaction costs of purchasing supplies in the market. Free-market competition gives us "the optimal amount of planning." Armen Alchian and Harold Demsetz extended Coase's work to encompass the advantages of team production, and Oliver Williamson showed the importance of "asset specificity," assets that have much more value if taken together than employed in separate lines of production, in determining firm size.

We now understand that there can be no over-riding tendency for the comparative size of firms to keep increasing indefinitely. There are economies of scale but there are also diseconomies of scale, and these just won't go away. Almost two centuries after Marx's prediction of the inexorable centralization of capital, US small businesses (under 500 employees) today account for over forty percent of output and over fifty percent of employment—this despite government policies which, on balance, favor the biggest corporations at the expense of smaller firms.

Historical Materialism

Classical Marxism gained a lot of its persuasive power from the doctrine known as historical materialism, which says that social change occurs by advances in technology ('forces of production') coming into conflict with economic and property rules ('relations of production'), leading to the adjustment of the relations of production, which then reshapes "the general character" of the whole culture, including politics, ideas, and values.

Historical materialism was effectively criticized over the years by many writers, including Mises in *Theory and History*. The most decisive criticism came with C.R. Hallpike's *Principles of Social Evolution* (1986). Hallpike did a study of numerous different cultures, measuring the correlation between mode of production and other institutions. He showed from this comparative analysis that mode of production is not a good predictor of other cultural features. Furthermore, Hallpike found that the more primitive a culture's technology, the more the technology correlates with social and cultural forms (p. 146). Thus, contrary to historical materialism, the forces of production do not look like primary determinants of changes in social structure in the stage of human development that most concerns Marxism, the last few thousand years, subsequent to the Neolithic Revolution.

And yet, there's an even more fundamental problem with Marx's position. Even if historical materialism were entirely correct, this could not support the claim that capitalism will be replaced by socialism. To reach that conclusion, we would need to show that socialism is more conducive to the development of the productive forces than capitalism is. Precisely on this point, both theoretical and practical developments have shown the opposite. The fullest development of the productive forces, in any industrial or post-industrial system, demands a functioning market. Any move toward central planning restricts and retards the productive forces and therefore tends to impoverish the population. The more advanced the industrial structure, the more devastation will ensue from trying to abolish 'commodity production'.

So successful has capitalism been in developing the productive forces—long after Marxists began claiming that capitalism had outlived its historic task—that today's Marxists no longer accuse capitalism of being a fetter on the productive forces. In the 1930s, Marxists claimed that the forces of production were not being allowed to develop as rapidly as they should, whereas now leftists are more likely to claim that the forces of production are developing far too rapidly. Today, at every turn, we see the Left opposing the development of technology and even opposing economic growth. It's somewhat ironic that the 'progressives' have now become the chief enemies of progress.

The End of Marx's System

Marx's economic theory (to which he devoted most of his mature years) is an inspired and impressive structure, yet it is based on demonstrable errors. His labor theory of value and the account of 'surplus value' that goes with it are seriously mistaken.

A fundamental weakness of the theory was brought out by the Austrian economist Eugen von Böhm-Bawerk. The famous contradiction between Volumes I–II and Volume III of *Capital* cannot be resolved. The mathematical expression of this contradiction, the 'Transformation Problem', is insoluble, but aside from this technical point, the attempt to deny that saved means of production make a contribution to the value of output is unsound and cannot be rescued.

Other devastating criticisms were made by the Unitarian clergyman, Dante scholar, self-avowed socialist, and brilliant economist Philip Wicksteed, who wrote a remarkable article on Marx's *Capital* in 1884 for the English socialist journal *To-Day*, which ultimately caused George Bernard Shaw to abandon his belief in Marxian economic theory.

In the last years of his life, Marx did no work on *Capital*, and it is not known precisely how aware he was of new theoretical developments in economics. He may or may not have known that economics was placed on a new basis with the 'marginal revolution' of the 1870s, which soon led to the theory of Marginal Productivity, and this may or may not have caused him to stop working on *Capital*. According to marginal productivity, all contributors to production are paid their marginal product. There is nothing left over; every contribution to output gets its share and there is no 'surplus'. The entire apparatus of labor-values and their 'transformation' into prices of production was a pointless, unnecessary, and intellectually makeshift distraction. Marginal productivity has been abundantly corroborated by a vast amount of empirical data—and marginal productivity theory makes numerous predictions not made by any alternative theory.

Peterson Misreads Marx

Peterson's own criticism of Marxist economics is marred by misunderstandings. To mention just one example, he criticizes the doctrine that the capitalist's income is surplus-value extracted from workers by noting that capitalists often perform useful functions in directing production (Žižek debate, 24.20). But Marx distinguishes management from capital. The capitalist hands over the work of direction and supervision to "a special kind of wage laborer," the manager (*Capital*, Volume I, p. 314).

When Marx talks about profit as surplus value, he is referring to what Austrian economists call pure interest, what neoclassical economists sometimes call 'normal profit', the rate of return on invested capital. If you inherit shares in a mutual fund from your grandmother, you can indefinitely pocket the proceeds without lifting a finger or even knowing anything about the production processes that yields those proceeds. You might be in a coma; the money still comes to you. Marx is entirely correct that there is a return to capital which is independent of the owner's current efforts. If the owner also works in the company as a manager, he will get wages of management in addition to his return on capital invested. Marx's position on this point is thus quite similar to that of an Austrian-school economist or a modern mainstream economist.

It's no defense of the income from capital to point to the labor of management or even to imaginative entrepreneurship, which can also be performed by someone hired by the owner, instead of by the owner (though there is entrepreneurial judgment in knowing whom to hire). The return on capital has to be defended differently, for example by the claim that people who save out of their income and place their savings at the disposal of a productive enterprise are entitled to a return on their savings. This return comes not from "unpaid labor," as Marx erroneously contends (any more than the worker's wage comes from 'unpaid capital' or 'unpaid electricity'). The return comes from the contribution their savings make to output: the savings purchase means of production, which increase output. Of course, the applied-ethical conclusion does not follow from the economic theory alone; it requires ethical premises. But the required ethical premisses are natural and intuitive.

Limitations of Lobsters

Communism as Marx envisioned it is not possible. One reason for this is Mises's point that an advanced industrial economy requires a price system, a price system requires a market, and a market requires private ownership in the means of production. (Private ownership here does not exclude ownership by worker's co-operatives or by voluntary communes, nor does it exclude a possible future non-capitalist free-market arrangement where business corporations have been supplanted by individual proprietorships and small partnerships.) Any serious attempt to take all industrial assets into ownership by 'the community' and dispense with monetary exchange must precipitate a catastrophic drop in output, and therefore in the real incomes of the masses.

But there is something else. In 1911 Robert Michels made a momentous intellectual breakthrough: he showed that all complex organizations give rise to a division between officials and ordinary members, or leaders and led. The greater the size and complexity of any organization, the wider the abyss between leaders and led. This is the 'iron law of oligarchy'.

Peterson argues against socialism that "hierarchy" is inevitable because of biological necessity, and to illustrate this brings in his much-ridiculed example of lobsters. Now, if we look at cultures with very simple organization, such as the BaMbuti pygmies or traditional Eskimos, we find very little 'hierarchy', almost none apart from a few distinctions based on age and sex. While we could quibble and say that we perceive some hierarchy in these cultures, they come quite close, in their comparative lack of hierarchy, to what Marxists at one time celebrated as 'primitive communism'. They are a pretty good refutation of the lobster argument for the inevitability of hierarchy.

The key here is complex organization. Marx's communism would involve the deliberate planning of production on a world scale. (It would thus be unlike Kropotkin's anarcho-communism, which, lacking the worldwide division of labor co-ordinated either by market or by plan, could only exist, as everyone now seems to agree, at a low level of real incomes.) Communist central planning would necessarily entail extremely large and complex organizations. These organizations can only be bureaucracies or oligarchies, pitted against the mass of producers, consumers, and voters.

Marx's conception of communism involves something that would later be called 'participatory democracy'. The great achievement of Michels was to show, in 1911, before the term 'participatory democracy' was even coined, that participatory democracy can never exist. The whole conception of a stateless society organizing production according to "a single vast plan" which somehow expresses the will of the world's population, is forever unattainable.

This leads to a more general conclusion. The attempt to organize industry by means of central planning will not only precipitate a huge reduction in output and therefore mass immiseration. The attempt must lead to an all-powerful and brutal state, just the opposite of what classical Marxists wanted or expected. Because of Michels's law of oligarchy, the officials of the central planning administration must become a new ruling class (or perhaps the front men for a new ruling class). The state cannot wither away, but can only expand mightily.

The socialist George Orwell expressed the fear that "economic totalitarianism," which he believed to be inseparable from socialism, must necessarily lead to political totalitarianism (Steele 2017, pp. 300–01) and we can now see that Orwell's fear was fully warranted. Friedrich Hayek made a related argument in "Why the Worst Get on Top," the celebrated chapter in his *Road to Serfdom*.

Classical Marxism aimed at a free and prosperous social order in which "the free development of each is the condition for the free development of all," and no public instrument of coercion would be necessary. But classical Marxism believed it could achieve this by abolishing the market and replacing it with "conscious" direction. Since any serious attempt at replacing the market with central planning requires an all-powerful state and the crushing of opposition, Marxists who succeed in gaining political power are faced with a choice. Either give up the attempt to abolish the market, or give up any hope for democracy or personal freedom. Western European social democrats took the first option, and continued to take it after 1917; the Bolsheviks took the second option.

Dictatorship of the Proletariat

Peterson somewhat obscures the exegesis of Marx's views by focusing on Marx's term, "dictatorship of the proletariat." (Peterson announces he will go by the *Communist Manifesto*, but keeps referring to the dictatorship of the proletariat, which is never mentioned in the *Communist Manifesto*.) The dictatorship of the proletariat is conceived as the brief transition from capitalism to communism. In communist society, there would, from the very outset, be no proletariat and no state. In Marx's view, the dictatorship of the proletariat is to be a democratic republic, like the Paris Commune, not a 'dictatorship' in the modern sense. Marx didn't think it would be run by a single political party. There would be no curbs on free expression of opinion and all elected positions would be revocable—it would be easy for voters to recall delegates (Hunt 1984, pp. 152–161, 326–336).

Marx studied Roman law and later in life read through the works of Aeschylus in the original Greek every year. The 'dictatorship of the proletariat' is a classical scholar's witticism: it combines two entities from ancient Rome: *dictatura*, a temporary emergency government to deal with crisis conditions; *proletariat*, the class of all those who own nothing except their children.

The economist Jean Charles Léonard de Sismondi had proposed in 1819 that the old Roman word 'proletariat' could be applied to the new class of industrial wage workers. In *The Eighteenth Brumaire of Louis Bonaparte*, Marx quotes Sismondi's remark: "The Roman proletariat lived at the expense of society, while modern society lives at the expense of the proletariat." Marx predicted in the 1840s that this new proletariat, still a minority in every country, would become "the immense majority" of the population and would be driven by the automatic mechanisms of capitalist development to overthrow the bourgeoisie and institute communism.

Another assertion by Peterson is that Marx and Engels advocated, not just a social revolution, but "bloody, violent" revolution. When Peterson said this in the debate with Žižek, there was mock cheering, presumably from leftists who believe that a bloody, violent revolution is desirable in the

US today. Peterson's assertion is a bit misleading, not merely because he interpolates the words 'bloody, violent' which are not in the *Communist Manifesto*. The *Communist Manifesto*, was written in 1847 and published in 1848, the 'Year of Revolutions'. Not a single European country in 1847 had an electoral system which would enable a majority of the population, even a very considerable majority, to exert any legal political influence, let alone to assume power. Many liberals, under those circumstances, considered an armed uprising the only way to get reforms, and of course, the attempted revolutions of 1848 were all liberal and 'national' uprisings, with no communist influence.

Marx and Engels tacitly excluded the US from countries where a "forcible overthrow" would be needed, and later, as effective democracy spread to more and more countries, they explicitly excluded the US, Britain, Holland, and France. These were countries where they believed the communist social revolution could be consummated by peaceful, legal methods. Marx and Engels denounced all violent political acts in democratic countries, and even in non-democracies, like Germany, as long as non-violent organization and political pressure were practically feasible (Hunt 1984, pp. 325–336). Later, Lenin and the Bolsheviks energetically obscured and misrepresented Marx and Engels's very solid commitment to peaceful, legal revolution.

Peterson associates bad outcomes with bad motivations. Thus, he concludes that the failures and atrocities of one Communist regime after another demonstrate that Marxism was motivated by hatred, not by love (2017, 1:11:10). But the road to Hell may be paved with good intentions, and when application of a theory repeatedly gives horrible results, this may simply demonstrate that the theory is faulty.

One of several things that Marx and Engels failed to take into account was the possibility that the great majority of the working class would become increasingly content with capitalism, and would never develop any desire for communism, seeing it as totally impracticable and irrelevant. Marx made serious intellectual blunders, and the world turned out very differently from anything he had imagined possible, but he no more intended anything like the Gulag than Jesus of Nazareth intended General Franco's *Terror Blanco*.

Was Bolshevism Excessively Rational?

Dr. Peterson likes to claim that we, in the modern world, are too much guided by rationality and should be guided more by "values" and "meaning" which we can find in ancient myths and other stories. Peterson says that Communism was the result of rational design, implying that it would not have been so disastrous if the Bolsheviks had been less reasonable and more open to non-rational influences. (This point is touched on in *12 Rules for Life*, p. 219, and more explicitly unpacked in *Maps of Meaning*, pp. 12–13).

The Bolsheviks, who changed their name to Communists in 1919, adhered to a specific set of beliefs: some remnants of classical Marxism combined with new theories which were at odds with classical Marxism. This set of beliefs implied that it was possible to construct 'socialism' in Russia and overtake the rest of the world in output per head and therefore income. The attempt to pursue this goal by collectivization of agriculture and central planning of industry was bound to lead to massive repression, mass murder, and the enslavement of the workers (as Stalin and the others recognized when they embarked upon it). Russia, which before World War I had been the world's fifth industrial producer and growing rapidly, fell further and further behind the West and by the 1980s had become a basket case for all the world to see. Soviet Communism, with all its repercussions throughout the world, retarded world economic development by approximately a century. All that blood and suffering was for nothing, or less than nothing.

The specific set of beliefs held by the Communists may be considered rational, but they rested on unfounded assumptions, some of them pointed out by critics from the outset. Many of the people slaughtered by the Bolsheviks in 1918–1920 were Mensheviks—Marxists who maintained that what the Bolsheviks were doing was contrary to Marxism. Mensheviks represent classical Marxism, social democracy, which proclaimed that a socialist revolution cannot succeed if it comes 'before its time' in a predominantly peasant country and cannot be imposed by a minority *coup* on an unwilling population.

The failure of a bad theory does not show the failure of all theories, much less the failure of rationality. The US founders in 1787 also had a theory. It was also rational, but it contained fewer errors. It may be too early to say, but so far the American experiment does not appear to have been as costly to humankind as the Soviet experiment. Peterson is mistaken to conclude that the experience of Communism shows the limitations of rationality and the need for reason to be supplemented by myth.

Peterson is very insistent that it is wrong to think that much can be achieved by a dramatic rise in everyone's material well-being, their real income. He thinks that Dostoevsky refuted Marx in advance, when he predicted that people with super-high incomes would smash things up just to create some excitement (Žižek debate, 30:25; Peterson 2017b, 1:20:05). This is a strange argument for Peterson to muster against Marxism, when he perceives the 'Communist' countries as being Marxist. The Communist countries were unable to raise people's real incomes, while the Western capitalist economies have been brilliantly successful at this.

Peterson maintains that pursuit of happiness is not a proper goal, and that more income does not give you more happiness. Yet pursuit of happiness is a recognizable goal in all cultures, and research indicates that more income is significantly correlated with more happiness (Diener and Oishi 2000). However, regardless of the soundness of Peterson's position on this point, it's inappropriate for him to bring this up when discussing the record of Soviet Communism. Whether Communism was right or wrong to aim at making people happier by raising their incomes, Communism was a wretched failure in this regard, because of the means chosen: attempted replacement of the market by central planning. Dostoevsky's prediction has not been borne out. If we look at the highest-income parts of the world: say, Sweden, Switzerland, or the highest-income counties in the US, we don't observe people randomly smashing things. Predominantly, we observe peace, harmony, very low crime rates, very low rates of mental disorder, deep satisfaction, and deep love of life. The trick is to get the rest of the world up to these income levels, and it is simply absurd to suppose that anything other than private property and a functioning market economy can accomplish that.

David Gordon and Ying Tang

Postmodern Neo-Marxism

Jordan Peterson often talks about "postmodern neo-Marxism." By neo-Marxism he mainly means the ideas of the Frankfurt School: Horkheimer, Adorno, Benjamin, and Marcuse. These writers revised Marxism after World War I because of the absence of socialist revolutions in the West and disappointing features of the new 'Marxist' state in Russia. They discarded certain assumptions previously embraced by Marxists, notably the unique role of the working-class in carrying through the socialist revolution. Yet they continued to maintain the fundamental assumptions of the Leninist variety of Marxism, including a hatred for the market economy, a conviction that 'commodity production' must be abolished, an acceptance that the analysis by Marx in *Capital* is correct, and the judgment that capitalism is inherently exploitative. They failed to grasp that advanced industrial production cannot be separated from the market economy. They lamented the rise of 'bureaucratic socialism' in Russia, without appreciating that this is the ineluctable result of any attempt to replace the market with central planning.

Instead of concluding that the workers were not becoming socialist because, objectively, socialism had nothing whatsoever to offer them, these neo-Marxists tried to discover ways in which capitalism was fixing the minds of the workers through ideological manipulation. They condemned the culture of capitalist societies because it failed to preach a uniformly anti-capitalist ideology. They despised popular culture because it was mass-produced by an industry which sought profitability, even though it immensely enriched people's lives.

In 1919 the Communist International (Comintern) was founded, instigating the formation of Communist Parties in every country, funded and tightly controlled by Moscow, and violently hostile to the democratic left. The Frankfurt neo-Marxists were free of Comintern control, and thus free to embrace things strictly forbidden by Moscow, such as Freud, Picasso, and jazz (though in fact they hated jazz as part of capitalism's culture industry). By assimilating Freud and returning to Hegel, they were able to break loose from scientific objectivity and indulge themselves in endless non sequiturs formulated in atrocious prose.

According to Peterson, Soviet Communism became impossible for French intellectuals to defend, because of the revelations about Soviet atrocities, especially by Solzhenitsyn, followed by the collapse of the Soviet Union, so Marxists regrouped and tried a different scheme. This account seems to attribute to conscious strategy what was probably more improvised, and it doesn't fit the timing very well. The Frankfurt School goes back to the 1920s (and so does Antonio Gramsci, who is often associated with neo-Marxism or Western Marxism). The philosophical ideas that would later come to be called postmodernism became trendy in France in the 1960s, a decade before *The Gulag Archipelago* became available to French readers and two decades before the abrupt end of the Soviet Union.

'Postmodernism' is usually attributed to Michel Foucault, Jacques Derrida, Jean-François Lyotard, and Jean Baudrillard, but these writers had no common program or platform, and probably mutually disagreed as much as they agreed. Although most French intellectuals shared in a leftist tilt heavily influenced by Soviet Marxism, postmodernism was not especially friendly to Marxism. An orthodox Marxist would be bound to denounce postmodernism, and some of the harshest critics of postmodernism have been leftists, not only orthodox Marxists such as Alex Callinicos, but many others, for instance Noam Chomsky, David Detmer, Terry Eagleton, and Alan Sokal. Aside from philosophical criticisms of postmodern epistemology, leftists as different as Chomsky and Žižek have diagnosed postmodernist discourse as a vehicle for sounding super-radical without actually doing anything to endanger the prevailing system of power.

What we now call postmodernism was sometimes earlier called post-structuralism, denoting those philosophers who rebelled against the French philosophical fashion of 'structuralism', represented by such thinkers as Saussure, Lévi-Strauss, and Althusser. Though these movements arose in a French context, structuralism and post-structuralism had some following among American literary theorists.

Peterson chooses to define postmodernism as the view that there is always an infinity of available 'narratives', with nothing to choose between them. This is quite close to another common definition: that postmodernism says there is no objective truth, only numerous incompatible interpretations. Yet another formula is that postmodernism rejects all 'grand meta-narratives', which would place postmodernism in stark opposition to Marxism.

Isn't the 'postmodernist' view that there is no objective truth a pernicious doctrine, and isn't Peterson right to oppose it with an insistence on 'truth'? Unfortunately, Peterson's views on truth are at least as wobbly as those of the postmodernists. Peterson frequently denounces 'lying' and praises respect for the truth. This has a nice ring to it. But Peterson's view of what constitutes truth (and therefore what constitutes lying) is different from that of most ordinary people and most philosophers.

There is a standard theory of truth, which has been accepted by humans for thousands of years, was given a classic statement by Aristotle in the fourth century B.C.E., is taken for granted in courts of law whenever witnesses promise to tell the truth, and is taken for granted in the evaluation of scientific research and many other areas. It's called the correspondence theory of truth; it says that a statement is true if and only if it corresponds to facts or to reality (a proposition, 'p', is true iff p). Peterson opposes this theory, and maintains a version of the pragmatist theory of truth, which says that a statement is true if it is useful. His own version of this theory is distinctively personal and we don't know of anyone who argued for it before Peterson (though it may be vaguely presaged in Nietzsche). Peterson's theory of truth says that "truth" is what contributes to Darwinian fitness.

According to Peterson, and any form of the pragmatist theory of truth, it can be 'true' to say something which describes reality inaccurately and 'false' to say something which describes reality accurately. If Peterson were to rigorously apply his own theory of truth, the Ninth Commandment, "Thou shalt not bear false witness against thy neighbor" would be translated as 'Tell that story about your neighbor which will maximize your reproductive chances'. No doubt Peterson wouldn't agree with this conclusion; he has not thought through the implications of his own definition, or definitions, of truth.

In addition to his pragmatist-Darwinist theory of truth, and logically quite independent of it, Peterson also insists that 'meaningful' stories, for example, the story of Cain and Abel are "true," even though what the story says never actually happened (and may not even be true by his pragmatist-Darwinist definition). In this broader sense a Bible story is 'true' for Peterson if it means a lot to him or to other people. It would be fine if Peterson were to say that such stories are metaphorically, or symbolically, or spiritually 'true', as distinguished from ordinary literal truth, but Peterson resists any such admission, and insists on saying that an account of something that did not, in point of fact, actually happen, can be 'more true' than an accurate account of something which really did occur.

Peterson has a feeble grasp on the notion of truth, and is not well-placed to criticize the postmodernists for their 'relativism' or indeed to reproach anyone for 'lying'.

Is Postmodern Neo-Marxism a Thing?

Peterson has adopted a definition of postmodernism (that there is nothing to choose between numerous competing narratives), which he applies to Derrida and (more dubiously) Foucault and then extends to other 'postmodernists'. Peterson talks as though postmodernism and Marxism are inherently favorable, but this isn't so clear.

Where Peterson seems to be right is that neo-Marxists, most of them now influenced by postmodernism, replace the class struggle between bourgeoisie and proletariat with a more general picture of a struggle between all oppressed groups and the dominant society. Thus the 'struggles' of blacks, gays, trans people, and other minorities can be arrayed against the racist, capitalist patriarchy.

The significant point here, carried over from earlier Marxism, is that there can be no resolution short of revolution. Thus, for instance, the neo-Marxist leadership of Black Lives Matter pointedly does not propose concrete practical measures to crack down on discriminatory behavior in police departments. They have no interest in improving inter-community relations or making the behavior of police officers more impartial. We will know that they are serious about combating racism on the day that they congratulate a police department for its excellent disciplinary policies. As of now, they only want everything to get worse until there is a general conflagration, out of which there will somehow emerge a new and wondrous form of society—with people just like them, they imagine, in positions of power.

In the Peterson-Žižek debate, Žižek made a big point of asking Peterson who these "Marxists" were, that he was always talking about. Peterson seemed at a loss for a clear answer, and this contributed to the impression that Žižek did somewhat better than Peterson in the debate. But here Peterson seems to have been on track.

To take the most conspicuous case, Judith Butler has been a huge influence on the vast armies of students who graduate each year in such subjects as Culture Studies, Gender Studies, Women's Studies, and Africana Studies (but *not* philosophy). Although Butler does not make an unhealthy fetish out of clarity or cogency, we can at least conclude from Butler's books that her thinking is a mixture of Frankfurt School 'neo-Marxism' and 'postmodernism'. The next most obvious example is Herbert Marcuse, a direct influence on Butler and also independently a powerful influence on faculty and students. Marcuse is a neo-Marxist, whose books are still selling briskly among students. Marcuse is not a postmodernist, but for some purposes Hegel will do as well as Derrida. The history of the intellectual origins of Wokishness has yet to be written (though James Lindsay has made a start), but it looks as if Butler and Marcuse must loom very large in it. We could easily pinpoint the postmodernist and neo-Marxist DNA of numerous lesser "second-hand purveyors of ideas," such as Kimberlé Crenshaw, Robin DiAngelo, or Gayatri Spivak.

And so, despite Peterson's inaccuracies about Marxism, and uncertainties about postmodernism and truth, postmodern neo-Marxism really exists, is growing in muscle with every Commencement ceremony, and is likely the biggest intellectual source for the ideology of the Wokish Left.

What Would Postmodern Neo-Marxists Do if They Came to Power?

A regime in which neo-Marxists, postmodernist or not, hold power has never existed, so any account of what it would be like involves some speculation. There would be no social revolution eliminating, at one stroke, racism, sexism, and everything upsetting to think about, because that is an unrealistic fantasy. There would be no outright attempt at replacing capitalism with a centrally planned system, because the Left has now lost all faith in any such project.

The most likely outcome is a battery of piecemeal attempts to attack various evils of capitalism, by interventionist programs, no doubt by hate campaigns against an endless succession of deplorable groups and individuals. Given the elitism of neo-Marxists, as illustrated by Adorno's withering contempt for popular culture and for the political opinions of ordinary Americans, the interventionism of a neo-Marxist regime would probably be unresponsive to plebeian tastes and would have no patience for the deplorable working class. Neo-Marxists have never displayed any undue concern for individual rights or liberties.

So, we can expect an authoritarian regime, heavily regulated yet retaining the basic functional elements of capitalism, which would soon abolish democracy and impose conformity on every aspect of intellectual life. Regrettably, the only word in common circulation to denote such a system is the rather imprecise term, 'fascism'. Jordan Peterson has rendered an outstanding service in alerting millions of people to this extremely real and extremely present danger.[1]

Bibliography

Adorno, Theodor W. 2019. *Night Music: Essays on Music, 1928–1962*. Seagull.

Adorno, Theodor W., Else Frenkel-Brunswik, Daniel J. Levinson, and R. Nevitt Sandford. 2019 [1950]. *The Authoritarian Personality*. Verso.

Alchian, Armen A., and Harold Demsetz. 1972. Production, Information Costs, and Economic Organization. *American Economic Review* 62:5 (December).

Böhm-Bawerk, Eugen von. 1959 [1884–1921]. *Capital and Interest*. Libertarian Press.

———. 1962. *Shorter Classics of Eugen von Böhm-Bawerk*. Libertarian Press.

---

[1] We're grateful to David Ramsay Steele for his many helpful suggestions for improving earlier drafts of this chapter.

Butler, Judith. 1997. *The Psychic Life of Power: Theories in Subjection*. Stanford University Press.

———. 2006. *Gender Trouble: Feminism and the Subversion of Identity*. Routledge.

Callinicos, Alex. 1991. *Against Postmodernism: A Marxist Critique*. Polity.

Carroll, Glenn R., and David J. Teece, 1999. *Firms, Markets, and Hierarchies: The Transaction Cost Economic Perspective*. Oxford University Press.

Coase, Ronald H. 1937. The Nature of the Firm. *Economica* NS IV. Reprinted in Coase 1988.

———. 1988. *The Firm, the Market, and the Law*. University of Chicago Press.

Chomsky, Noam. 1995. Noam Chomsky on Postmodernism. <http://bactra.org/chomsky-on-postmodernism.html>.

Courtois, Stéphane, et. al. 1999. *The Black Book of Communism: Crimes, Terror, Repression*. Harvard University Press.

Detmer, David. 2003. *Challenging Postmodernism: Philosophy and the Politics of Truth*. Prometheus.

Diener, Ed, and Shigehiro Oishi. 2000. Money and Happiness: Income and Subjective Well-being across Nations. In Diener and Suh 2000.

Diener, Ed, and Eunkook M. Suh, eds. 2000. *Culture and Subjective Well-being*. MIT Press.

Eagleton, Terry. 1996. *The Illusions of Postmodernism*. Blackwell.

Engels, Frederick. 1987 [1878]. Anti-Dühring: Herr Eugen Dühring's Revolution in Science. In *Karl Marx Frederick Engels Collected Works*, Volume 25. International.

———. 1989 [1880]. Socialism Utopian and Scientific. In *Karl Marx Frederick Engels Collected Works*, Volume 24. International.

Gordon, David. 1986. *Critics of Marxism*. Transaction.

———. 1991 [1990]. *Resurrecting Marx: The Analytical Marxists on Freedom, Exploitation, and Justice*. Routledge.

———. 2020. Wicksteed on Surplus Value. *Mises Wire*. Mises Institute <https://mises.org/wire/wicksteed-surplus-value>.

Hallpike, C.R. 1986. *The Principles of Social Evolution*. Oxford University Press.

Hayek, F.A., ed. 1935. *Collectivist Economic Planning*. Routledge.

———. 2017 [1944]. *The Road to Serfdom*. University of Chicago Press.

Held, David. 1980. *Introduction to Critical Theory*. University of California Press.

Horkheimer, Max. 1972. *Critical Theory: Selected Essays*. Herder and Herder.

<http://bactra.org/chomsky-on-postmodernism.html>

Horkheimer, Max, and Theodor W. Adorno. 1972 [1944]. *Dialectic of Enlightenment*. Herder and Herder.

Hunt, Richard N. 1974. *The Political Ideas of Marx and Engels I: Marxism and Totalitarian Democracy 1818–1850*. University of Pittsburgh Press.

———. 1984. *The Political Ideas of Marx and Engels II: Classical Marxism 1850–1895*. University of Pittsburgh Press.

Kotkin, Stephen. 2017. *Stalin: Waiting for Hitler, 1929–1941*. Penguin.

Lindsay, James. 2020. The Truth about Critical Methods. <www.youtube.com/watch?v=rSHL-rSMIrohttps://www.youtube.com/watch?v=rSHL-rSMIro>.

———. 2020. Woke Utopia: The End of the West and a New Cult. <www.youtube.com/watch?v=dE8p-mcFdNg>.

Marcuse, Herbert. 1971. *An Essay on Liberation*. Beacon Press.

———. 1989. *Counterrevolution and Revolt*. Beacon Press.

———. 2007. *The Essential Marcuse: Selected Writings of Philosopher and Social Critic Herbert Marcuse*. Beacon Press.

Marx, Karl. 1970 [1876]. *Capital: A Critical Analysis of Capitalist Production*. Volume I. Progress.

———. 1972 [1894] *Capital: A Critique of Political Economy*. Volume III. Progress.

———. 1979 [1852] The Eighteenth Brumaire of Louis Bonaparte. *In Karl Marx Frederick Engels Collected Works*, Volume 11. International.

———. 1989 [1873]. Critique of the Gotha Programme. In *Karl Marx Frederick Engels Collected Works*, Volume 24. International.

Marx, Karl, and Friedrich Engels. 1976 [1848]. Manifesto of the Communist Party. In *Karl Marx Frederick Engels Collected Works*, Volume 6. International.

McInnes, Neil. 1972. *The Western Marxists*. Library Press.

Michels, Robert. 1966 [1911]. *Political Parties: A Sociological Study of the Oligarchical Tendencies of Modern Democracy*. Collier-Macmillan.

Mises, Ludwig Edler von. 1920. Die Wirtschaftsrechnung im sozialistischen Gemeinwesen. *Archiv für Sozialwis-senschaften und Sozialpolitk* 47:1 (April).

———. 1935. Economic Calculation in the Socialist Common-wealth. Translation of Mises 1920. In Hayek 1935.

———. 1966 [1949]. *Human Action: A Treatise on Economics*. Regnery.

———. 2007 [1957]. *Theory and History: An Interpretation of Social and Economic Evolution*. Ludwig von Mises Institute.

———. 2015 [1944]. *Omnipotent Government: The Rise of the Total State and Total War*. Ludwig von Mises Institute.

Peterson, Jordan B. 1999. *Maps of Meaning: The Architecture of Belief*. Routledge.

———. 2017. Identity Politics and the Marxist Lie of White Privilege.
<www.youtube.com/watch?v=8u3aTURVEC8&t=1561s>.

———. 2017b. Existentialism: Nietzsche, Dostoevsky, and Kierkegaard.
<https://m.youtube.com/watch?v=4qZ3EsrKPsc&t=4734s>.

———. 2018. *12 Rules for Life: An Antidote to Chaos*. Random House Canada.

———. 2021. *Beyond Order: 12 More Rules for Life*. Penguin.

Peterson, Jordan B., and Slavoj Žižek. 2019. Slavoj Žižek Debates Jordan Peterson.
<www.youtube.com/watch?v=qsHJ3LvUWTs&t=1790s>.

Sokal, Alan, and Jean Bricmont. 1999. *Intellectual Impostures: Post-Modern Philosophers' Abuse of Science*. Profile.

Steele, David Ramsay. 1992. *From Marx to Mises: Post-Capitalist Society and the Challenge of Economic Calculation*. Open Court.

———. 2005. Life, Liberty, and the Treadmill. *Liberty* 19:2. Reprinted in Steele 2019.

———. 2017. *Orwell Your Orwell: A Worldview on the Slab*. St. Augustine's Press.

———. 2019. *The Mystery of Fascism: David Ramsay Steele's Greatest Hits*. St. Augustine's Press.

Tupy, Marian L. 2017. 100 Years of Communism: Death and Deprivation. *Cato Institute Commentary*. <www.cato.org/commentary/100-years-communism-death-deprivation>.

Turnbull, Colin M. 1988 [1962]. *The Forest People*. Simon and Schuster.

Wicksteed, Philip Henry. 1884. *Das Kapital*: A Criticism. *To-Day* (October). Reprinted in Wicksteed 1933, Volume II.

———. 1933 [1910]. *The Common Sense of Political Economy*. Two volumes. Routledge.

Williamson, Oliver E. 1983 [1975]. *Markets and Hierarchies: Analysis and Antitrust Implications*. Collier-Macmillan.

———. 1985. *The Economic Institutions of Capitalism: Firms, Markets, Relational Contracting*. Collier-Macmillan.

[4]
Does Jordan Peterson's Appeal to Authenticity Make Him a Hypocrite?

MADELEINE SHIELD

What is your 'authentic self'—is it something that you design and create, or something to be discovered within yourself? At present, the philosophical literature remains somewhat divided on this question. This lack of consensus is also reflected in popular culture; in fact, ordinary appeals to the notion of an authentic self often involve diverse, if not contradictory, views on selfhood (Taylor 1992; Ferrara 1998). Just as authenticity is invoked when appealing to the idea that the self is *innate* (discovering your authentic self), it is equally present in arguments which characterize the self as *acquired* (creating your authentic self). These opposed notions can even coincide within the same worldview—a case in point being the argument for authenticity made by Canadian author and professor Jordan Peterson.

As we will see, Peterson's different ideas about selfhood demonstrate how this conflict underlies popular discussions on authenticity, and highlight some of the metaphysical and moral challenges that often accompany it. While viewing the self as constrained in some aspects, yet autonomous in others, is not inherently contradictory, it seems as if understandings of the self as *exclusively* either innate or acquired are metaphysically opposed to one another. That is to say: if one is true, then the other must be false. Furthermore, as Simon Feldman (2015) has pointed out, using authenticity to support a range of different perspectives is potentially problematic because it renders the concept less about being 'true' to oneself, and more of "an alluring pretext for convincing people to adopt quite varied visions of the good life" (p. 163). For this reason, he asks that we consider closely whether it is *really* authenticity that is being valued in a given contemporary context, or whether the term is merely being deployed—rather inauthentically—in support of a particular worldview.

Why Peterson Says We Should Be Authentic

Jordan Peterson's *12 Rules for Life: An Antidote to Chaos* promotes personal authenticity on the basis that it is necessary to the wellbeing of both the individual and the state. The concept appears in Rule 6, titled "Set your house in perfect order before you criticize the world" (p. 112), and also in Rule 8: "Tell the truth—or, at least, don't lie" (p. 146). Here, Peterson rails against inauthentic behavior, which he defines as continuing "to perceive and act in ways [one's] own experience has demonstrated false" (p. 152). As the chapter titles indicate, for him this mostly involves an avoidance of truth and personal responsibility; thus, he frames authenticity as a practice of honesty and accountability.

Throughout the book, Peterson appeals to authentic living as an effective means of strengthening one's ability to overcome various challenges and thereby to improve one's enjoyment of life. "Have you cleaned up your life?" he asks. "If the answer is no, here's something to try: *Start to stop doing what you know to be wrong* . . . begin to say what you really think" (p. 117). He associates this kind of honesty with a range of benefits, some more obvious than others: "Your life will become simpler and less complicated. Your judgment will improve. You will untangle your past. You will become stronger and less bitter. You will move more confidently into the future. You will stop making your life unnecessarily difficult" (p. 118).

Peterson also ascribes wider, much more serious consequences to inauthentic behavior. He argues that there is a direct causal relationship between the individual proclivity "to falsify [one's] own day-to-day personal experience" and social totalitarianism (pp. 152, 155). Just as inauthenticity corrupts the soul, it also corrupts the state—hence Peterson's contention that it is "deceit that still threatens us, most profoundly, today" (pp. 155, 118). So how does one embody the authentic, under Peterson's view? As we'll see, his characterization of the journey toward personal authenticity is complicated by his contradictory understandings of selfhood. This reflects the common tension underlying appeals to authenticity—that is, whether one's authentic self is something to be *discovered* or *created*.

'Creating' Peterson's Authentic Self

Peterson's characterization of the authentic self as entirely self-determined occurs through his valorizing of individualism and social autonomy. Although he does not specify a target audience for his book, it is no secret that the readers of *12 Rules for Life* are primarily white, middle-class men (Burton 2020; Bryant 2018). This is unsurprising given Peterson's brand of self-help advice, which has been described by *The Guardian* as a "tough-love, stern-dad" style, and by *The New York Times* as "stern fatherly lectures to young men on how to . . . grow up and take responsibility for their own lives." (Lynskey 2018: paragraph. 4; Brooks 2018: paragraph 2). As these characterizations indicate, Peterson's work carries a strong emphasis on personal accountability and self-reliance. In line with this, he frames the practice of authenticity as the individual's responsibility to account for their own failures and to achieve their own success. He asks his readers: "Are you working hard on your career, or even your job, or are you letting bitterness and resentment hold you back and drag you down?" (p. 117). An authentic response to this, Peterson argues, consists in recognizing that personal failure lies in having had the wrong aim or methods, while an inauthentic one blames that failure on external factors, such as other people or the unfairness of the world (pp. 152, 118).

Peterson also believes that we have a wider social responsibility to enact this kind of authentic behavior. He imagines a scenario in which the reader's 'power-hungry' colleague begins to introduce counterproductive and inconvenient rules into the workplace. Refusing to speak up in this situation, contends Peterson, would be an example of inauthenticity which contributes not only to the corruption of the authentic individual's 'soul', but to a much wider "process of bureaucratic stagnation and oppression" (p. 152). Under his view, to act authentically in this scenario would instead be to either complain, so as to elicit the change one desires, or to simply "find a job somewhere else" (p. 75). This characterization of authenticity implies that one always has the capacity, and therefore the responsibility, to choose one's path in life.

By appealing to individualism and social autonomy in his framing of authenticity, Peterson's argument presupposes that one's authentic self is something to be created, rather than discovered. It is because of his insistence that individuals are not dependent on external factors to achieve success that Peterson has been labeled "The twenty-first century's most vocal proponent of self-reliance" (Burton 2020, paragraph 1). Since, on Peterson's view, assuming personal responsibility is central to acting authentically, it is unsurprising that he frames the authentic self as being entirely free and self-determined. In line with this, Peterson's advice concerning authenticity is prescriptive only insofar as it states that one must be honest, with oneself and with others, and that one must not deny one's social autonomy. In apparently all other aspects, he urges his readers to follow their own standards of judgment in life. "You can rely on yourself for guidance," he writes. "You don't have to adhere to some external, arbitrary code of behavior" (p. 117). Here, the individual appears to be entirely free to choose their own conception of an authentic life—as long as it agrees with the notion of free will in the same way Peterson does.

For him, the shape that one's authentic self takes is therefore personally determined—not predestined by any kind of inner 'essence' within oneself. Inauthenticity, as an avoidance of truth and personal responsibility, consists in a failure to recognize this freedom. As he writes: "Someone living a life-lie is attempting to manipulate reality . . . so that only some narrowly desired and pre-defined outcome is allowed to exist" (p. 149). Peterson is clear about the moral responsibility that attends one's personal freedom, arguing that inauthentic behavior cannot be blamed on the unconscious or on repression, but only on the individual. "When the individual lies, he [or she] knows it. [They are] . . . conscious, in the present, during the commission of each error, and the omission of each responsibility" (p. 152). According to this view, authenticity—and therefore success and well-being—is always a matter of personal choice. Despite this, however, Peterson simultaneously appeals to the idea of an authentic self which is *not* self-determined, but fixed.

'Discovering' Peterson's Authentic Self

Appealing to evolutionary psychology, Peterson contends that the current social hierarchies of the West are naturally rooted in biology, and are therefore both inevitable and justified (pp. 26–28, 74, 205–07). Underlying Peterson's various pieces of advice in *12 Rules for Life* is thus the notion that social inequality is an unfortunate but unavoidable aspect of human existence. For him, the principle of unequal distribution is not restricted to the domains of finance and creative production, but applies to all aspects of society. In Peterson's dualistic worldview, observes Tara Burton (2020), "there are winners and losers, males and females, alphas and omegas" (paragraph 5).

Peterson argues for the inevitability of social hierarchy on the basis that it is a natural phenomenon. Here, he frames hierarchical structures in terms of competence rather than privilege, arguing that societies are inevitably stratified according to the natural difference in abilities between the individuals within each society. As he writes: "the collective pursuit of any valued goal produces a hierarchy (as some will be better and some worse at that pursuit no matter what it is)" (p. 205). But what determines who is better, and who is worse?

To answer this question, Peterson relies on a brand of biological essentialism. This is essentially the idea that humans have evolved to possess intrinsically different characteristics from one another, determined by biological factors such as their identified sex (*see* pp. 27–28, 46–47). Peterson invokes evolutionary psychology to support the notion that our current social order is thus biologically derived and, therefore, fixed. He somewhat infamously argues that the social organization of lobsters, with whom we share a common evolutionary ancestor, offers a suitable analogy for that of humans. Like us, claims Peterson, lobsters exhibit dominance hierarchies (p. 28).

The most powerful males rise to the top through aggression, where they are rewarded with prime real estate and their pick of females. According to Peterson, this evolutionary continuity demonstrates that current human hierarchies are natural and, by extension, inevitable; in other words, an essential and unchangeable feature of human biology (pp. 205, 211). The further implication of Peterson's claim is that these hierarchies are therefore justified. He writes: "Hierarchies . . . are incredibly ancient, evolutionarily speaking. Do male crustaceans oppress female crustaceans? Should their hierarchies be upended?" (p. 211). He finds further justification for this viewpoint in appealing to the historical aspect of human hierarchies.

Peterson defends his biologically essentialist view of social hierarchies by appealing to their long-standing existence in human societies. Throughout his work, Peterson makes consistent appeals to the merits of (Western) cultural tradition (pp. 117, 156, 205, 211). Although his emphasis on individualism and social freedom is unwavering, his one allowance in terms of reliance on external principles appears to be the conventional guidelines of a given person's culture. "The wisdom of the past was hard-earned," he writes, and it is "reasonable to do what other people have always done, unless we have a very good reason not to" (p. 156). More often than not, he argues, it is an ignorant assumption to think that we know better than our "ancestors." Peterson uses this appeal to tradition to argue that social hierarchies are justified. "Of course," he writes, "culture *is* an oppressive structure. *It's always been that way*. It's a fundamental, universal existential reality" (p. 205).

This emphasis on the role of cultural tradition is not at odds with Peterson's biological essentialism. Rather, it is precisely *because* he conceives of human nature as attributable to biological factors, and therefore as stable and fixed, that he views traditional social conventions as such reliable "guidelines" (p. 117). This line of reasoning is implied when Peterson brings together his appeals to evolutionary psychology and tradition in discussing his lobster analogy: "Why is all this relevant? . . . [Because it] means that dominance hierarchies have been an essentially permanent feature of the environment to which all complex life has adapted" (p. 28). According to this account, social hierarchy is an inevitable biological aspect of human existence, based on the evolutionary continuity of certain male and female traits.

By positing human nature as biologically predetermined, Peterson appeals to a view of the self as a stable and given entity which cannot be freely determined by the individual, but must be discovered within themselves. He hints at the notion of an inner, authentic essence throughout *12 Rules for Life* when he refers to the individual as being guided by their 'soul' (pp. 20, 48, 87). For example, he writes: "There is an unspeakably primordial calculator, deep within you"; and again: "Your entire Being can tell you something that you can neither explain nor articulate . . . we all contain wisdom that we cannot comprehend" (pp. 31, 117). It follows from this essentialist understanding of the self that being authentic involves the discovery and expression of one's inner essence. Peterson clearly appeals to this view when he asserts:

> If you will not *reveal yourself* to others, you cannot reveal yourself to yourself. That does not only mean that you suppress *who you are*, although it also means that. It means that so much of what you could be will never be forced by necessity to come forward. (p. 150, my emphasis)

This view of the self as innate clearly provides a stark contrast to Peterson's earlier framing of selfhood as being acquired—a contradiction which carries not only metaphysical, but moral, implications.

The Conflict in Peterson's Authenticity

As I've suggested, Peterson's notion of the self as biologically fixed does not sit comfortably with his narrative of the individual's capacity for self-determination. Such inconsistency has not gone unnoticed by scholars. Steven McGregor (2018) claims that the "reference to a [primordial] calculator shows Peterson's hand, his tendency to speak more about success when it would seem that he is more interested in the soul" (p. 20). In a similar vein, Tara Burton (2020) observes that

"Peterson's ideology has always involved a very particular mixture of valorizing social freedom (*you're on your own, kid*) and biologically rooted determinism (*but it's in your DNA*)" (paragraph 6).

While it is not inherently contradictory to regard the self as constrained in some aspects and free in others, Peterson's work seems to lack a clear account as to how these opposing ideas are to be reconciled. Instead, he switches between them as two metaphysically incompatible extremes, ultimately arguing for an authentic self that is at once freely chosen by the autonomous individual *and* genetically predetermined by biological forces. This position is clearly problematic: believing in the latter heavily undermines the potential for the former to be true. Given their close relation to the notions of free will and moral responsibility, these differing interpretations of the self also carry significant moral implications.

Framing the authentic self as freely chosen by the individual overemphasizes their level of personal responsibility, while viewing it as fixed underemphasizes it—and both extremes neglect social considerations. As many philosophers know, there is evidence to suggest that the individual is constituted by social factors. The human self is socially embedded because it exists in constant relation to others; in other words, we are both shaped by society and contribute to its development in return. It is for this reason that the authentic self involves an important social dimension; as Bernard Williams says, "we need each other in order to *be* anybody" (2002, p. 200, my emphasis). Peterson's account appears to neglect this element of intersubjectivity.

Neither one of his interpretations of selfhood recognizes the extent to which the self is constituted, and therefore constrained, by social factors. His narrative of social autonomy, for example, frames the individual as entirely independent of social constraints, picturing the self as always being 'free' to choose. In actuality, we are all restricted by the social aspect of our existence, in the sense that our selfhood relies on it. Moreover, some of us are even further restricted in that we are socially marginalized. This points toward the fact that the 'abstract' individual invoked by Peterson when valorizing social freedom is, in fact, not universal but—to borrow Sandra Bartky's (1990) description—"specific and quite privileged ... [having] escaped the characteristic sorts of psychological oppression on which modern hierarchies of class, race, and gender rely so heavily" (p. 97). Given that the relationship between society and the individual is one of reciprocal influence, it follows that these hierarchies are, at least in part, culturally constructed. However, Peterson's biological essentialism, which frames the self as genetically fixed, also neglects this social element. It severely limits the individual's capacity for any kind of autonomous decision-making, which in turn restricts—if not totally precludes—any moral responsibility their actions can be said to carry.

Given this, Peterson's two understandings of the authentic self are not only contradictory, but clearly problematic from a moral point of view. On the first account, external constraints are ignored and the individual is thus held overly accountable; on the second, external factors are overemphasized, with the consequence that the individual can in no way be held accountable. This begs the question—how are such disparate and conflicting ways of seeing the authentic self able to co-exist within Peterson's work?

Reconciling Peterson's Authentic Selves

There is *one* sense in which Peterson's mismatched visions of the authentic self can be considered compatible, and that is if they are applied to a particular kind of privileged individual. As I have explored, his combined emphasis on social autonomy and biological determinism appears to be metaphysically contradictory, since it requires that the self is at once fixed and changeable. For many people, understanding themselves as framed by their biological make-up would conflict with the notion that they are entirely free as individuals to determine their path in life. However, if the individual in question is someone whose biology *itself* supposedly entails a capacity for freedom and autonomous decision-making, then these views become much easier to reconcile.

It's not difficult to guess who would qualify for such criteria under Peterson's framework of biological essentialism; his frequent references to the natural power and authority of the male crustacean provide one obvious hint. Peterson's view of gender roles is centered on man's innate capacity for dominance over others and his free will. This is clear when he expresses views such as: "Women's proclivity to say no, more than any other force, has shaped our [men's] evolution into the creative, industrious, upright, large-brained (competitive, aggressive, domineering) creatures that we are" (p. 47).

Thus, Peterson's two versions of the authentic self only make sense together if the individual they refer to is someone who fits this image; someone with a 'natural' propensity for self-determination. Burton (2020) recognizes this when she observes that, under Peterson's masculinist doctrine, "All a man needs to be transformed from an unemployed slacker incel[1] into an impressive professional with a clean room and a girlfriend is a Schopenhauerian will *and* to embrace his primal nature" (paragraph 5). Men—particularly white, cisgender, middle-class men—can thus simultaneously identify with Peterson's notion that authenticity requires the discovery and expression of their true (biological) essence, *and* with his contention that their authentic self is something they are able to create for themselves.

This argument put forward by Peterson is one which serves to both uphold and defend the current social order, in which men are seen as biologically privileged over women. Given that Peterson himself is a beneficiary of this status quo, we would therefore do well to heed the advice of Feldman; that is, to consider whether it is *really* authenticity that is being valued in Peterson's work, or whether he is merely using the concept—rather inauthentically—to support his particular worldview. If this were true, it would appear that Peterson is prescribing for others a practice of authenticity in which he himself does not partake.

The Ambiguous Ideal

An increasingly popular cultural idea, 'authenticity' is invoked within popular culture in support of a range of different philosophical positions. In particular, the concept fea-

---

[1] For readers who are unfamiliar with it, the word 'incel' stands for 'involuntary celibate'. The term refers to young men who belong to an online subculture that is based around an inability to attract women, despite having a desire to do so.

tures in interpretations of selfhood as both innate and acquired—two notions which, when adopted exclusively, are not only metaphysically opposed, but also have competing moral implications. Jordan Peterson's *12 Rules for Life* offers a fitting example of this problematic use of authenticity; his worldview is one in which these conflicting views of the self coincide. At the same time as Peterson's biological essentialism presupposes a self that is genetically fixed, his simultaneous appeal to social autonomy frames the self as entirely self-determined.

Peterson fails to provide a clear account of how these metaphysically inconsistent ideas are to be reconciled—perhaps because for his predominantly white, middle-class, male readership there is no need: their social position is such that it renders his particular blend of ideas somewhat compatible. By switching between these interpretations of selfhood as two extremes, Peterson neglects the extent to which the self is both socially constituted and constrained, ultimately failing to accommodate important metaphysical and moral considerations—and, it seems, failing to embody authenticity himself.

Works Cited

Bartky, Sandra. 1990. *Femininity and Domination: Studies in the Phenomenology of Oppression*. London: Routledge.

Brooks, David. 2018. The Jordan Peterson Moment. *The New York Times*. <www.nytimes.com/2018/01/25/opinion/jordan-peterson-moment.html>.

Bryant, Ben. 2018. Why Do Young Men Worship Professor Jordan Peterson? <www.bbc.co.uk/bbcthree/article/f1d7fed0-4ddf-4a8a-94b9-ea05f913cdd2>.

Burton, Tara. 2020. Jordan Peterson's Perfectly Petersonian Health Scare. *Religion News Service*. <https://religionnews.com/2020/02/18/jordan-petersons-perfectly-petersonian-health-scare>.

Feldman, Simon. 2015. *Against Authenticity: Why You Shouldn't Be Yourself*. London: Lexington.

Ferrara, Alessandro. 1998. *Reflective Authenticity*. London: Routledge.

Lynskey, Dorian. 2018. How Dangerous Is Jordan B Peterson, the Rightwing Professor Who 'Hit a Hornet's Nest'? *The Guardian*. <www.theguardian.com/science/2018/feb/07/how-dangerous-is-jordan-b-peterson-the-rightwing-professor-who-hit-a-hornets-nest>.

McGregor, Steven. 2018. Jordan Peterson's Third Way. *The New Criterion* 37:1 (September).

Peterson, Jordan B. 2018. *12 Rules for Life: An Antidote to Chaos*. Toronto: Random House Canada.

Taylor, Charles. 1992. *The Ethics of Authenticity*. Cambridge: Harvard University Press.

Williams, Bernard. 2002. *Truth and Truthfulness: An Essay in Genealogy*. Princeton: Princeton University Press.

[5]
Not an Anti-Feminist Per Se

**LUIS FELIPE BARTOLO ALEGRE AND
FABIOLA VALERIA CÁRDENAS MALDONADO**

J o Coburn asked Jordan Peterson, in an interview, whether he thinks that a trans woman is a real woman. Not before objecting to the nature of the question, he replied, "No, because I think women are able, generally speaking, of having babies, and they have female genitalia, and they have an XX chromosome, and I think biological markers are relevant" (Coburn 2018). This was neither the first nor the last time that Peterson openly stated that there's a distinctive characteristic of women's nature: something that fundamentally differentiates women from men and even from those who fail to "fit easily into a gender category," as he suggested trans women do in that same interview.

Peterson's remarks about women's nature aren't restricted to their physical constitution. As a public intellectual, he has highlighted how some biological factors explain some differences between men and women in terms of their behaviors and in social outcomes. With this, he was pushing back against explanations that only conceived these differences as products of culture or as social constructs. His point, however, isn't that everyone always behaves (or should behave) according to their biological sex. A man may have a 'womanly' vocation, like nursing, and still be a man. Conversely, a woman may have a 'manly' personality trait, like physical aggressiveness, and still be a woman. As he told

Anne McElvoy when she asked him, "Who is the average woman? Am I the average woman?": "Well, in some ways probably, in other ways not" (McElvoy 2018).

His point, instead, is that the amplification of these differences does not have to be regarded as a bad thing, since "if you maximize free choice, then you also maximize differences in choice between people," which for Peterson is precisely "the purpose of setting up a society that offers maximal equality of opportunity" (Skavlan 2018). But if Peterson doesn't expect a person to behave according to his or her condition of being a man or a woman (or something else), then why does he take great pains in noting these differences? Why precisely him, who regards individual sovereignty as the "great discovery in the West" (Rogan 2017)? Why not simply talk about persons as individuals, and leave the average man and woman for the statisticians?

We think that Peterson's insistence on inborn differences between men and women could be taken as an invitation to rethink women's (and men's) liberation also— although for Peterson perhaps mainly—as a project of understanding our biological dispositions and taming them for our own interests.

So, You're Saying . . .

From a simplistic perspective, and regardless of the rigor of their arguments, there are two opposing views on the differences in behaviors, interests, attitudes, and outcomes between men and women. On the one side, there are those we might call cultural determinists, who dismiss the influence of biological factors and reduce the differences between the sexes to socio-cultural constructs. On the other side, there are those we might call biological determinists, who claim that most important differences between men and women are determined only by our biological constitutions.

In the extreme forms in which we have described them, these views are much more present among politicians, activists, journalists, and public thinkers than among scholars and scientists. In fact, as the science popularizer Pere Estupinyà says, the only properly academic extremism we can find in this discussion is from "some circles that deny any biological influence and claim that sex is only a cultural construct" (Estupinyà 2013, pp. 50–51). On the other side, although much can be said on the exaggerations of the biological approach, there doesn't seem to exist a scientist worthy of that name who denies the importance of socio-cultural factors in the shaping of men's and women's differences.

If the extremes seem to be clearly identified in science, why do they blur when brought into wider public debate? This may be partly due to the media's tendency to misrepresent scientific findings when they report them. It is enough to come up with a provocative headline and mention the word science to get thousands of clicks and in the process spread inaccurate or outright false information about our species. The most heated and least productive debates are often the result of the confusion produced by these news stories (*see* for example Kreimer 2020b). The mediatization of knowledge seems to overshadow the rarely appreciated labor of scientists and good scientific popularizers, who are often misquoted or misinterpreted in the name of simplification or clicks.

Only Two Reasons Men and Women Differ?

The reader may be understandably skeptical towards the assertion that some social and behavioral differences between the sexes may be explained by biological factors to a greater extent than they may be by socio-cultural factors. After all, isn't it true that some models of masculinity and femininity are—intentionally or not—transmitted to us since we are kids through education, socialization, media, and so forth? Well, there are some ways in which scientists can discriminate which of our behaviors and social structures are probably not mainly determined by culture. In an interview, Peterson explains one of these ways in relation to the differences of temperament and interests between men and women:

> You offer men and women well validated tests of preference and of personality, and you do that all across the world with tens of thousands of people in multi-country samples, and then you look at the differences between men and women and you rank-order that by . . . egalitarian social policy. And what you find is, the more egalitarian the society, the more different the men and women become. (Skavlan 2018, 7:59)

We see then that, in countries with more egalitarian social policies like Denmark and Finland, the differences in preference and personality between men and women are greater rather than lesser, contrary to what a cultural determinist would expect. This shows, according to Peterson, that these differences are rooted mainly in biology rather than in culture, since for him "there's only two reasons that men and women differ: one is cultural, and the other is biological. And if you minimize the cultural differences, you maximize the biological differences" (Skavlan 2018). In other words: if it's not culture, it must be biology. However, is this disjunction accurate?

Although Peterson's argument justifies us in believing that some differences between the sexes—those studied in the research alluded to—are not mainly a product of sexism, it doesn't immediately justify that they're a product of our biological constitution. There's the misconception that human behaviors, interests, and so forth are either products of our biology, which includes our genetics and is very difficult to change, or of culture, which is made up by somewhat arbitrary conventions that, in certain circumstances, can be changed very fast. There's more to this story, though.

Apart from our given biological dispositions and our somewhat arbitrary cultural conventions, there's what the philosopher Daniel Dennett calls "forced moves" or "good tricks" (1995, section 16.4). A particular pattern or tendency found in all societies could be, indeed, deeply rooted in our genetics such as an infant's tendency to prefer different types of toys according to their sex (Jadva, Hines, and Golombok 2010). Some patterns or tendencies, though, cannot be immediately traced to our genes, since some of them may just be easy or good strategies for tackling problems that humanity can find in some or all contexts. For example, the cross-cultural tendency of assigning men to occupations that require an intense use of physical strength, like soldiers or constructors, could be due to this being the optimal form of labor division (at least for less technologically advanced societies) rather than to there being an instinct to perceive men as destined to these occupations.

Not only physical conditions might bear forced moves, but these may also be triggered by some cultural or social situations. For example, Nicholas Christakis has speculated that, due to the current COVID-19 pandemic, some of the progress made by women in the labor market may be undone (Harris 2020). In a post-pandemic world with fewer jobs, the result may be that the best economic strategy for heterosexual couples might be for the man to work and the woman to stay home given that men earn more than women around seventy five percent of the time. In this case, the return to classical gender roles would not occur because of a genetic propensity to return to them whenever we have the occasion to, but because of the different conditions that men and women have in society. Those different conditions, of course, do not necessarily reveal that sexist discrimination is at the bottom of this tendency, for many studies have shown that several factors other than sexism account for most of the gender pay gap (this is very nicely explained in Wheelan 2014, Chapter 11). What those different conditions reveal, instead, is that if we minimize the differences due to sexist discrimination, we do not immediately nor necessarily maximize the differences due to our biological constitution.

How Men and Women Differ

The above might also hold for the paradoxical fact that in countries with more gender-equality there are more women choosing to become nurses and men choosing to become engineers. Although it's reasonable to attribute those differences in preferences to our inborn predispositions, some of the studies reporting this paradoxical fact also report that there are more women who are apt and would enjoy following a career in STEM (Science, Technology, Engineering, and Math) than those who finally graduate in those fields (Stoet and Geary 2018, p. 10). This shows that there may be some circumstances preventing them from specializing in those fields other than their biological dispositions. Hence, although the current research seems to point in the direction of there being innate behavioral dispositions explaining our average differences, we should always be open to the possibility that there may be more complex explanations giving culture a greater role in the account of our differences.

However, even if the explanation of our differences were not mainly genetic, Peterson's point against the cultural determinists would remain valid. After all, these differences would not be explained mainly by sexist discrimination or indoctrination, but by some forced moves to which cultural innovation is bound in a given context, or even in general. On the other hand, though, there are several sources that give support to the claim that these differences are strongly associated to our biology. (For a scientifically informed philosophical discussion on sex differences, to which we are highly indebted, we recommend checking Kreimer 2020a.)

The first source comes from extensive social studies, especially those where data on differences in preferences and behavior are collected, classified, and ranked according to how likely that behavior was influenced by sexism. This is the very kind of research showing that in countries with more gender-equality the occupational preferences of men and women differ more according to the typical stereotypes. But this is also confirmed by similar studies that rank the data by socio-economic status and find that, in socio-economic strata with less economic pressures, the differences in occupational preferences also tend to increase in agreement with the stereotypes. Moreover, there are also cross-cultural social studies where women consistently self-report higher neuroticism (which isn't a bad thing per se), agreeableness, warmth, and openness to feelings, whereas men self-report to be higher in assertiveness and openness to ideas (Costa, Terracciano, and McCrae 2001).

Another source is composed of psychological and behavioral studies. For example, it has been found that females have a greater interest in persons than in things, whereas the opposite holds for males (Su, Rounds, and Armstrong 2009). This would explain part of the differences in our occupational choices, for nursing is more related to caring for people rather than dealing with things and the opposite holds for engineering. Similarly, as we have advanced, studies of infants provide strong evidence that our stereotypical preferences for certain kinds of toys and colors are hardly just a product of socialization (Jadva, Hines, and Golombok 2010).

Continuity between Us and Animals

A very special kind of source is neurological studies. These studies go beyond social and psychological studies in attempting to explain part of our behaviors from how our brains are structured. Hence, part of the behavioral differences between men and women are explained in these studies by the average physical differences existing between males' and females' brains. For instance, the larger number of androgens (like testosterone) in males' brains with respect to females' brains—one of our most important neurological differences—seems to account for many of our behavioral and psychological differences. In this line, some studies show that female children who are exposed to above-average amounts of androgens in a prenatal stage are more likely to show and engage in stereotypically male interests and activities (Berenbaum 2018).

Studies on sex reassignment corroborate the hypothesis that many of our attitudes are not just a product of socialization. The very rare condition called cloacal exstrophy causes male newborns either to have a defective penis or not have one at all. It was perhaps the idea that gender identity depends on upbringing that made some doctors suggest sex-reassignment surgery for these male-born children to physiologically transform them into females. The results, however, were not what the doctors expected (Reiner and Gearhart 2004). First, out of fourteen genetic males surgically reassigned as female—whose ages ranged from five to sixteen years old—eight identified themselves as male. More importantly, though, is that all of them showed, although in different degrees, male-typical interests, behaviors, and attitudes, despite having been raised as females.

We can gain a layer of depth by adding ethological studies as a further source. Here, instead of comparing human behaviors just cross-culturally, we can compare behaviors in cross-species studies. Some interesting results are summarized by the philosopher Roxana Kreimer. First, we see that both human and chimpanzee male offspring tend more than female offspring to spend time away from their mothers, which might mean that they are more prone to risk. Also, there's evidence that both human and monkey females might have a greater social interest than males. In that respect, it has been reported that female baby monkeys of two-three weeks old look more at the face, specifically to the eyes, than do male babies, and that they establish more contact with caregivers between the fourth and fifth weeks. Finally, even the atypical case of female hyenas, which are more aggressive than their male counterparts, gives support to what we have been saying; they have more testosterone than do the males (Kreimer 2020a, p. 11). They are female, but female hyenas' brains are more 'male-like' in this respect.

The significance of ethology for our understanding of human behavior is related to Peterson's claim that "anthropomorphization with animals is generally the appropriate tactic unless you have reason to doubt it . . . because there's continuity between us and animals rather than discontinuity" (Lewis 2018). Our belonging to the animal kingdom, though, also implies that the principles of natural selection must apply to us. Darwinian analysis, then, can also be a source of hypotheses on the differences between males and females, including on the lack of equality of outcome, as suggested by philosopher Peter Singer:

If Darwinian thinking tells us that we have been too ready to assume a fundamental difference in kind between human beings and nonhuman animals, it could also tell us that we are too ready to assume that all human beings are the same in all important respects. . . . Darwinian thought . . . gives us grounds for believing that since men and women play different roles in reproduction, they may also differ in their inclinations or temperaments, in ways that best promote the reproductive prospects of each sex. Since women are limited in the number of children they can have, they are likely to be selective in their choice of mate. Men, on the other hand, are limited in the number of children they can have only by the number of women they can have sex with. If achieving high status increases access to women, then we can expect men to have a stronger drive for status than women. This means that we cannot use the fact that there is a disproportionately large number of men in high status positions in business or politics as a reason for concluding that there has been discrimination against women. For example, the fact that there are fewer women chief executives of major corporations than men may be due to men being more willing to subordinate their personal lives and other interests to their career goals, and biological differences between men and women may be a factor in that greater readiness to sacrifice everything for the sake of getting to the top. (Singer 1999, pp. 17–18)

Not an Anti-Feminist Per Se

None of the differences noted, though, have the character of some inescapable fate, let alone of necessary conditions for the definition of manhood and womanhood. All we wanted to point out here are some average differences between human males and females, from which all of us deviate to different extents. The average man and woman do not exist but as idealizations that would help us understand the main tendencies of our interests and behaviors, as well as their manifestations in larger social tendencies. On the other hand, Peterson himself has pointed out that scientific advances like the birth control pill have even "changed the fundamental biological nature of women and men" (Sommers and Crittenden 2020), and more advances may even result, as Yuval N. Harari suggests, in there not being sexes or genders in the future (Scott 2015).

But provided sexes exist and we are unable to prevent genetics from influencing our preferences and attitudes, we need to understand how our differences as male and females impact us as individuals and in society. The whole feminist project depends on that. As with Jordan Peterson, we don't regard ourselves as "anti-feminist per se," for we agree with him that "the idea that the world would benefit from the movement of talent from both sexes into the workplace as rapidly as possible is something that anyone with any sense should share given the rarity of talent and the necessity for utilizing it" (Jones 2019). This is where it seems that, despite all his criticism to radical feminism, Peterson seems to espouse some form of feminism after all. But what is feminism really?

Feminist philosophy is often defined as a set of ideas that comprises a normative and a descriptive claim (McAfee 2018). According to the normative claim, all people are worthy to the same rights, respect, and opportunities regardless of their sexual or gender identity. The descriptive claim states that women are not fully treated as if they were so worthy, but are disadvantaged in relation to men due to sexism or the way society is structured. Any feminist who regards the descriptive claim as essential to feminism, would be committed to change the current state of the relationship between the sexes. But to do so, this feminist would need to ask herself first what is this current state and what aspects can and should we change? Knowing the answer to an important question like this can be bittersweet, for we may suddenly become aware of a reality that doesn't fit our intuitions or those prevailing in our social circles.

However, it seems that some conceptions of feminism are more committed to the descriptive claim than to the normative claim. Without even being aware of it, they may be more committed to their own theories of the relations between the sexes or genders than to improving the opportunities of women in a given society. An effective commitment to change, as opposed to just moral posturing, requires making our best efforts to know the truth, unless we don't really care about making things worst for both men and women.

But even if after doing your best to know the truth you're not convinced by the theses on the differences between the sexes here expounded, it is never wise to disqualify the hard work of the scientists who put them forward, let alone giving them such an ignominious label as 'neurosexist' (as Fine 2010 does). Science is neither friend nor enemy of feminism per se, but a provider of knowledge that could be used for (or against) feminist causes.

Thanks to empirical inquiry, as we advanced, we have discovered that several factors other than sexism are behind the gender pay gap (Bertrand, Goldin, and Katz 2010), and that we can control some of them to an extent, like the pressure of motherhood on women's lives (Budig and England 2001). All of this has suggested measures such as parental leave and childcare policies which have contributed to a serious reduction of this gap and to a wider participation of women in the workplace (Misra, Budig, and Moller 2007). In sum, although there's no need for a descriptive claim—there's no need for a feminist theory of the world—the struggle for equality of opportunity between the sexes or genders can and should benefit from science, even when it doesn't fit some feminist narrative.

For all that said, feminism could benefit from Peterson's emphasis on the fact that certain female propensities, like being too agreeable, may be putting them at a disadvantage when negotiating certain working conditions compared to men; and this, by the way, also holds for men who are too agreeable. On the other side, Peterson has also insisted that some of the things that women purportedly feel to be more important than men do, like having a family, are also of a great importance for men. In this respect, he talks from personal experience: "What I've experienced in my life, although I have a very productive career, a very interesting career, it's definitely been the case that my family has been more and more important to me as I've got older, and I don't think that

that's an uncommon experience" (Holt 2019). Hence, whereas women may be, on average, disadvantaged when negotiating their working conditions, so are men when deciding their priorities in life. This is but the other side of the coin of our inborn propensities.

Now, back to women's behavioral tendencies. We do not deny that societies have implicit or explicit mechanisms for stimulating the adoption of certain social behaviors and the prohibition of others in the upbringing of men and women. Hence, someday we may discover that these social dynamics account for more of the explanation of the differences in our propensions than we can recognize from the current state of scientific research. Hence, women's tendency to be more empathetic and kinder may be the result of patriarchal oppression or sexism after all, or perhaps even the result of some 'evil trick'. But whatever the answer may be, there's no gainsaying that women have been entering fields that were mostly or exclusively represented by men, which they often did—by the way—not by being very kind.

One of these areas is comedy, previously occupied almost exclusively by men. This noble profession often involves making someone uncomfortable for a good laugh's sake. A difficult situation for the average woman to cope with, but one that has slowly been mastered by a number of talented female comedians in recent years. We want to end quoting Whitney Cummings, one of these talented comedians, in a film where she portrays a neuroscientist who had a hard time accepting the neurological differences between men and women. Almost at the end of this film, which she also co-wrote and directed, she tells us why our differences should not be regarded as the product of an evil trick nor as something that implies the denigration of women:

> After years of research, I found that the male and female brain is wired very differently. Frankly, I was disappointed by the results because they didn't feel like social progress. So, I kept looking for a bias. I re-did the studies over and over again and I did find a bias after all. A very problematic and subjective bias. And that bias was

me. I went into all this thinking that girls being emotional, sensitive, hypervigilant was a bad thing because our society makes us feel so ashamed of it. I viewed these qualities as weaknesses. But that was a flaw in my approach. And in many ways, my life. The truth is that these stereotypical female qualities are actually strengths: nurturing, passionate, tenacious, supportive, and resilient. These don't seem that bad. And even though the female brain can, at times, be complicated and confusing, nobody can deny our ability to get back up. Every day our brains tell us there is a lot to be afraid of. But even though we're hardwired to avoid danger, we're also wired for courage. So, when it comes to fight or flight, flight is always easier. But every now and then you come across something that's worth fighting for. (Cummings 2017)

References

Berenbaum, Sheri A. 2018. Beyond Pink and Blue: The Complexity of Early Androgen Effects on Gender Development. *Child Development Perspectives* 12:1
<https://doi.org/10.1111/cdep.12261>.

Bertrand, Marianne, Claudia Goldin, and Lawrence F. Katz. 2010. Dynamics of the Gender Gap for Young Professionals in the Financial and Corporate Sectors. *American Economic Journal: Applied Economics* 2:3
<https://doi.org/10.1257/app.2.3.228>.

Budig, Michelle J. and Paula England. 2001. The Wage Penalty for Motherhood. *American Sociological Review* 66:2
<https://doi.org/10.2307/2657415>.

Coburn, Jo. 2018. Conversation with Ayesha Hazarika and Jordan Peterson. *Daily Politics*. BBC Television.
<https://bbc.co.uk/programmes/b0b3kq88>.

Costa, Paul T., Antonio Terracciano, and Robert R. McRae. 2001. Gender Differences in Personality Traits across Cultures: Robust and Surprising Findings. *Journal of Personality and Social Psychology* 81:2
<https://doi.org/10.1037/0022-3514.81.2.322>.

Cummings, Whitney. 2017. *The Female Brain*. IFC Films.

Dennett, Daniel C. 1995. *Darwin's Dangerous Idea: Evolution and the Meaning of Life*. New York: Simon and Schuster.

Estupinyà, Pere. 2013. S=EX2: La Ciencia del Sexo. Madrid: Debate.

Fine, Cordelia. 2010. *Delusions of Gender: How Our Minds, Society, and Neurosexism Create Difference*. New York: Norton.

Harris, Sam. 2020. A Pandemic of Incompetence: A Conversation with Nicholas Christakis. Making Sense Podcast <https://samharris.org/podcasts/222-pandemic-incompetence>.

Holt, Hayley. 2019. Jordan Peterson Says Young Men Attend His Talks to Turn Their Lives Around. *Breakfast Today*. 1 NEWS <https://youtu.be/VICsw43SOV8>.

Jadva, Vasanti, Melissa Hines, and Susan Golombok. 2010. Infants' Preferences for Toys, Colors, and Shapes: Sex Differences and Similarities. *Archives of Sexual Behavior* 39:6 <https://doi.org/10.1007/s10508-010-9618-z>.

Jones, Tony. 2019. Jordan Peterson Destroys Q&A. *Q&A*. Melbourne: Australian Broadcasting Corporation. <https://abc.net.au/qanda/2019-25-02/10811138>.

Kreimer, Roxana. 2020a. Is It Sexist to Recognize that Men and Women Are Not Identical? A Critical Evaluation of Neurofeminist Rhetoric. *Disputatio: Philosophical Research Bulletin* 9:13 <https://doi.org/10.5281/zenodo.3567201>.

———. 2020b. Verdades Para Crédulas. <https://youtu.be/qenahT2N3I>.

Lewis, Helen. 2018. Jordan Peterson: There Was Plenty of Motivation to Take Me Out. It Just Didn't Work. B*ritish GQ*. <https://youtu.be/yZYQpge1W5s>.

McAfee, Noëlle. 2018. Feminist Philosophy. Stanford Encyclopedia of Philosophy, ed. Edward M. Zalta. Metaphysical Research Lab, Stanford University.

McElvoy, Anne. 2018. Jordan Peterson on Gender, Patriarchy, and the Slide Towards Tyranny. *Intelligence Squared*. <https://youtu.be/7QRQjrsFnR4>.

Misra, Joya, Michelle J. Budig, and Stephanie Moller. 2007. Reconciliation Policies and the Effects of Motherhood on Employment, Earnings, and Poverty. *Journal of Comparative Policy Analysis: Research and Practice* 9:2 <https://doi.org/10.1080/13876980701311588>.

Reiner, William G., and John P. Gearhart. 2004. Discordant Sexual Identity in Some Genetic Males with Cloacal Exstrophy Assigned to Female Sex at Birth. *New England Journal of Medicine* 350:4 <https://doi.org/10.1056/NEJMoa022236>.

Rogan, Joe. 2017. Jordan Peterson and Brett Weinstein. *Joe Rogan Experience*. <https://youtu.be/6G59zsjM2UI>.

Scott, Michael. 2015. Yuval Noah Harari on the Myths We Need to Survive. Royal Geographical Society: *Intelligence Squared*. <https://youtu.be/UTcgioiHM0U>.

Singer, Peter. 1999. *A Darwinian Left: Politics, Evolution, and Co-operation*. New Haven: Yale University Press.

Skavlan, Fredrik. 2018. Full Interview with Jordan B. Peterson. *Skavlan*. SVT/TV2. <https://youtu.be/_iudkPi4_sY>.

Sommers, Christina Hoff, and Danielle Crittenden. 2020. The Jordan Peterson You Don't Know. The Femsplainers Podcast <https://youtu.be/O4IBh-MgvFc>.

Stoet, Gijsbert, and David C. Geary. 2018. The Gender-Equality Paradox in Science, Technology, Engineering, and Mathematics Education. *Psychological Science* 29:4 <https://doi.org/10.1177/0956797617741719>.

Su, Rong, James Rounds, and Patrick Ian Armstrong. 2009. Men and Things, Women and People: A Meta-Analysis of Sex Differences in Interests. *Psychological Bulletin* 135:6 <https://doi.org/10.1037/a0017364>.

Wheelan, Charles. 2014. *Naked Statistics: Stripping the Dread from the Data*. Barnes and Noble.

Part II

The Storyteller

[6]
Clean Up Your Theory!

David Ramsay Steele

Dr. Jordan Peterson has many claims to fame, but perhaps the most significant is his claim to reveal the meanings of stories, especially Bible stories such as Adam and Eve and occasionally stories from popular movies like *The Lion King*.

When Dr. Peterson was surfing his first great wave of celebrity, he went on the road with Dave Rubin, and addressed huge crowds in packed halls across the world. Peterson would make a presentation from the stage, talking for two and a half hours at a stretch, largely extempore, explaining the meaning of a single story.

Stories as Entertainment and as History

Stories are told and listened to for many reasons. One of them is the sheer thrill and fascination of the story itself. When we read an Hercule Poirot mystery, we usually don't think it has something profound to teach us; we read it for its own sweet sake. In such cases we're inclined to say that the message of the story is the story. Although stories always do convey many other things, there are some stories where the reader is not primarily interested in those other things, but only in the story itself.

Another motive for reading or listening to stories is that they're taken to be literal historical accounts of what actually happened. Millions of people still take the story of Adam and Eve in this way, and if we do view it like that, then any search for a further meaning may seem less important, though we might be curious about some details of the story not disclosed in *Genesis*.

Stories with Lessons

There are also stories which, while assumed to be fiction, quite unmistakably carry a more general message. The simplest case is where the 'lesson' of the story is perfectly blatant and well recognized by everyone. We all instantly get the point of the story about Brer Rabbit and the briar patch; it captures the common human situation where a person pretends to be averse to something he devoutly wishes for. You will occasionally hear the briar patch alluded to in discussions of national politics.

Allusions to some such stories have entered into the language. We all know what's meant by 'sour grapes', the response of someone who finds themselves unable to get what they wanted, and therefore consoles themselves by saying that it was probably not worth wanting. This comes from one of Aesop's Fables, from around 600 B.C.E. Each of his Fables ends with an explicit 'moral' or lesson. And so we have the expression, 'the moral of this story'.

The moral, or meaning, or message Peterson finds in various stories are not like this. Their truth is not self-evident, even after they are pointed out, and the assumption is that it takes unusual insight to dig them up. Peterson conveys the impression that he's doing something difficult and important by refamiliarizing his audience with these stories and then explaining what they mean. But how could it be so important?

Three Puzzles

There are three main puzzles here. First, since the meaning Peterson gives a story usually isn't obvious but obscure and debatable, how do we know when we've got the right meaning? Second, a related point but not quite the same, what does it actually mean to say a meaning is the correct one? Is the correct meaning the meaning intended by the originator of the story, or imputed by people who heard the story when it first started circulating, or by someone who has studied a lot of stories, or by someone who has cracked a code which unlocks the secrets of all stories? If none of these, then what? Third, since we can, after a lot of trouble, decipher the meaning of the story, we must be able to state the meaning without the story, so why do we still need the story? Does the story itself add anything to the bare meaning, except a bit of entertainment?

Peterson has stated that he didn't understand the story of Adam and Eve until he read *Paradise Lost*. This remark reveals a couple of things about Peterson's presuppositions. First, it assumes that the story of Adam and Eve has one specific meaning, which is other than that it actually happened (Peterson agrees that it didn't). Second, this meaning must be difficult to identify; it must be non-evident to the ordinary reader, since Peterson, like most of us, has been familiar with this story since childhood, and didn't know its meaning until he read *Paradise Lost*. Thirdly, the meaning Peterson has now arrived at is not something in the mind of the original author, or of the compiler who decided to include this tall tale in *Genesis*, or of any of the thousands of people who learned and studied this story for many centuries after that. We know this because the cosmology and theology of John Milton, the English Puritan who wrote *Paradise Lost* in 1667, are violently at odds with the cosmology and theology of the writers and compiler of the *Torah* and of the *Torah*'s devotees, especially pre-Exile devotees.

Nearly all Christian and some Jewish interpreters of this story believe that the serpent was Satan—this is implied in the *New Testament* (for instance, *Revelation* 12:9; 20:2). But 'Satan' means something utterly different to Christians than it does to Jews. In Christian teaching Satan is an archangel who rebelled against God and became the source and sovereign of Evil. Christians call him Lucifer, but there's no such person in the *Tanach* (the *Old Testament*). "Lucifer," in a Latin translation of *Isaiah* 14:12, signifies the Morning Star, a metaphor for the Neo-Babylonian Empire, about to be replaced by the Persian Empire. It doesn't by any stretch of the imagination refer to a rebel angel. In the *Tanach*, Satan is a servant of God who acts, in accordance with God's instructions, to lead humans into sin—see especially the book of *Job*.

This reflects the deeper division that in ancient Judaism, God purposely creates evil as well as good (*Isaiah* 45:7), whereas in Christianity, probably influenced by Zoroastrianism, God creates only good, and evil comes from the evil god, Lucifer or the Devil, who wages continual war on the good God. In *Paradise Lost*, Satan establishes the city of Pandemonium ('all the demons'), his base of operations to invade the human world. *Paradise Lost* comprises twelve books, and the Garden of Eden appears only in the ninth book! What precedes that ninth book draws upon *Genesis*, but places everything in the context of the evil god Lucifer, unknown to *Genesis*.

Then there's original sin, which Peterson reads into the story (37:50). In Christianity, especially Protestantism, the story of Adam and Eve is bound up with original sin (all humans have inherited a sinful nature from Adam), but there's no place for original sin in Judaism. Islam too, like Judaism, accepts the story of Adam and Eve while rejecting original sin. Original sin is a peculiarly Christian coinage, propounded by Augustine of Hippo and taken to the extreme by John Calvin. If you understand the story of Adam and Eve as involving original sin, you place yourself in opposition to the writers of *Genesis*, your only source for this story. Peterson seems to acknowledge that original sin is exclusively Christian (*Maps of Meaning*, p. 314), but he doesn't recognize any incongruity in finding this thoroughly un-Jewish notion in a Jewish story.

The Null Hypothesis

It's not that all talk of meanings in stories is pointless. It's that we ought to be clear about what we mean when we claim that a story has a meaning, especially a meaning unknown to most people familiar with the story. The thing we have to account for is the claim that the supposed meaning of the story has some special status because it's the 'correct' interpretation of the story. If I say to you, 'Indecision can be costly, so don't overthink your actions', this might possibly be sound advice, but is it any sounder, does it carry any more weight, if I tell you that in my opinion this is the 'real meaning' of *Hamlet*?

There is a 'null hypothesis' in all this talk about the meanings of stories by Peterson and other Jungians. It is that Peterson, or whoever is doing the interpreting, finds an amenable moral, dictated by his twenty-first-century secular liberal worldview (in Peterson's case with a dash of Protestantism) that has some broadly plausible derivation from the story in question. This is as arbitrary as it is facile. We can easily come up with dozens of possible meanings that can be read into any story, and then pick the one we find most congenial to our own ethical outlook.

A defender of Peterson might retort: 'Who's to say that Dr. Peterson isn't entitled to find a moral message in some story or other and then deliver that message, with the story thrown in as entertainment value?' Yes, of course he's free to do this. Out of all the many meanings that could be conferred on a story, Peterson picks one that tickles his fancy. For Peterson, stories are Rorschach tests. His interpretation tells us something about Peterson and nothing about the story. No problem! Until Dr. Peterson informs us that this is objectively the real meaning of the story, and something of urgent importance for putting people's lives in order and saving civilization.

God Said to Abraham, Kill Me a Son

One Bible story where the real meaning is seen as puzzling and controversial is the story about Abraham being ordered by God to get ready to kill his son Isaac as a sacrificial offering (*Genesis* 22). At the last moment, God changes the plan, and tells Abraham to sacrifice a ram instead. Peterson says, "The story ends happily," though the ram might have had a different opinion.

Many theologians have puzzled over this story, as God's behavior looks difficult to defend morally. Immanuel Kant maintained that Abraham could not be certain that God was talking to him, but could be certain that what he was being commanded to do was immoral. Kant's view was clearly not that of the storyteller, the author of this part of *Genesis*.

Peterson offers two different solutions of his own to this puzzle. In his first solution, he maintains that ancient humans did not sufficiently appreciate the need to make sacrifices to get a future return (*12 Rules*, p. 170; "The Great

Sacrifice," 38:57). The story brings home the message that we have to sacrifice something now to get something more in the future. So the point of the story is to give people what economists call lower time preference. He has also appealed to this theory to explain the story of Cain and Abel ("Cain and Abel," 3:49).

This interpretation has a serious problem. There's plenty of evidence that, thousands of years before the supposed time of Abraham (very roughly, 2000 B.C.E.), humans were routinely delaying gratification, making sacrifices for the future—they were saving and investing. The making of stone hand axes goes back to a time long before our hominin ancestors had evolved into humans. Fire-hardening clay to produce ceramic goes back around thirty thousand years, and building kilns to greatly improve the fire-hardening goes back at least eight thousand years.

For another perspective on the historical timing, *Genesis* tells us that Abraham hailed from the city of Ur. Whether this be true or not, the city states of Mesopotamia, had, by the supposed time of Abraham, already enjoyed many centuries with an elaborate system of cost accounting, credit, interest, banking, mortgages, and negotiable debt instruments. They no more needed to be cryptically informed about saving and investment than today's Wall Street floor traders.

One source of fatally flawed theories about early humans is the assumption that they were stupid or afflicted with a kind of childish simplicity. In fact, we can find no reason to doubt that humans even (say) fifty thousand years ago had IQs roughly as high as humans today, perhaps higher. The key difference between them and us is that we possess more capital, including human capital or accumulated knowledge. This is on top of the fact that people fifty thousand years ago were enduring a glaciation, with much of the world's land surface covered in kilometers-thick ice sheets. Anyone of average IQ can just *see* that it pays to sacrifice a lot now to get a return on this investment in the future. No one, or at least no community with a typical range of IQs, has to be tricked into learning this palpable fact by some coyly coded narrative.

Arguing that saving for the future is a difficult notion to grasp, Peterson asserts that wolves eat all they can once they have a kill, and don't know how to make provision for the future ("The Great Sacrifice," 37:37). You might suppose that someone from the wilds of northern Alberta would have heard that wolves routinely go to the trouble of burying the meat they can't eat immediately, preserving it for later occasions. Perhaps wolves don't understand the reason for their own behavior, but hominins observing wolves and many other animals making provision for the future would have understood it.

Dr. Peterson's alternative, and utterly different, solution to the puzzle is to liken Abraham's willingness to kill his son with the willingness of parents to 'sacrifice' their children by allowing them to leave home ("The Great Sacrifice," 1:00:56). Loosely speaking, they are both cases of giving up our children. Peterson identifies Abraham's willingness to slaughter his son with parents' willingness to see their children move out and make their way in the world, in other words justifying a troubling piece of apparent evil by vaguely analogizing it to something utterly different which happens to be amenable to cozy bourgeois sentiment. There's also the point that research into human happiness (known in the trade as subjective well-being or SWB) finds that parents become happier when their children move out, so in the typical case it's not even loosely a sacrifice. The empty nest syndrome is one of those myths of the present day, like the prevalence of a midlife crisis, which is contradicted by empirical research.

So what's the 'real meaning' of this story? I see no reason to look further than the obvious interpretation, that it is morally required to submit yourself totally to the commands of God, even to the point of killing your children. We tend to find this repugnant; the writers and compilers of the *Torah* didn't. The story, along with other biblical references, reflects an awareness of child sacrifice as a customary practice that prevailed, or had recently prevailed, among the Israelites and other Canaanite cultures.

Peterson's Theory of Myths

Peterson has given us a clear explanation of how and why he thinks stories are important in Chapter 1 of *Maps of Meaning*, his first book, published in 1999. Peterson occasionally makes remarks showing that he still agrees with this explanation.

Here is Dr. Peterson's theory. The world is both a "forum for action" and "a place of things." Each of these is necessary; we can't do without both "modes of construal" (p. 1). The place of things is knowledge of facts and the forum for action is knowledge of values. Science can give us information about facts but it can't give us information about values (ethnology can tell us about the values people have in fact embraced, but it cannot recommend to us the values we ought to embrace).

The way Peterson talks about this, it seems as though only science can give us information about objective facts. But long before there was what we would call 'science', there was everyday knowledge of objective facts, what we might call common-sense knowledge (I am taller than my brother; eating this kind of berry will give you tummy ache; village y is further away from here than village x). Any human in any culture has a vast store of such knowledge. All human cultures include a folk physics and a folk biology, which consist of factual assertions about objective reality. For that matter, many non-human animals know a lot of objective facts and some couldn't survive without this knowledge. I had a cat who knew that a certain sound (a can opener) indicated she would soon get food—this is knowledge of objective reality. Science is a refinement and elaboration of human common-sense knowledge; human common-sense knowledge is a refinement and elaboration of animal knowledge. These all refer to the world of objective, physical reality, as well as to the world of subjective states of mind.

Peterson tells us that science can't help us in the forum for action, because that requires values; facts alone are insufficient. We're informed about meaning or value from myths, stories which communicate values and meaning. In the modern world, we have the factual knowledge given to us by science, but we lack the meaning and values given to us by myth. Mythic stories, then, are "maps of meaning." By becoming more acquainted with these stories and their correct interpretation, we will possess a guide to action: we will have a better idea of what to do, how to live our lives. (A lot of the time, Peterson in effect assumes that 'meaning' and 'value' are more or less the same thing, which I think is a mistake. To save space, I won't pursue this minor point here.)

Peterson correctly asserts that facts alone cannot logically imply any course of action. Facts by themselves cannot motivate. But he doesn't seem to notice that the counterpart is also true. Values by themselves can never motivate. They always have to be combined with beliefs about facts. Both beliefs about facts and judgments of value are required to motivate any purposive action. So, there can be no "forum for action" which excludes beliefs about facts.

Peterson seriously holds that there was a time in human history when there was no "notion of objective reality" (p. 1). Rather surprisingly, but quite unmistakably, he believes that this was the case up until the seventeenth century! (p. 5) Peterson maintains that "The 'natural', prescientific, or mythical mind is in fact primarily concerned with meaning—which is essentially implications for action—and not with 'objective' nature." And he asks, "How, precisely, did people think, not so very long ago, before they were experimentalists?" (p. 3).

As we will now see, humans, like all mammals, have always been experimentalists, and awareness of objective facts about the physical world must always precede the construction of myths.

The Baby as Scientist

If a baby shortly after birth is shown a succession of white balls, followed by a red ball, the baby will look longer at the red ball than it did at the preceding white ball. This, and thousands of other experiments made possible by plentiful videotape and extremely accurate timing, have helped to propel a revolution in what is known about the mental processes of infants. Peterson sometimes cites Jean Piaget, who closely observed children beginning in the 1920s, but Piaget didn't have videotape and we now know from more rigorous and more numerous observations by Alison Gopnik and her colleagues that most of his conclusions were mistaken (*Words, Thoughts, and Theories*, pp. 2, 220–21).

An implication of the new research is that babies are like scientists; they continually pay close attention to the physical world and develop their own theories about it. A baby is programmed by its genes to find out about the world of material objects, by a process of adopting theories and then revising or rejecting them in the light of new observations. The essential points of this revolution are summed up in the already-classic book, *The Scientist in the Crib*, first published in 1999. As *The Scientist in the Crib* puts it, "Human children in the first three years of life are consumed by a desire to explore and experiment with objects" (p. 86).

This shouldn't be too hard to accept, since we easily observe that kittens and puppies are obsessed with finding out about the physical world by experimental trial and error. It's harder to see with human babies because they have a longer period of near-immobility, but in this immobile period we now know that they are observing closely and drawing conclusions from their observations.

Parents often bewail the fact that their toddlers are 'into everything': they're driven by an instinct more powerful than hunger to understand the workings of the physical world. At the same time as they're learning about the world of physical objects, babies are also learning about other people, their minds and motivations. And we now know, for example, that a baby understands that they are a separate person, an independent self, at least at eighteen months and possibly earlier.

Dogs, cats, chimps, and humans are all born with some innate theories about the physical world (or, more strictly, with innate pre-programming to create such theories when stimulated by experience), and all of them revise these theories from practical experience in the first weeks, months, and years. After a few months outside the womb, dogs, cats, chimps, and humans have acquired a considerable amount of knowledge about the objective facts of the physical world. But then something happens which opens up a wide gulf between humans and other mammals: humans acquire a language capable of describing the world and arguing about it. This acquisition of a language also arises from an innate predisposition, revised and elaborated by practical experience.

Once they have acquired the rudiments of a language, humans can listen to stories and make up stories. And now they are ready to imbibe myths. When they start to learn about myths, their knowledge of objective facts about material objects is already extensive. It could not be otherwise. The story of Icarus can mean nothing to you unless you already know something about the Sun, flying, heating, melting, and falling.

The Alchemist as Scientist

Peterson frequently mentions alchemy, and follows Jung in seeing alchemy as essentially a non-empirical, magical pursuit, which reveals aspects of the collective unconscious, a kind of genetically programmed folk wisdom (*Maps of Meaning*, pp. 417–446).

Alchemy, in the West, began in the third century C.E. and flourished in Europe from the twelfth to the eighteenth century C.E. (*The Secrets of Alchemy*, p. 4). Alchemy was not mystical or spiritual. It was chemical science, though naturally it embodied many chemical theories we now consider to be mistaken. No one had a satisfactory method for distinguishing elements from compounds. Techniques of purification were primitive, and many recorded alchemical experiments only worked because of impurities, along the lines of "Stone Soup" (pp. 141–43).

Alchemists were often concerned with trying to change one substance into another, most notoriously to turn lead into gold. Alchemists believed that all metals are compounds, not elements, and therefore there had to be a way to reshuffle the elements to change one metal into another. 'Alchemy' and 'chemistry' meant the same thing until about 1700, when a division appeared, due to social and political pressures, for example the fear that being able to make gold from lead might undermine the currency and wreck the economy.

Alchemists believed that their knowledge should be kept secret from everyone except a few wise adepts. They therefore wrote their books in elaborate codes, in which mythological or symbolic figures were employed to represent physical entities. In an example cited by Lawrence Principe, a book of alchemy might include a drawing of a dragon attacking an eagle, signifying 'Let the red dragon devour the white eagle'. The red dragon means nitric acid; the white eagle means ammonium chloride. The red dragon devouring the white eagle signifies the chemical reaction of these two substances. This kind of symbolism was an encryption device, to keep knowledge of chemistry from falling into the wrong hands ("Learning about Alchemy with Larry Principe").

In the mid-nineteenth century, by which time alchemy was considered a thing of the past, a movement of popular thought arose, a rebellion against established beliefs, both science and Christianity. This new 'occult underground' or counter-culture (which over a century later would be called New Age) embraced Eastern religion, magic, spiritualism, and all forms of occultism. Since alchemy was being dismissed by conventional opinion and by official science and religion, and seemed to be mysterious and profound, the occult underground was attracted to alchemy, and interpreted it in terms of spirituality and self-transformation. The fact that alchemy was dismissed, by those who knew very little about it, as a mishmash of mysticism and magic, only recommended it to these new occultists. (The author of *The Occult Underground* gives us fascinating information about the popular new occultism which took hold in the mid-nineteenth century, but he, like Dr. Peterson, gets alchemy exactly wrong.)

Many books appeared, rooted in magical or spiritual thought, 'explaining' alchemy in this fashion, and since neither scientists nor historians of science were at that time much interested in alchemy, this erroneous explanation went unchallenged. It was copied from book to book, and became almost the only readily available theory of what alchemy had been. Then the Freudians and the Jungians arrived, and recast the magical or spiritual forces as forces in the unconscious mind. All these interpretations of alchemy as something other than experimental chemistry are still being copied from book to book for popular readerships, and all these books are endlessly reprinted, as though this interpretation had not been comprehensively demolished. Finally, along came Dr. Jordan Peterson, without taking the precaution of looking into any works on the history of chemistry published in the last fifty years, and repeated the old, thoroughly refuted, but still widely popular conception of alchemy.

For more than a half-century, historians of science have been carefully analyzing the alchemical texts, reproducing the experiments described, and building up a precise picture of the alchemical theories. They have shown that alchemy was a discipline dedicated to explaining the physical world by experimental and theoretical means. Among outstanding scientists who were committed alchemists were Tycho Brahe, Isaac Newton, and Robert Boyle. Historians of science have now re-introduced the old term, chymistry, to apply to both chemistry and alchemy, emphasizing the fact that (up until 1700) these were two names for one discipline.

Historical investigation of alchemy shows that Dr. Peterson is dead wrong. Alchemy was experimental science, and it went back more than a thousand years. But there's worse to come for Peterson's theory of myths.

Ancient Science

The first civilization to invent writing was Sumer, in what is now southern Iraq. No doubt there was science before Sumer, but it could not be permanently recorded. Sumerian civilization began around 4000 B.C.E., and was conquered by neighboring Akkad around 2300 B.C.E. Sumer and Akkad were eventually replaced by Babylon and Assyria. All these civilizations enabled and nurtured science. Their scientists could, for example, calculate the volumes of solid objects of various shapes, apply geometry and algebra to physical processes, and accurately predict the positions of the planets many hundreds of years into the future.

Science flourished in Egypt and in Greece, and then tremendous advances were made in the Greek-speaking world following the conquests of Alexander. Archimedes (third century B.C.E.), was one of the greatest scientists, greatest mathematicians, and greatest engineers of all time, with a large number of original discoveries, still incorporated into today's science. All ancient scientists knew that the Earth is a sphere, but in the second century B.C.E. Eratosthenes calculated the circumference of the Earth, correct to within two hundred miles.

With the rise of Rome, according to Richard Carrier, science continued to progress for a while, and reached a level roughly equal to that which would be re-attained by Europe in the sixteenth century. Roman scientific progress ceased after about 250 C.E., followed by centuries of retrogression. The revival of science in Europe beginning in the fourteenth century C.E. involved the recovery of ancient science, which had been largely destroyed within Christendom, but partially preserved by Islamic scholars writing in Arabic.

In China, independent of the West, there was spectacular philosophical, scientific, and technological progress in the period of 'warring states', 475–221 B.C.E. Then China was unified under a single government staffed by a formally educated bureaucracy with a single ideology, neo-Confucianism. Philosophical progress ground to a halt; scientific and technological progress were slowed to a snail's pace (and perhaps there was actual retrogression). Europe preserved its political disunity and later became the dynamo of progress. A condition of progress is that there be no powerful centralized state enforcing conformity of thought over a wide territory.

Aside from experimental science itself, the objective nature of physical reality has been discussed in more general terms for thousands of years. Pre-Socratic philosophers (sixth and fifth centuries B.C.E.) were able to discuss issues like the nature of time, space, and matter, often entirely naturalistically. Some of them were pure materialists, maintaining that everything in the universe, humans included, consists of nothing but physical matter. Later there were works like Aristotle's *Metaphysics* (fourth century B.C.E.) and Lucretius's *On the Nature of Things* (first century B.C.E.). Like his predecessor Democritus, Lucretius held that nothing at all exists except "atoms and the void."

Dr. Peterson's contention that thinking about nature as objective and non-supernatural goes back only four hundred years is a breathtaking howler.

The Myth of Archetypes

Peterson often appeals to Carl Jung's theory of archetypes. Jung noticed that very often the same story patterns appear in different cultures and in the utterances of mentally disturbed persons. Jung concluded that there are 'archetypes', unconscious predispositions in all humans, to produce the same story patterns in conscious thought. It's essential to the Jungian theory that these archetypes are genetically programmed, not merely transmitted through the culture.

Peterson uncritically swallows this theory and thinks that the archetypes generated by our unconscious have important things to tell us about meaning and values. This would buttress his claim that, when interpreting a story, he's finding something actually there in the story that can provide us with authoritative guidance about how to live our lives.

The archetype theory is unfalsifiable—how might the entire range of known stories be any different if there were no archetypes? There's no way to rule out alternative explanations for similarities in many stories: first, the stories could have been spread by cultural contact; second, there's a limited range of possibilities in human experience for basic story patterns; third, the stories could have been selected for by appeal to our aesthetic faculty (there are plot elements, known to Aristotle, Alexandre Dumas, and Joss Whedon, which make for an appealing story).

Archetypes are just a myth.

Is and Ought

Jordan Peterson relates his view of the need for myths to the philosophical problem of 'is and ought'. He sees the problem he perceives in many people not finding a meaning or a purpose in life as being associated with what he calls "the age-old problem of deriving the *ought* from the *is*" (*Maps of Meaning*, p. 13).

This is a serious misunderstanding about the history of philosophy. The problem of is and ought (or fact and value) was raised by David Hume in 1739. It then went unnoticed even by most of Hume's readers for well over a hundred years. Only in the mid-twentieth century did philosophers seriously begin to tackle this question.

The problem may be put like this. You can write down any number of sentences describing purely factual states of affairs, but you cannot logically derive from these statements, by themselves, any judgment about the morally right course of action. For instance,

1. An injection of substance *x* administered to person *A* will kill that person (a purely factual statement).

2. I ought not to give an injection of substance *x* to person *A* (a moral or ethical judgment).

Statement #2 does not logically follow from statement #1. But it would follow if we added the statement 'I ought not to do anything which will kill person *A*'—a moral judgment, not a factual statement. It would also follow from some such moral judgment as 'No one ought to kill any human being except under certain conditions', plus a factual statement that killing person *A* would not fall under those conditions.

Hume's question is purely conceptual and does not readily arise in everyday life, because we all normally take many goals or purposes for granted. If I tell you 'This building's on fire', I can assume you'll want to leave the building. I do not have to add 'I guess that you, like me, would prefer not to undergo a painful death by smoke inhalation and multiple burns, at least not this afternoon, and therefore the fact that the building is on fire, when combined with your system of values, implies that you should get out of here.' All that can be left unsaid.

Hume's problem of 'is and ought' is a serious philosophical development, but it has almost no direct application to practical matters, because we virtually never encounter situations where people can't bring themselves to make moral judgments, along with other value judgments. Quite the contrary, the worst atrocities usually happen, in part, because people are far too ready to make confident value judgments.

The human baby is born with extremely strong preferences or 'values': it prefers to avoid discomfort and it prefers to get approval from the other humans it encounters. As human infants absorb ideas from the culture, they develop further values. We simply never observe, in any time or place, a whole bunch of people who spontaneously abstain from making value judgments and therefore can't decide what to do.

So, when Peterson says that "an impassable gulf divides what is from what should be" (*Maps of Meaning*, p. 1) this is true (if Hume is right) of the logical relationships among sentences, but is not true of actual human thinking and doing (as Hume was well aware).

Hume's problem of is and ought has little bearing on Peterson's problem of whence we get our values. And Peterson's problem is misconceived from the get-go because knowledge of objective facts always necessarily comes before knowledge of myths.[1]

Bibliography

Carrier, Richard. 2017. *The Scientist in the Early Roman Empire*. Pitchstone.

Dewrell, Heath D. 2017. *Child Sacrifice in Ancient Israel*. Penn State University Press.

Gopnik, Alison, and Andrew N. Meltzoff. 1997. *Words, Thoughts, and Theories*. MIT Press.

Gopnik, Alison, Andrew N. Meltzoff, and Patricia K. Kuhl. 1999. *The Scientist in the Crib: Minds, Brains, and How Children Learn*. Morrow.

Hume, David. 1985 [1739]. *A Treatise of Human Nature: Being an Attempt to Introduce the Experimental Method of Reasoning into Moral Subjects*. Penguin.

Lindberg, David C. 2007 [1992]. *The Beginnings of Western Science: The European Scientific Tradition in Philosophical, Religious, and Institutional Context, Prehistory to 1450*. Second edition. University of Chicago Press.

Neher, Andrew. 1996. Jung's Theory of Archetypes: A Critique. *Journal of Humanistic Psychology* 36:2.

Peterson, Jordan B. 1999. *Maps of Meaning: The Architecture of Belief*. Routledge.

———. 2017. The Great Sacrifice: Abraham and Isaac. <https://www.youtube.com/watch?v=-yUP40gwht0&t=2772s>.

———. 2017. Cain and Abel. <www.youtube.com/watch?v=vMJnpwwpytg>.

———. 2018. *12 Rules for Life: An Antidote to Chaos*. Random House Canada.

———. 2021. *Beyond Order: 12 More Rules for Life*. Portfolio.

Principe, Lawrence M. 2011. Learning about Alchemy with Larry Principe. <https://www.youtube.com/watch?v=MbCol-h_ql0>.

---

[1] I thank David Gordon, Ray Scott Percival, and Barry Smith for criticisms of drafts of this chapter.

————. 2013. *The Secrets of Alchemy*. University of Chicago Press.

Russo, Lucio. 2004 [1996]. *The Forgotten Revolution: How Science Was Born in 300 BC and Why It Had to Be Reborn*. Springer.

Temple, Robert. 1986. *The Genius of China: 3,000 Years of Science, Discovery, and Invention*. Simon and Schuster.

Webb, James. 1988 [1974]. *The Occult Underground*. Open Court.

[7]
Stone, Stone-Soup, and Soup

MARC CHAMPAGNE

THE COLLECTOR: I've studied that trinket through every scientific means available, and it is my considered opinion that [this Infinity Stone is] nothing more than a worthless hunk of polished glass!

THANOS: I'm not surprised to hear you say that, old friend. To open this jewel's hidden secret requires great imagination.

—JIM STARLIN, *The Thanos Quest, Book Two: Games and Prizes* (1990)

To dislodge powerful intuitions, one needs tools commensurate with the task. Whatever else he may be wrong about, Jordan Peterson is surely right that stories, not arguments, are what ultimately move (most) people (most deeply). I thus want to introduce my argument by juxtaposing three stories, one fictional, the others not.

The tale of the "stone soup" has murky origins in European and Asian folklore. It can be found in different variants, but the core narrative is about a stranger who goes around promising to make soup from a stone. Intrigued and hungry, the various people he encounters provide him with a pot and some water to boil the stone. As the stranger prepares his wondrous dish, he remarks that the flavor would come out more fully were a dash of seasoning added. His spectators oblige and the seasoning is added. After a sip to test whether the broth is ready, the stranger suggests that it might benefit from having a few vegetables thrown in, for good measure. Farmers eager to taste the soup provide the stranger with root vegetables, celery, and so on. Finally, when the liquid has become a genuine soup, a ladle is used to fills bowls, and everyone—including the stranger—gets their fill. In some versions, the satisfied stranger leaves with the stone, while in other versions he hands over the stone to the villagers, so that they may reproduce the culinary miracle whenever needed.

Let us now switch to the non-fictional stories. The city of Mecca in Saudi Arabia is home to one of the most important pilgrimage sites in the world. A trip to Mecca that occurs during a specific five-day window of the lunar calendar is known as the Hajj, while at other times of the year such a trip constitutes the lesser Umrah. The pilgrimage site itself is built in a concentric fashion. At the outer rim, we find hotels meant to accommodate the millions of tourists who travel there every year. The next ring within is a mosque, the Masjid al-Haram, one of the largest buildings in the world. Inside, we find a large open-air space with white marble flooring, where devotees slowly spiral barefoot toward an almost-cubical structure. This structure must be circled seven times (counterclockwise). One corner of the cubical structure houses a black stone which, it is believed, came from heaven. Pilgrims jostle to kiss or touch this stone. Those who cannot get near enough point in the direction of the stone while proclaiming God's greatness.

I suppose one could draw an explicit conclusion from this juxtaposition. But, if you have to spell out the moral of a story, you haven't picked a potent enough story. The foregoing juxtaposition should thus become especially telling when we consider the third story—the shortest of the bunch: In 2017, Peterson gave a series of lectures on the Psychological Significance of the Biblical Stories. His first lecture lasted two hours. In that time, Peterson managed to cover only a single line from the Bible. The end.

The lopsided gloss-to-text ratio just recounted provides a startling fact: one can understand Peterson's lectures without having read (or "believing in") the Bible. Hence, the critique I want to develop, which might be called the stone-soup objection (Champagne 2020, pp. 137–38), comes in two versions. The weak version says that if the principles of a proper life can be intelligibly discussed in purely natural terms, then one *can* forgo supernatural origins and treat the Bible as a fully-human document (it should be obvious that this applies to more than just the Bible). The stronger version says that one *should* forgo supernatural origins and treat the Bible as a fully-human document. Clearly, the stronger objection is only feasible if the weaker version is. I will argue for both. Discarding supernatural baggage is not just a matter of being more parsimonious, but of avoiding the dogmatism that comes with infallibility. Let me explain.

Detecting Profundity in Manifest Simplicity

Peterson believes that the Bible contains a special kind of ageless wisdom that must be unlocked by a process of interpretation. This is nothing new. What is striking, though, is how much insight and depth he claims to discern in even the simplest Biblical lines. Peterson is a psychologist, not a priest, so he transforms all the components of his target text into tenets that seem more plausible to his audience (and which conveniently connect with his ideas in psychology).

We can illustrate this by parsing the Book of Genesis's first line. In Peterson's hands, the phrase "In the beginning . . ." supposedly means the state of disorder that humans confront, before their consciousness and language imposes some sort of cognitive order (Peterson 2017a, section 3). The next word, ". . . God . . ." supposedly means the guiding principle behind hierarchies of competence, presented in a personified form so as to give us an ideal "of what it means to be a properly functioning, properly social, and properly competent individual" (2017a, section 3). The verb ". . . created . . ." supposedly means the capacity of consciousness "to be aware and to communicate" what(ever) is before it (2017a, section 5). Finally, ". . . the heavens . . ." supposedly means an "image of perfection" that represents the possibility of our ideals and our current state—". . . and the earth"—"coming together in some sort of communication" (2017b, section 6).

Putting these segments back together, we might say that the environmental stimuli received by conscious awareness and categorized by language give rise to distinctions and orderings that can be refined and that those refinements, when communicated to others, foster better living conditions. Agree or disagree, this is clearly different from saying "A long time ago, a perfect being built everything that we now know as the universe," which is arguably the paraphrase many (or at least I) have in mind when reading the verse.

Is this psychological account found in the Bible—or on the stage of Toronto's Isabel Bader Theatre? Peterson says that "There is more to this [Biblical] story than I understand or can understand. I am laying out what I can understand and then making it rational, but . . . one thing I have found about digging into these stories is that the deeper you dig, the more you find. And that's . . . one of the things that convinced me that there was more to them than I had originally suspected" (2017a, Q&A, my transcription). Crediting simple (and often simplistic) stories with complex insights amounts to crediting a stone with flavoring a soup.

Cooking a Soup around the Stone One Grew Up With

Stripped of all priming and partisanship, a sentence like "In the beginning God created the heavens and the earth" (Genesis 1:1) is actually quite plain. We may interpret this simplicity as a strength or a flaw. Let us assume, as Peterson does, that it is a strength. Such a gloss leads to two problems. First, we must explain why we privilege this particular statement. After all, another old book could just as confidently assert that "The heavens and the earth were never created and had no beginning." This is arguably just as profound-sounding, so why is such a contrary claim not revered? In the absence of reasons, we are told, we must have "faith." Faith, however, is an attitude that can be directed at anything but cannot be directed at everything. Hence, we need to be told why we give a free pass to some claims and not others (the answer "Because my parents did so" is rarely found satisfying).

Detecting profundity in manifest simplicity generates a second problem. If a sentence that takes five seconds or so to enunciate can be understood only after two hours or more of interpretation, what are we actually interested in: the sentence—or the elaborate gloss we build around it? This distinction matters, because lectures like the ones given by Peterson do not pretend to have any Divine origin, whereas the Biblical text does. This origin in turn matters, because ideas that are Divine cannot be wrong, whereas ideas arrived at by humans can be mistaken and thus possibly revised. Peterson claims that the Bible is the culmination of millennia of observations, but no amount of observations will provide one with a religious level of certainty.

Peterson is no doubt correct that "find[ing] out what the [religious] stories are about can aid our self-understanding" (2017a, section 3). Yet, when he says that "Without the cornerstone provided by that [self-]understanding, we're lost" (2017a, section 3), we have to be clear about what exactly is bearing the load. Fortunately, the question of whether something is load-bearing can be tested: one simply removes a posit and sees whether the sense-making structure erected around it still stands. Performing that test, we may ask: does getting together at a specific location with people who share a sense of belonging enhance one's life? Certainly. First-person reports of those traveling to Mecca, for example, amply establish this (Alnabulsi et al. 2020). Would these psychological and social benefits vanish if the object(s) or text at the center of such gatherings were revealed to have a purely natural/human origin? Done with gradual cultural adaptation, future generations could get accustomed to the idea that their beliefs rest on an entirely natural foundation (in fact, many religious followers may currently feign belief in front of their peers, to avoid opprobrium). Similarly, I do not think the intelligibility and merit of Peterson's Biblical lectures are diminished by accepting that he addresses—and is an active participant in—a human creation.

Hastening the Erosion of Religion by Prizing Intelligibility and Practicality

Peterson explains that his motive for assessing the Bible "is to extract out something of value that's practical. One of the rules that I have when I'm lecturing is that I don't want to tell anybody anything that they can't use. I think of knowledge as a tool" (2007a, section 4). Tools, however, are distinguished by their function and functions can be realized by different things. It does not matter, for example, if a garlic presser is made of copper, aluminum, or stainless steel. If it presses garlic, then it is a garlic presser. Why doesn't Peterson direct his interpretive prowess toward, say, Islam's Quran or Thelema's Book of the Law—also cryptic tomes allegedly originating from a divine source and thus ripe for a Petersonian treatment? Tradition gives ideas a head start, but what book should one consult to tell one what book one should consult? We humans are responsible for our claims, arguments, and interpretations, so it is an abdication of our responsibility to credit a text with ideas that we have formulated ourselves.

So what if, instead of listening to a-Peterson-lecture-about-the-Bible, people listened to a-Peterson-lecture, full stop? We would likely still hear about evolution, Jung, Nietzsche, Dostoevsky, ideology, motivation, consciousness, lobsters, dragons, chaos, order, hierarchies, the hippocampus, Piaget, parenting, Nazis, psychedelics, dreams, gulags, and Solzhenitsyn. The Bible would doubtlessly show up too, if and when appropriate. But, with the specter of infallibility gone, that text would receive interpretive charity, not credulity. Importantly, large portions could be skipped.

All texts, religious or otherwise, must be interpreted. But, interpretation is something *we* (humans) do, so its practice, no matter what the intent, risks exposing the non-divine roots of religions. Fanatics may prefer literal interpretation, but for the mainstream Western public, the authority of the Bible is no longer a given. Peterson notes that one of his favorite thinkers, Friedrich Nietzsche, "believed that the Catholicization of the phenomena of life and history produced the kind of mind" capable of maximal coherence and thereby "capable of transcending its dogmatic foundations, and concentrating on something else" (2017a, sect. 1). Nietzsche had in mind medieval philosophy/theology, but the Protestant Reformation's emphasis on individual readings also contributed to this intellectual shift. Whatever the historical details, a lot of people found that they could make soup (live a moral and rewarding life) without any stone. In this way, "Nietzsche believed that Christianity died of its own hand" (2017a, section 1). It's nevertheless hard to let go, so salvage attempts like Peterson's attract a lot of attention.

The irony is that, the more Peterson makes sense, the less you have to read the Bible. The stone-soup is thus a transitional stage in an unfinished learning curve. So, while Peterson and his followers see themselves as champions of religious belief, they are actually hastening its erosion. Indeed, Peterson's explanatory prowess risks exposing the Bible as *dispensable*.

Many Christians celebrate Peterson's work, but leaders of other faiths, knowing better, would see his engagement with religious ideas as subversive (for instance al-Andalusi 2019). Peterson thinks "part of the reason that Islam has its back up with regards to the West" is that it realizes the "questioning mind of the West poses a tremendous danger to the integrity of their culture, and it does. Westerners, us—we undermine ourselves all the time with our searching intellect" (2017a, section 1). By prizing regular standards of intelligibility and practicality, Peterson is at the forefront of this undermining.

Foundations that Were Under Our Feet All Along

Is this gradual transition from stone-soup to soup something to be feared or celebrated? According to Peterson, Nietzsche "knew that, when we knocked the slats out of the base of Western civilization by destroying this representation—this God ideal—we would destabilize, and move back and forth violently between nihilism and the extremes of ideology" (2017a, section 1). Two things are worth noting.

First, unless we cherry-pick historical events, it is by no means obvious that things are currently worse. As a social scientist, surely Peterson ought to know that, if secular collectivist regimes resulted in atrocities (Cheng 1995; Solzhenitsyn 2018), it's inconclusive to blame secularism as the culprit. Not only is the sample geographically and historically tiny, a contrast is required with secular *individualism*—which is quite another story. In any event, Peterson undercuts his own arguments when he defines "God" as whatever one values most (in Paikin et al. 2009, minute 18), since this permissive definition would entail that there has never been a Godless society, Communist ones included.

Second, even if one could somehow link secularization with selected atrocities, an oscillation between apathy and militancy ensues only if the corner stone is not replaced with something better. Make no mistake: better replacements *are* possible. One may take issue with the particular account put forward by Nietzsche, but there is no valid inference from the premise 'A viable replacement of x did not work in this first attempt' to the conclusion 'No replacement of x is possible.'

"Nietzsche's idea," Peterson says, "was that human beings were going to have to create their own values" (2017a, section 1). Peterson believes that this cannot be done, but—in keeping with his claim (Peterson 1999, p. 73) that we act out ideas long before we notice and verbalize them—he is blind to the fact that creating values is exactly what he does when he weaves his various sources together on stage. His audience members nod approvingly, not because they have reached some universal bedrock, but because they have heard the stories in childhood. Going back to the sentence parsed earlier, another group raised on "The heavens and the earth were never created and had no beginning" would presumably feel an equally strong simpatico connection with this contradicting claim. Things sound intuitive only because they were implanted in our minds before our critical thinking faculties hit puberty. He who controls education controls imagination.

Ideas indeed play themselves out in historical time. But, precisely for that reason, assessing whether an idea is worthwhile depends on when we render the verdict. Atheism is a relatively recent arrival. So, on an elongated timeline, it is too early to tell. Luckily, one does not have to convince the whole globe in order to gauge whether something is true. On a personal scale, the verdict can come much sooner. Peterson has an unfortunate tendency to set up a false alternative between theism and anything-goes nihilism, but those bereft of theistic conviction (like the people documented in Everett 2009) are doing just fine, both morally (Saslow et al. 2013) and existentially (Lacewing 2016).

This should come as no surprise. The supernatural, being unreal, has no causal effect on the world apart from our actions and choices. That is why stones need actual ingredients. So, whatever measure of control we have over our destiny is already there. We do not need any kind of grand leap in our nature, since we have been the discoverers of the insights all along. What remains is for us to own up to this (scary but emancipatory) fact.

Playing the Game of Life Without Any Trump Card

Because the stone that prompts cooking sessions is merely a prompt, one might be tempted to view it as harmless. Alas, things are not that simple because, even if we remove a stone, we do not thereby remove its need. On his daughter Mikhaila's podcast (2021, minute 36 onward), Peterson recognizes that humans "have a profound religious impulse. I am not saying that it is good or that it is bad. I am saying that something has to be done with it." I agree. Unlike me, however, Peterson describes himself as "a rather staunch admirer of traditional Christianity . . . in its Catholic form" because this is supposedly "as sane as people can get" (my transcriptions). Yet, as his daughter immediately pointed out, some Catholic doctrines are "a little 'out there'." Indeed.

In reply, Peterson acknowledges "the strange irrationality that goes along with a religious belief," but he insists that "we need something structured and irrational to protect us from even less structured and more irrational beliefs." Judging from the conversation, meaninglessness and fear of death are the main threats we must protect against. To keep these at bay, "[w]e cannot live in a fully rational world because we are not smart enough. We need something to fill in the gaps." If Peterson's account is correct, it can never be soup all the way down.

I am sympathetic to (and have in fact defended) the claim that the non-rational elements of our lives cannot be fully eradicated, even in principle (Champagne 2015; Champagne 2019). Hence, nothing in the rejection of religion commits one to a triumphant belief in the exhaustive powers of reason. Yet, while reason has limits, we should not stuff our hopes and fears into the residual gap. A worthwhile distinction should thus be made between the non-rational (unrelated to reason) and the irrational (against reason). Accepting the former does not entail accepting the latter.

According to Peterson, "[t]he advantage of codified religion is that there is a unifying force behind it," whereas "what you get now [in secular society] is this fragmentation and search for replacement for religious values" (Mikhaila Peterson podcast). It is tautologically true that traditional ideas enjoy wide(r) social dispersion. There are obvious advantages to this. Yet, what Peterson's account neglects to mention is that, when the cornerstone of a tradition is considered sacred, it drags with it something that his commitment to open inquiry and dialogue ought to shun, namely dogma. Despite warning in his book *Beyond Order* (2021, p. 29) that established social structures can become tyrannical once contestation/revision is removed, Peterson informs us that some religious stories "cannot be improved upon" (p. 54). This is where he and I part ways.

The idea of a "supreme value" beyond the reach of all human reasoning may sound noble, but it can be (and routinely is) invoked to justify any action. No matter how important a thing is—girls receiving an education, wearing (or not wearing) what one wants, making a living in an office tower without being smashed by a plane—the Divine will always be more important. Many people may think that the 9/11 hijackers misunderstood God's message, but this exact objection is mirrored, since those hijackers thought many people misunderstood God's message. Of course, no one can verify what God wants, so objections can always be met with an appeal to mystery. God is the ultimate trump card.

The fact that adherents of some religious traditions are more peaceful than others is a comparison liable of changing depending on the circumstances. Such score-keeping may be historically significant, but it is not philosophically significant. Importantly, the looming possibility of belief-sanctioned violence is not present in secular discourse. No one has ever been beheaded for penning a negative movie review or publishing a drawing of Pinocchio. Horrible acts do happen. But, when we acknowledge that the soup comes from *our* ingredients, we acknowledge our ability to be wrong and/or do evil. No secular account of human nature can accommodate a concept like "Papal Inerrancy" or "Infallible Imams" (and the edicts that such concepts license).

Peterson says that "the Bible exists in that space that is half into the dream and half into articulated knowledge" (2017a, sect. 3). This is true—not because the Bible enjoys some special status—but rather because *all* human experience is part dream and part articulate knowledge. Surely psychology has taught us that. Peterson is also correct when he states that interpreting stories "can aid our self-understanding" (2017a, section 3). Discussing a good movie after a viewing also has that effect. Peterson would be ill-placed to deny this since, in his hands, even Disney movies become further evidence of his psychological theories—minus, of course, the looming possibility of blasphemy.

Peterson's arguments invoke many truths then infer conclusions far stronger than what those premises allow (see the excellent analysis of "Jesus-smuggling" by Woodford 2020). The concepts of value hierarchy and topmost value can be brought down to Earth and made compatible with our ability to err. All one needs to do is match the religious devotee's enthusiasm while acknowledging that one's yearning for a full life, no matter how ardent, cannot guide one about what to do next. That, like most things, requires fallible inquiry.

A Learning Curve that One Must Learn

The stone stage, which I have barely touched upon, rejects inquiry in favor of literal interpretation. If a text says that the universe was created by someone in six days, then the universe was created by someone in six days. If a text says that seventy-two perpetually-virgin wives are waiting for one in another world, then that is indeed what awaits one in another world. Why, one might wonder, should anyone believe such outlandish claims? Literal interpretation has an answer to that too: the text insists that it is saying the truth. Problem solved.

Most religious traditions have this auto-certifying feature, so comparison with competing creeds is usually frowned upon. However, even if you ban everything that might lead you to think otherwise, you cannot ban your own mind. The "stone-soup" stage thus begins with the realization that implausible tenets need to be interpreted non-literally. One way to transition while saving face is to consider the previous stage, not wrong, but "extremist" or "fundamentalist." As Peterson's success shows, many Christians are currently in the stone-soup stage. There are early indications that others may be taking baby steps into it as well:

> What does it mean to be Shi'i? How should believers see themselves, the texts that they read and the contexts in which they live? More critically, what is the relationship between our rational faculty and knowledge, and how does the Imam with his infallible knowledge intervene in the epistemic process? . . . Two central issues remain . . . .: that proper rational inquiry needs to be critically engaged in evaluating intellectual traditions . . . and that the revelation in the words of both the Qur'ān and the *hadīth* [or record of the Prophet Muhammad's words and actions] directly addresses our reality both within and without. Out of these two methods a hybrid version will probably emerge that seeks to integrate philosophical inquiry about the nature of existence, selfhood and knowledge with a deep contemplation of the texts transmitted from the Imams. The primary task of that hybrid will be to articulate a clear and coherent hermeneutics that can effect this reintegration. (Rizvi 2012, p. 503)

It's only a matter of time before this "hybrid" project sees the emergence of a homegrown Peterson.

In the stone-soup stage, comparisons with other texts are not frowned upon but encouraged. Differences in specific religions notwithstanding, what is common to all humans who believed in religions is that a. they were humans and b. they believed. So, one reads a book like *Maps of Meaning* (Peterson 1999) or *The Hero with a Thousand Faces* (Campbell 2004) and discovers "that there were similarities between messiah stories in different religions and that throughout human history, civilizations produced religion and the structures of religion, which were human attempts at dealing with the challenges of life" (DeWitt 2013, pp. 188–89). This is a big concession—bigger, as we shall see, than initially realized. But, for a person at this stage of the learning curve, adopting a more plausible "stance on religion was a saving grace. By grasping the concept that there were very human motivations for the rise of religion, I could promote religion and spirituality not on the basis of its truth but on its benefits to humans" (DeWitt 2013, p. 189). It is okay to believe if the belief works. Or so one thinks.

Transition to a stoneless soup gets ushered in, quite quietly, with a simple question: *why* does the belief work? It is a pesky question, to be sure. But, it is not a question that will go away. If a literal interpretation was wrong, then surely the practical success of a belief cannot be miraculous. By that point, all that remains is to realize/accept that an adoption of secularism has *already* occurred. Unbeknownst to one, the shift to a stone-soup was actually a shift to soup.

For a host of reasons, coming to terms with this can take time. There are many closets we can hide in—and more often than not we are hiding from ourselves. To ease the coming out process, the curiosity and respect for truth that prompted one to question the stone stage must be nurtured and encouraged. It also helps to have irreligious families and communities around—to break the volunteer's dilemma and witness first-hand that living a 100% human life does not result in spontaneous human combustion. Still, even in ideal circumstances, only individuals can decide, at their own pace.

Learning as a Personal, Not Social, Trajectory

A rationale is discernible in the progression from stone, stone-soup, and finally soup. What gets this learning curve into gear is the fact—and it is very much a fact—that stones have no nutritional value. Unpacking that analogy, *vague and unjustified platitudes surrounded by brilliant glosses remain vague and unjustified platitudes*. Hence, if Peterson's lectures contain something of value, then it is he, not the Bible, that deserves credit.

Some religious believers pre-empt critical investigation by simply reciting/chanting their preferred text, over and over. This is not what Peterson does. Instead, his university background is on full display. As a result, one can comprehend a Peterson lecture without ever having read the Bible. This is likely the case for many attendees and online viewers. Since it only takes a modicum of self-awareness to realize that the stone can be removed without loss, rationally explicating the irrational is an untenable venture, destined to unravel.

When I say "destined" to unravel, I mean this in a logical sense, not a historical sense. Patterns can be discerned in time (Champagne 2016), but there is nothing inexorable about history (Popper 1961). Aside from truisms about inheriting a culture and language, collective trends are largely irrelevant, since individuals are the only agents of change and only individuals undergo experiences. So, whereas a book like *Maps of Meaning* (Peterson 1999) makes sweeping historical claims, commentators like Sandra Woien prefer to drag Peterson onto safer terrain by insisting that, in his lectures, "Peterson is not trying to provide a religious or inductive justification [...]. Instead, he is simply trying to show that Biblical stories have a psychological or prescriptive significance that should not be ignored" (Woien 2021, p. 150). Like a placebo, the stone at the heart of this stone-soup certainly does a lot of psychological work. But, here too, a gradual disrobing of falsehoods can ensue—to the extent that one decides to think.

Jerry DeWitt, once a Pentecostal pastor, describes how he began with the belief that "God *loves* everyone." This feelgood belief obviously clashes with the needless suffering we witness around us, so DeWitt weakened it to "God *saves* everyone." According to this revised view, the suffering experienced in this world is merely transitional, since God will finally apply his benevolence at full capacity in the afterlife. Of course, the main drawback of this account is that it is supported by no evidence whatsoever. So, he eventually switched to saying that "God is *in* everyone." This cleverly obviates the search for evidence by asking us to instead look inward. Of course, once we look inward, we eventually conclude that "God is everyone's *internal dialogue*." Healthy adult humans can indeed monitor their own actions and choices. In other words, they have a conscience. Yet, how plausible is it that, when you cogitate, you are conversing with an all-powerful deity? DeWitt (2013, pp. 235–260), recounts that, by that point, it was just a matter of time before concluding that "God is a *delusion*" (in the strict non-judgmental sense of delusional belief).

Now What?

It may be irrational to believe in a placebo after its status has been revealed, but it is entirely rational to seek the benefits it once provided. No human can tolerate meaningless-ness (for long), so if nothing of substance is offered to replace the psychological and societal function(s) previously served by religious beliefs, those beliefs will come back gal-loping—often in even less healthy forms. Achieving a ten-able alternative to religion therefore "requires (among other things) a viable theory of *values*, a viable theory of *consciousness*, a viable theory of *meaning*, and a viable the-ory of *aesthetic experience* and *ritual*" (Champagne 2020, p. 181; emphasis added). Unlike religion, there is no reason to expect or demand that these components come from a single source.

By addressing narratives that have shaped Western imaginations, Peterson is tapping into something truly pri-mordial. Those who disagree with Peterson should therefore take notice, since countering his outlook without proposing a replacement narrative simply won't make a dent.

If we put aside preconceptions and pay close attention (Champagne forthcoming), we realize that all the mater-ials for a non-dogmatic drama about our challenging but exalted place in the universe are already here, in this world. DeWitt recounts that, after letting go of religious belief, he was able to satisfy his desire to help people "all without pretending that I was someone who I wasn't or pre-tending to know all the answers" (2013, p. 241). Try it your-self: a bowl of soup without a stone tastes the same—and weighs less.

We've heard other-worldly tales for millennia, so natu-rally stories built solely from this-worldly materials are bound to sound new. Yet, familiarity is a byproduct of par-enting and enculturation, so what counts as "traditional" or "established" can change with time. Secular mythologies and narratives may have thus far failed to rival the popular influence of religions, but this does not make their devel-opment any less important or urgent. As was said at the outset, a good story can only be dislodged by a *better* story. I cannot think of a nobler task than to essay a worldview that retains the enchantment of religion while avoiding its drawbacks. Can this be done? My own life and household attest that it can. As for a larger scale, the only way to find out is to find out.

References

Alnabulsi, Hani, John Drury, Vivian L. Vignoles, and Sander Oogink. 2020. Understanding the Impact of the Hajj: Explaining Experiences of Self change at a Religious Mass Gathering. *European Journal of Social Psychology* 50:2.

Al-Andalusi, Abdullah (real name Mouloud Farid). 2019. Should Muslims Be Left-wing or Right-Wing? Why Muslims Don't Need Dr Jordan Peterson. abdullahalandalusi.com blog post, July 16th.

Campbell, Joseph. 2004. *The Hero with a Thousand Faces*. Princeton: Princeton University Press.

Champagne, Marc. 2015. Don't Be an Ass: Rational Choice and Its Limits. *Reason Papers* 37:1.

———. 2016. Diagrams of the Past: How Timelines Can Aid the Growth of Historical Knowledge. *Cognitive Semiotics* 9:1.

———. 2019. Consciousness and the Philosophy of Signs: A New Précis. *American Journal of Semiotics* 35:3–4.

———. 2020. *Myth, Meaning, and Antifragile Individualism: On the Ideas of Jordan Peterson*. Exeter: Imprint Academic.

———. Forthcoming. Putting Aside One's Natural Attitude— and Smartphone—to See what Matters More Clearly. In *Phenomenology and Phaneroscopy*, edited by Mohammad Shafiei and Ahti-Veikko Pietarinen. Cham: Springer.

Cheng, Nien. 1995. *Life and Death in Shanghai*. London: Harper-Collins.

DeWitt, Jerry. 2013. *Hope After Faith: An Ex-Pastor's Journey from Belief to Atheism*. Boston: Da Capo.

Everett, Dan. 2009. *Don't Sleep, There are Snakes: Life and Language in the Amazonian Jungle*. New York: Random House.

Lacewing, Michael. 2016. Can Non-Theists Appropriately Feel Existential Gratitude? *Religious Studies* 52:2.

Paikin, Steve, Justin Trottier, Kathy Shaidle, Gretta Vosper, Jordan B. Peterson, and Rob Buckman. 2009. Advertising Atheism. *The Agenda with Steve Paikin*, TVO television program, originally aired February 19th.

Peterson, Jordan B. 1999. *Maps of Meaning: The Architecture of Belief*. New York: Routledge.

———. 2017a. Biblical Series I: Introduction to the Idea of God. Lecture given at Toronto's Isabel Bader Theatre, May 16th.

———. 2017b. Biblical Series II: Genesis 1: Chaos and Order. Lecture given at Toronto's Isabel Bader Theatre, May 23rd.

———. 2021. *Beyond Order: 12 More Rules for Life*. Toronto: Random House Canada.

————. Peterson, Mikhaila, Mark Manson, and Jordan B. Peterson. 2021. *The Mikhaila Peterson Podcast*, Episode 54. February 7th. <www.youtube.com/watch?v=dGDF2tTq6xw&t=1318s>.

Popper, Karl R. 1961. *The Poverty of Historicism*. New York: Harper and Row.

Rizvi, Sajjad H. 2012. 'Only the Imam Knows Best': The Maktab-e Tafkīk's Attack on the Legitimacy of Philosophy in Iran. *Journal of the Royal Asiatic Society* 22:3–4.

Saslow, Laura R., Robb Willer, Matthew Feinberg, Paul K. Piff, Katharine Clark, Dacher Keltner, and Sarina R. Saturn. 2013. My Brother's Keeper? Compassion Predicts Generosity More Among Less Religious Individuals. *Social Psychological and Personality Science* 4:1.

Solzhenitsyn, Aleksandr. 2018. *The Gulag Archipelago*. With a foreword by Jordan B. Peterson. London: Penguin Random House.

Woien, Sandra. 2021. Review of *Myth, Meaning, and Antifragile Individualism: On the Ideas of Jordan Peterson*. *Reason Papers* 42:1.

Woodford, Stephen. 2020. Jesus Smuggling: Is Jordan Peterson Guilty? *Rationality Rules*, February 11th. <www.youtube.com/watch?v=on0Lziov00Y&t=197s>.

[8]
The Masculine and Feminine of God

KATIE SKURJA

When our son was not quite three-years old, you could almost see the thought bubbles form over his head when he was making a connection about some important concept. At times, announcing his astute observations could be socially awkward. On one such occasion, our friends Mark and Cynthia were visiting when I watched a thought bubble form in the air as we stood talking in the kitchen. I noticed he had been staring at them intently as they leaned against our counters. Suddenly, he lunged toward Cynthia with a finger pointing at her lower mid-section and proclaimed, "Lou have a china!" Turning toward Mark, he proudly said, "Lou have a penis!" (He couldn't yet pronounce his y's, so *you* became *lou*.) Even though our friends were both casually dressed in loose-fitting jeans and neither is a paragon of god-like sexuality, a child barely out of toddlerhood could proudly tell the difference between a man and woman. How much easier for a child to distinguish male and female when the sex-typical features are more pronounced? And yet, this is the issue at the heart of what catapulted Jordan Peterson onto the international stage.

In 2016, Peterson released a video explaining why he would refuse to comply with Canada's proposed Bill C-16 on gender identity rights. His objection had to do with the compelled speech aspect of the law, which would require state employees to use preferred pronouns of individuals including made-up words for newly minted genders. Though his

119

detractors accuse of him of extremist ideas, his greatest "sin" is rooted in standing for free speech and the self-evident truth of the biological differences between men and women. In doing so, he became a lightning rod in the culture wars.

As if that wasn't daring enough, Peterson had the audacity to discuss the differences that tend to show up in personality between men and women. Though he freely says men and women are more alike than different, he does not back down from research showing tendencies of women falling on one side of the median and men on the other in various ways. Take the area of interests. Women tend to be drawn toward people and men have a proclivity to be more interested in things. Of the Big Five Personality traits, the biggest difference tends to show up in the trait of agreeableness in a 60-40 split between men and women respectively. Women also tend to score higher in the traits of openness and neuroticism, the latter of which is understood as negative emotions, such as sadness and fear.

These differences, Peterson often explains, are most pronounced on the extremes of the spectrum. While most of us fall somewhere in the middle of the bell curve, displaying varying degrees of agreeableness and its counterpart of disagreeableness, the most disagreeable people tend to be men. This is evidenced by the huge disparity of men in prison for violent crimes, representing the far end of that spectrum. Though disagreeableness may sound like a negative trait on face value, especially if it leads to behaviors that can land one in prison, Peterson reminds us that every trait has a positive and a negative expression. The more a trait is overemphasized, the more its shadow side, or negative impulses, are expressed. However, the existence of shadow sides does not negate the positive aspects of a trait. Some of the favorable aspects hidden within the disagreeable trait include self-starter, thinking outside the box, and courage.

At the other end of that spectrum, the most agreeable people tend to be women. For several years, I was part of a prison ministry team at our local women's prison. As women shared their stories, a common theme emerged. Many of the women were in prison because of their willingness to go along with the schemes of the boyfriend. Though it may sound positive to be high in the agreeable trait, there is a dark side when used out of proportion. Some of the shadow sides of being too agreeable include people-pleasing, co-dependency, and passivity.

When trying to pigeon-hole him as an extremist on various positions, many interviewers have accused Peterson of being anti-woman for standing by research showing these tendencies of men and women in the various traits. Unwilling to be backed into a corner, Peterson often draws on examples from his clinical experience helping those who are too agreeable become more assertive. Both women and men who suffer from an excess amount of any given trait need to face their fears in order to become more balanced.

In speaking about men and women, I have heard Peterson on more than one occasion allude to the idea that to say *male* and *female* is not the same as saying *masculine* and *feminine*. What that difference is, I have not yet heard him specifically articulate. This absence of clarity from someone who can talk circles around most speaks to the complexity of the subject. It is far easier to talk about biological differences between men and women than the expressions of those differences in personality. Given a room of a hundred people, even a young child could successfully sort the males from the females. Distinguishing the difference between masculine and feminine is a bit trickier, providing fodder for confusion.

Of Lions and Lambs

Part of the problem is rooted in our language. By the very words, *masculine* is equated with *male* and *feminine* is equated to *female*. In one psychology journal article from 1974, words such as *compassionate, gentle, childlike, shy,* and *tender* were used on a list to describe feminine. Included in the list was the word *feminine* itself, as if it was self-evident of what that means. By contrast, words used to describe masculine included leader, *assertive, dominant, independent*, and *self-reliant*. Given this list of descriptors, a biological male who relates more to the *feminine* traits may feel like there is something wrong with him. In the same way, a biological female whose personality is better described as *masculine* might believe she is defective. Such people might even be susceptible to the idea that they were born in the wrong body.

From my own experience, I can understand the difficulty of trying to tease out the nuance of talking about the difference between the biology of male and female from the psychology of masculine and feminine. However, I want to submit there is a way to talk about these differences that even a child can understand. I stumbled on this concept after unintentionally kicking a hornet's nest while teaching about the masculine and feminine sides of God in a seminary class back in 2004.

The main premise of the spiritual formation class is about embracing paradox as the key to a healthy spirituality because the very nature and character of God is paradoxical. A paradox is a bigger truth that holds together two seemingly opposing truths. All the big "T" Truths that we see in Christ, the image of the unseen God, are paradoxical: truth and grace, justice and mercy, human and divine, servant and leader, to name just a few. To say that Christ is one or the other of these polarities is to fall into an untruth. Because our minds have a tendency to think in binary, black-and-white ways, the concept of paradox is very elusive to us. Like balancing on the top of a teeter-totter, holding paradox is not easy. We human beings seem to find comfort in sitting firmly with our feet on the ground of one side or the other, regardless that it is only a half-truth.

After getting some pushback from both the conservative and the progressive ends of the spectrum, I experimented with using the language of *Lion* and *Lamb* to refer to masculine and feminine respectively. Christ, as the image of God, embodies both of these natures. It was a breakthrough in the conversation, uniting both sides of the spectrum! What I discovered is we can talk freely about the Lion and Lamb sides of God, and thus of ourselves, in a way that transcends the language barriers of masculine and feminine. I found that I could talk with a big, angry Marine about his need to embrace his Lamb side without him flinching. Had I suggested he needed to face the feminine side of God, he would have stormed out of my office and never looked back. In the same way, I could talk with a mousy, petite, and fearful woman about her need to embrace her Lion side without scaring her away. If Christ, who is the image of the unseen God, is both Lion and Lamb, then so are we who are created in the image of God.

The Mouths of Babes

When I was first introduced to Peterson's work, I was smitten by the fact that he transcends the divide of the psychological and the spiritual. He is able to find the nuggets of truth in the extremes of the various polarizing topics, but then rises above them to embrace the bigger truth, the paradox. In referencing the spark of the divine in every human, he was speaking my love language. The notion of being created in the image of God is a central theme in my work. I refer to it by the Latin name, the Imago Dei. Though I believe the image of God within, the Imago Dei, is much more than a spark of the divine, I was thrilled to hear Peterson repeatedly refer to this important distinction in human beings.

Though originally Peterson was taking a stand in defense of the freedom of speech in 2016, the reason his protest video catapulted him onto the international stage was because the issue was tied to human sexuality. Because of this, many of the interviews, debates, and forums in which he participated in the ensuing few years would become embroiled in the topic of male and female. Time and again, as he would try to explain how men tend toward disagreeable and women toward agreeable on the Big Five personality traits, an interviewer would try to put words in his mouth, accusing him of being anti-woman or promoting toxic masculinity. Oftentimes, I have found myself willing him to use the language of Lion and Lamb as a means to rise above the limitations of *masculine* and *feminine*. To use the metaphors changes the conversation, taking it out of the emotionally and politically charged boxing ring.

Even children as young as five-years old can tell me which of their parents is the bigger Lion. It is not always the dad. They can tell me the positive aspects as well as the negative traits (shadow sides) of each side. The mouths of babes can discuss the benefits of the Lion and Lamb learning to play nicely together on the inside (paradox). Children can also easily tell you which one they relate to more and why they are afraid of the other side (shame). Amazingly, children can apprehend and describe concepts like paradox, shadow sides, and shame with ease. I have said to many a wise young cherub in my office, "I need you to come and help me teach my class because you get this better than most adults." Indeed, we can let the children teach us if we have ears to hear.[1]

Seemingly child-like metaphors, Lion and Lamb, transcend language barriers and allow us to discuss difficult concepts without the cultural baggage. These metaphors can hold and represent many characteristics in an objective, non-judgmental way. Though we tend to equate *male* with Lion qualities and *female* with Lamb qualities, there are female lions and male lambs in the natural world as well as among humans. In the animal kingdom, lions and lambs do not co-exist nor do they need to learn from each other in order to live happy lives. For us humans, it is imperative for these two sides to learn how to work together lest we wreak havoc in the world.

The Diamond Inside

In his 2018 interview with psychiatrist Iain McGilchrist, Peterson was intrigued to hear his guest describe the left brain thinking like a predator animal and the right brain thinking like a prey animal. It is almost like we are innately double-minded. As predator and prey sides of ourselves, these opposing forces tend to be at odds within the human soul. When not working as an integrated whole, each side develops its corresponding shadow sides. Powerful Lion types who reject their Lamb side can become tyrannical bullies, while sweet, gentle Lamb types can become manipulative and passive-aggressive. Our tendency to over-identify with one side and judge it as better than the other creates a split in the paradox of what is meant to be a synergistic whole, a yin yang of sorts. As one side rejects the other, shame creeps in. Shame acts in opposition to paradox, pulling the strands of DNA apart until they mutate and become something no longer resembling the original source. Shame, rooted in judgment, is a powerful force and is the counterpart of grace, rooted in acceptance.

---

[1] To get a glimpse of the brilliance of young children, check out the interview of children discussing these concepts: <www.youtube.com/watch?v=W9PELJQOfXg>. Here is a shorter version: <www.youtube.com/watch?v=hVTBnl5iEEg>.

A metaphor I often use to discuss these split strands of DNA, the beauty of the Imago Dei and the brokenness of humanity is . . . a Peanut M&M. Metaphorically speaking, the peanut represents the Imago Dei, the image of God inside every human being. The chocolate layer of the Peanut M&M represents our shame, the aspects of ourselves that we do not like or have deemed unworthy. The candy coating represents the many masks we all wear to hide the undesirable parts of ourselves. It is hard, shiny, and attractive enough to obscure the mess of the chocolate layer.

When teaching this concept, I use a large, diamond-shaped prism to represent the peanut, the Imago Dei. Like each unique human, every diamond is slightly different, yet made of the same beautiful substance. Every human has intrinsic value by virtue of the fact that we are all created in the image of God; everyone has a Diamond inside, even if it is not apparent at first. To represent our shame, the chocolate covering the Diamond, I use brown-colored play dough called "poo dough." As any child can tell you, no amount of poo can change the value of the Diamond. For the candy-coating layer that hides our poo mess, I use a large, shiny plastic egg. Together, these create the layers of the Peanut M&M. Now we can talk about each layer as they exist within the individual.

Bully Lions and Manipulative Lambs

Dominant Lamb people tend to judge the Lion side by its worst impulses, which it views as mean, angry, and intimidating. In other words, they see them as disagreeable and believe it is not a good way to be. Dominant Lion people judge the Lamb side as weak, naive, and helpless. To a strong Lion person, the trait of agreeable is synonymous with powerless and is not something to embrace. The bigger the judgment toward one side, the more it is hidden in the shame-bound poo layer. The more a part of us is hidden, the more it controls us in covert and maniacal ways. As Peterson points out, these differences are most pronounced in the extreme ends of the bell curve distribution.

While it's popular these days to refer to the masculine as *toxic*, children instinctively know that neither men nor women make good Lions. Too much Lion side in anyone can make a person become a mean, angry, and controlling bully. Ironically, some of the most infamous interviews with Peterson have been with women displaying toxic levels of Lion behavior who appear more bent on drawing blood than having an honest conversation. For example, in her hit piece for the UK *Times*, Decca Aitkenhead repeatedly accused Peterson of toxic masculinity in spite of the fact that he broke down in tears multiple times during the interview. As he described his painful health journey, she listened with a detached coolness devoid of compassion (Aitkenhead 2021).

Children intuitively understand the perils operating from either end of the Lion and Lamb spectrum. When people lead with their Lamb side and are afraid of their Lion side, they will be fearful, weak, dependent, and manipulative. Both men and women can err on either end of the spectrum and thus show the shadow sides; toxic behavior can show up in many different forms and is no respecter of persons. And yet, as Peterson reminds us, there is still a difference. A strong Lion personality in a large, muscle-bound male body fueled by high levels of testosterone is going to be different than a strong Lion personality in a petite woman's body fueled by estrogen. On a physical level, there would be no contest between the two. Though the toughest female martial arts fighter could win a match against a slew of slightly built, less-trained, or out-of-shape men, she would not stand a chance in the ring against the strongest male counterpart.

In previous generations, before the industrial revolution, these physical differences were much more of a mitigating factor for women in the workplace and other areas of life. Peterson frequently points out the relatively recent advent of birth control and its impact on women's ability to compete in jobs that are not dependent on physical strength. Though male and female Lions may be able to compete in positions of management and leadership, men still occupy the most physically grueling and dangerous jobs in the world. In many of those thankless, but necessary types of jobs, women are not even trying to compete.

Sugar and Spice

During the past century, the women's rights movement fought to expand what it means to be a female beyond the confines of "sugar and spice and all the things nice." In the early 1930s Katherine Hepburn shocked the world by wearing pants at a time when women could still be arrested for doing so in public because they were "masquerading as men." There were efforts to break down the stereotypes, making it acceptable for girls to like "snakes and snails and puppy dog tails" without denying their biology. Alternatively, there were efforts to provide boys with the chance to play with dolls as well as trucks. It became widely accepted that toys and clothes do not define the person. Yet, close to a century after Katharine Hepburn first donned slacks on the silver screen, we find ourselves in a Twilight Zone of sorts where little boys are presumed to be girls if they like dolls and dresses, while girls are suspected to be boys if they are interested in trucks and guns.

As Peterson has alluded to, there is something innately problematic about the following equations: male = masculine and female = feminine. These equations can wreak havoc on psychological, spiritual, and physical growth now even more so than a century ago. At one level, these equations are a matter of confusing hardware with software. Hardware is akin to the body, whether one was born with a vagina or a penis. Software is about the soul, Lion and Lamb. Hardware is about biology and is immutable, while software has to do with the psychological and spiritual aspects of a person and is malleable.

Anyone with more than one child knows children are born "bent" if you will, toward one or the other in varying degrees. Some kids come out of the womb with a big Lion personality and some come out docile and sweet little Lambs. These variations occur regardless of biological hardware. To reinforce these as static or permanent is to deny possibility for spiritual or psychological growth, creating the layers of the M&M covering the Imago Dei. For a Lion-leading person, the Lamb side becomes hidden in the shame-bound *poo* layer, while the dominant Lamb person hides the scary Lion side deep in the dungeons of the soul in hopes it will never see the light of day. To believe these personality leanings are hardware requires the acceptance of the accompanying shadow sides for each of the animal personalities. The expectation of such a person sounds something like this: *If you*

*really loved me, you would endure my bad (Lion or Lamb)
behavior. It is just who I am.*

On the one hand, if we adhere to these equations, male =
masculine and female = feminine, we can become too defined
by the body. If you are born with a vagina, you must be a
Lamb: cute, cuddly, sweet, and a good follower. If you were
born with a penis, you must be a Lion: tough, assertive, independent, and a leader. Under such a paradigm, we accept the
shadow sides of each and chalk up angry Lion behavior as
"boys being boys" or depressed passivity as "being a girl." In
this worldview of men and women, those whose software does
not conform with the hardware are shamed, ostracized, or
medicated. In one way or another, there is an expectation to
deny one's instincts in order to match the interior world to
the body.[1] On the other hand, adhering to these equations
can lead one to be overly defined by the software, how one
feels on the inside. In this way of thinking, people become too
defined by the soul. Irrespective of hardware, a person born
bent towards the Lamb side must be a girl. In the same vein,
a person bent toward the Lion side must be a boy, even if the
hardware came in the form of a female body. Though we
would never consider software permanent for our technological devices, this paradigm suggests the software of the soul
is immutable and the most important "truth" of our being.

Several years ago, a friend sent me an article about a
woman in Texas whose youngest son preferred dresses and
dolls to cowboy boots and guns like her other three sons.
After resisting it for a bit, the mother finally accepted that
her youngest son must actually be a girl. My friend compli-
mented me on my open-mindedness, saying she hoped I
would be this open if such a family came to see me. I wrote
her back saying that if the little boy came into my office, I
would talk to him about Lions and Lambs. I would bet money
that not only would he tell me he is more of a Lamb than a
Lion, but his parents and siblings would likely say the same.
The hardware of such a young person doesn't need to be
denied or changed to fit the internal software. To do so
ignores the fact that software changes over time and needs
to be updated. If hardware is changed to match a faulty
understanding of software, there is an assumption the software is permanent.

When working with a Lamb-leading person of any age, male or female, the path toward health is to face fears of the Lion side within. For the Lion-leading person, the path to greater freedom is to uncover the treasures hidden in the Lamb side. Trying to manage the anger of a dominant Lion person without facing the fears of vulnerability will only take the person so far. When the poo hits the fan, the anger will still rule the unintegrated person. As Peterson often says, facing into your worst fears is the path forward. Exposure therapy works for all manner of fears, making a way for integration to occur with the two disparate energies.

Like most things that exist on continuum of opposing sides, the Truth is found in a paradox that is bigger than either end of the spectrum. Having the spark of the divine, the ineffable beauty of the Imago Dei within, is the one thing we all have in common. If that is the starting point, we can have very different conversations when it comes to difficult topics. Often writing about the importance of non-dual thinking, Richard Rohr suggests if we start with how we are the same, we can discuss how we are different. But if we start with how we are different, it is almost impossible to discuss how we are the same (Rohr 2018).

Transcending the Divide

From a Christian perspective, Jesus *is* the face of God. He is the Logos, as Peterson likes to say. We know about the nature and character of God by looking to Christ as the image of the unseen God. So, what does Christ tell us about masculine and feminine? Christ transcends not only the divide of masculine and feminine, but every other polarity we find ourselves debating: Greek or Jew, slave or free, rich or poor, black or white, Republican or Democrat, etc. The spirit of Christ is the preeminent example of synergy; the whole is greater than the sum of the parts. The synergistic spirit of Christ allows us to transcend the many divides plaguing our society.

In various interviews and in subtle and not-so-subtle ways, Peterson has declared the existence of the transcendent in each person to be the most important discovery in the history of the human race. When the Imago Dei, the Diamond inside each of us, is the starting point for what it means to be human, we can live in the synergy of a third way, a higher way. The Diamond can shine through humans regardless of male or female, black or white, able-bodied or not. The housing of the Imago Dei is not unimportant, but it alone does not define who we are—only the Diamond can do that. The whole is *always* greater than the sum of the parts.

On first blush, it can seem simplistic to speak of the complexities of human beings in terms of a Peanut M&M or having Lion and Lamb sides hidden within the Diamond. However, if Peterson can spend a whole lecture on the deep metaphorical truths of Pinocchio, then maybe I am in good company. Perhaps we need metaphorical truths to help us find our way forward from the current morass in which we find ourselves.

References

Aitkenhead, Decca. 2021. Jordan Peterson on His Depression, Drug Dependency, and Russian Rehab Hell. *The Times* (January 30th).

Peterson, Jordan. 2018. The Master and His Emissary: Conversation with Dr. Iain McGilchrist. February 17th
<www.youtube.com/watch?v=xtf4FDlpPZ8>.

Rohr, Richard. 2018. Parts of a Whole. Daily Meditations. August 16th.
<https://cac.org/category/daily-meditations/2018/08/page/2>.

[9]
Biblical Lilliputians Meet Gulliver

RON DART

In the beginning was the myth.

—HERMANN HESSE, *Peter Camenzind*

We have, in the last few decades, in both book and film versions, been immersed in epic myths: *Star Wars, Lord of the Rings, The Hobbit*, and *Harry Potter* to name but a few. There are also the often redone Robin Hood and King Arthur myths. And comparative mythographers, Joseph Campbell, Robert Bly, and Carl Jung have held the attention of many for different reasons.

Jung has had a multitude of interpreters, including Jordan Peterson, who drop their buckets in the wells of his wide ranging and comparative work on myth. The prolific publications of Robert Graves's books on myth and Frazer's *The Golden Bough* are all part of the archive of the turn to myth. Why such a compelling and attractive turn?

The Western Tradition, within the Enlightenment ethos of the eighteenth to twentieth centuries, waged an internal family squabble. The right-of-center wing of the Enlightenment committed itself to an empirical, rationalist, logical, positivist approach to thought and the notion of objectivity. Such an ideology had many an affinity with certain types of science and it tended to be imperialistic in scope and vision, thereby colonizing other legitimate ways of knowing and being. Needless to say, within the Rationalist branch of the Enlightenment tribe, there was opposition to such a one-

131

dimensional and single-vision way of interpreting the self, the larger material world, and our all too human journey— such was at the heart of the Romantic rebellion and counter-culture within the Enlightenment clan.

The Romantic opposition to the Rationalists held high the significance of intuition, imagination, narrative, and myth as a way of being and knowing. Such a tension and dynamic, of course, has roots in the Classical Tradition, a certain interpretation of "logos" and "mythos" at the heart, as Nietzsche noted, between "Apollo" and "Dionysius." The centrist, via the Humanist voice within the Enlightenment, took the position that both the Rationalist-Apollonian-logos and Romantic-Dionysian-mythic ways of knowing both revealed and concealed significant elements of the human soul and society, hence the task of the Enlightenment Humanists, was to synthesize the best of the Rationalist-Romantic ways of knowing while exposing their significant blind spots and aberrations.

There can be no doubt, though, that the turn to myth in the West, in the last few centuries, has had much to do with a conscious questioning of a narrow way of knowing that excludes much insight, wisdom, and goodness. It's significant that Jordan Peterson's initial tome, *Maps of Meaning*, dealt with this tension and the implications of being unduly critical of a simplistic rationalist and scientific way of knowing. Peterson's turn to Jung and Jung's turn to Nietzsche (*Jung's Seminar of Nietzsche's Zarathustra* are significant in understanding Peterson and myth, although Peterson draws from many other sources in his mythic journey. But, what does this turn to myth have to do with Peterson and the *Bible*?

The Bible: Secularism and Literalism

There have been two extremes when approaching the *Bible* in the last few centuries. There has been a form of hard or aggressive secularism (to some degree, the first-born child of empirical and scientistic rationalism) that argues and assumes humanity is evolving beyond the need for such a primordial and dated text, hence no real need to study or ponder the *Bible* other than an outdated archive of our undeveloped past. Such an approach consistently highlights the violence, inconsistencies, notions of God that are but projections of the human unconscious, and also assumes that most events in scripture are incapable of being either verified or falsified. The nineteenth century brought a form of textual cynicism and thinkers such as Freud, Marx, Nietzsche, and Darwin played roles in both disenchanting those who tenaciously clung to the sacred and the texts that supported such world-views. Such a notion of secularism was, obviously, at odds with approaching the *Bible* in other than an uber-critical and dissecting way, science versus religion the dualism, science the new god that judged and dismissed the claims of religion.

The overreaction to hard and aggressive secularism was, ironically enough, indebted to many secular principles and premises and went in two directions. The first approach was to justify the claims of the *Bible* in an empirical manner: archeology, anthropology, and other academic disciplines as means of highlighting how Biblical names, places and sites demonstrated the validity of the *Bible*. The underlying ideology that defined such an attitude was that the *Bible* was the inspired, inerrant, and infallible Word of God, hence it could not be wrong. This tendency could lead to fideism (fundamentalism or conservative evangelicalism) or various forms of sixteenth-century protestant exegesis that were committed to historical, grammatical, linguistic, and more literalist reads of the authoritative and inspired text.

The second approach was very much a rigorous and vigorous attitude to the text in which higher and lower criticism was applied, and yet again the text an object to be studied and dissected as a scientist would study trees, bees, and stars. Protestant exegesis split over the more liberal stream that went in one direction, the text increasingly deconstructed, and the alternate stream with more moderate leanings. But, both groups accepted a more scientific approach to the text and a deeper application of it off the radar beyond a rather simple devotionalism. Again, we might ask, what has this to do with Jordan Peterson and his turn to the *Bible*? And, why is his turn hailed by many within the Christian Tradition and yet many within such a complex and layered family tree remain suspicious of him, given his more mythic read of the *Bible*? Much hinges, of course, on what is meant by myth.

The *Bible* and Myth: *Genesis*

There is a popular and rather immature notion of myth as falsehood, fantasy, deceit, and distortion of reality. This, of course, is not what myth means in a more mature, subtle, and sophisticated manner. Myth, at a deeper level, has much to do with perennial and timeless truths wrapped in the garment of multiple stories and narratives. But, for those who insist on a historic verification of the hard facts of history, myth eludes them. Are *Star Wars, Lord of the Rings, The Hobbit, Harry Potter* and many other myths grounded in historic reality? Of course not! Does this mean they do not convey truths about the human condition and journey? It would simply be foolish and silly to ignore that myths embody epic truths. Hence, there is a frequent clash between those who see history as the only real facts and those who understand that myth conveys real facts in a different way. And, those committed to myth quite rightly argue that the way historic facts are interpreted and applied is also a form of myth.

It is this mythic exegesis by Peterson that both offends the secularists and the Biblicists. Peterson takes the *Bible* seriously which irritates the secularists and reads the *Bible* in a mythic manner that disturbs the more literal Biblicists. Peterson's in depth mythic read of *Genesis* is a needful portal into his read of the *Bible*. The fact that the initial chapters of *Genesis* deal with, inevitably so, the creation-evolution debate, from a more historic, literal and empirical perspective, means Peterson is, out of necessity, drawn into a debate that animates many. Yet for Peterson, such an approach misses the deeper meaning and significance of *Genesis*. Are the initial chapters in *Genesis* about being committed to a young Earth notion and, if so, how does such a read square with science and evolution? Do the creation days create contradictory problems for those who think in a literal, sequential and logical manner? Does "day" mean a literal day? And, a few chapters later, was the flood a worldwide flood or a local flood? If Noah lived and his family was on the ark, is it possible to verify his existence by finding remnants of the ark on Mt. Ararat?

Needless to say, such an approach to *Genesis* has little interest for Peterson. Peterson's mythic exegesis is somewhat baffling to both the aggressive secularist and Biblical literalist (both, in their different ways, addicted to an empirical and literal read of *Genesis*, the former group jettisoning the text for its lack of basic scientific credibility, the latter clan pleading for a literal, historic and empirical read of the text sans solid evidence or alternate science). But, for Peterson, such narrow-minded quibbling misses the larger and more layered understanding of how a sacred text is to be read and different literary genres in such an interpretive reading. Let us now turn to Peterson and his more subtle approach to exegesis that bypasses the hard-core secularist literalist and Biblical literalist.

Peterson very much sees himself as a scientist. As a scientist who judiciously weighs the facts in both the external and internal spheres of life, he takes seriously, the evidence of evolution in both the biological and psychological areas of life, and as a clinical psychologist, he is interested on how the wisdom of human unfolding is stored and passed on from generations to generations. The fact that Peterson is indebted to Carl Jung's ideas of both the collective unconscious and archetypes means that he draws from a plurality of sources, not to mention a variety of civilization myths; additionally significant is that Peterson considers the *Bible* as a type of repository and library which speaks to the human experience. Taken together, this combination of experience and vision can reveal much concerning the best and worst of the human journey.

In 2017 Peterson gave twelve lectures on *Genesis* at the University of Toronto from May to August. These lectures were well attended and spoke much about an alternate read of the *Bible* that addressed the audience, in an existential way, in their all too human journey. Peterson mined *Genesis* in his twelve lectures, and each lecture bored into the perennial and timeless themes waiting to be drawn forth. What are the motifs Peterson drew from *Genesis* that seemed to be such a new approach for those who attended the lectures or watched them on YouTube?

The lectures were entitled *The Psychological Significance of the Biblical Stories* and Peterson's fuller vision was to traverse much of the *Bible*, but since beginnings must be made, *Genesis* was the logical place to start. Lectures #1–3 were less concerned, as mentioned above, with dating the Earth's history but more concerned with the underlying themes of the early chapters dealing with the origins of the human journey. The main theme Peterson turned to was the tensions and clashes within the human journey in the creation account between chaos and order, free speech and true speech, archetypes of the male-female (their distortions and ideal types). When order, structure, and form are negated, chaos and fragmentation ensue. When language is used in a true way, meaningful communication occurs but when speech only focuses on free speech sans truth, chaos occurs yet again. Such, in many ways, is our modern dilemma as are confused notions of gender archetypes.

Lecture #4 addresses the perennial Adam-Eve tension between picking the fruit on the tree of the soul of certain desires but being wary of indulging other appetites and how evil often clothes and conceals itself as an angel of light. Evil often appeals to the human longing for meaning and purpose and yet the places turned to slake such a hunger often betray the very hunger. The issues Adam and Eve faced are as much with us today as then, these myths the foundation of all myths.

Lecture #5 confronts the issue of sibling rivalry in Cain-Abel and the vindictive reaction by one brother, Cain, who feels slighted and rejected for his aggressive will to power tendencies (my will be done) rather than knowing how to be still and receptive like the more contemplative and shepherd, Abel. The perennial Cain-Abel is played out today between the secularized protestant work ethic *vita activa* types in oft opposition to the more *vita contemplativa* Abel vocations, and Cain continues to marginalize and kill (metaphorically) the Abels in our ethos, the rivalry never ending. If Adam and Eve embody increasing distance from the Eden of the inner and outer life, Cain embodies willpower without virtue and Abel the victim of such a drive. Abel, a type of Christ, is crucified by those who bear the mark of Cain on their addicted souls.

Lectures #6–7 deal with Noah, the deterioration of society, the flood of cleansing (type of baptism), and the renewal of the earth (dove type of Christ leading Noah and family into the renewed Earth). Noah, unlike Abel, is not killed by the Cain-like Sodom and Gomorrah culture, but Noah, like

Abel, embodies a life of virtue and integrity, vice and virtue ever in conflict in our east of Eden existence.

Lectures #8–12 deal with Abraham, the founder of faith for Jews, Christians, and Muslims alike. He is, for Peterson, an ideal archetype that furthers the Abel-Noah vision that is willing to risk for higher truths, is generous to strangers, and knows life is a pilgrimage through time. His potential sacrifice of Isaac, at a deeper level, portrays a decision of weighing a good and finite love against a better and best infinite love. Abraham, also, faced many challenges, much opposition, many betrayals, was ever faithful to his nephew Lot, knew significant disappointments yet ever soldiered on never indulging inclinations to cynicism or vindictive and vengeful attitudes. What is the take away? We all have a deeper calling to heed and hear, a vocation longing to live. Abraham reflects the sacrifices needed to be made to live such costly grace, a life of faithful openness to the risk of higher challenges.

Peterson's reading of *Genesis* 1–12 touches on myths that speak across the mountains of time. Although the remainder of *Genesis* is, at a literal and historic level, the origins of the Jewish religion, Abraham as an archetype transcends both Judaism, Jewish ethnicity, and chosenness by God—-such is the mythic way that speaks to one and all across cultures, civilizations and, when heard and read aright, addresses our age and ethos both at the level of soul and society.

Jordan Peterson and Northrop Frye

There can be no doubt that Northrop Frye (considered by many to be one of the most important literary theorists of the twentieth century) has a literary, cultural, religious and historic depth and breadth Peterson simply lacks, but Peterson has a psychological and applied approach that is lacking in Frye. However, both men focus on more in-depth ways of interpreting the *Bible*.

I was fortunate, when Frye was alive, to correspond with him about his read of William Blake when compared with Allen Ginsberg and Kathleen Raine's read of Blake (who I corresponded with also). Frye's four key books that deal with how to read the *Bible* are *Creation and Recreation* (1980),

The Great Code: The Bible and Literature (1982), *Words with Power* (1990) and *The Double Vision* (1991). *The Great Code* is Frye's summa that highlights the various genres and forms of speech that inform and shape Biblical thought. Hence, knowing how language-genres work produces more mature means of reading and interpreting this text that has, for good and ill, informed most of Western culture and literature and, in a global sense, world and comparative literature.

For Frye and Peterson, merely reading the *Bible* without knowing how to read it leads to all sorts of puerile interpretations that have dogged and distorted Biblical interpretation. Frye, in his classic tome, *The Great Code*, divides the book into Parts 1–2. Part I delves into "The Order of Words", and, in this section, language, myth, metaphor, and typology are dissected in order. In Part 2 "The Order of Types," he reverses the order. Needless to say, Peterson never approaches the *Bible* with the sophisticated range of Frye, and Frye does not factor substantive in his thinking even though both men focus on the *Bible* and myth as a golden key to reveal truths that a more simplistic, literalist approach conceals. I think it can be reasonably suggested that Peterson's approach to both myth and the *Bible* would be enhanced and enriched by a thorough going immersion in Frye's more layered and subtle approach to his code of interpretation. Frye's high noon was pre-Peterson, but both men are Canadians and have called University of Toronto their educational home, Frye in the English Department, Peterson in the Department of Psychology.

Peterson, as I mentioned above, has had a commitment to comparative mythology and he has applied such an approach, as a clinical and practicing psychologist, to his work with those who tend to be disoriented and seeking maps of meaning in an age and ethos that flatters itself on deconstructing maps of meaning (yet but another map of meaning). Peterson has in his lectures on the *Bible* reflected on more than *Genesis*, but he has taken deeper dives into *Genesis* than other books. He has promised lectures on *Exodus* and *Proverbs* but nothing of substance has been delivered yet. Peterson has also, in his various lectures and published books, referred often to the *New Testament* but has done no systematic exegesis. Yet, there can be no doubt, Peterson has a greater commitment to wedding mythic reads of the *Bible* to a form of existential, personal and individualist application in a way Frye does not. Frye is more committed to the epic vision and its interpretation of culture, religion, politics, education and religion. It is important, though, to note that Frye and Peterson turn to myth as the key to interpreting the *Bible* although Frye's understanding of myth links affectionate hands with type, metaphor, and language in a way that Peterson turns to but does not develop in the same fullness as Frye. As mentioned above, Peterson's approach to the Bible would have a more comprehensive range if he had been in dialogue with Frye.

The *Bible* and Classical Exegesis

The Classical Greek tradition, when reading Homer or Hesiod, could read both men in a simple literal manner. If this were done, the thoughtful would be obviously offended by the immoral behavior of the gods and their engagement with humanity. It was this more literal read that so irritated Plato, hence his objection to the poets and their myths. But, needless to say, Plato created his own myths. There were many other Greek philosophers (pre-Socratic and the Classical phase) that read Homer-Hesiod and the panorama of Greek myths in a more allegorical, figurative and tropological way. This approach meant the Greek epics and myths had perennial significance beyond the dilemmas raised by a literalist approach.

The *Iliad*, when understood this way, signified that life was a battle and be wary of uncritically welcoming Trojan Horses into the soul or society. The *Odyssey,* when read similarly, highlighted the fact that life is a journey in which many are the lures and temptations (think of the Sirens, Scylla, Charybdis, and Calypso for instance) and the voyage through time in the ship of the soul and society must be navigated in a wise, wily, and discerning way, the goal (Ithaca—home of the soul) ever the destination. Life is full of unpredictable trials. We are ever at odds with one another and yet there is need for unity.

It was this more layered and nuanced way of reading the Greek and Roman classics that, for example, shaped the thinking of the Jewish philosopher, Philo of Alexander, in his reading of the Jewish *Septuagint* (Greek version of the Hebrew Bible). It was never, of course, an either-or contrast —the literal was respected and honored but there was a sense that when the rind of the literal was peeled off, the sweet fruit of the allegorical mythic read of the text yielded the more substantive transformative insights. Or, to alter the metaphor, when the hard shell of the literal was cracked open, the tasty kernel was the gift. This more subtle and complex understanding was at the center and core of the Alexandrian Christian vision. Alexandria was a center and hub of a thriving cosmopolitan culture, so Alexandrian exegesis of both Classical Greek myths and, also, the *Bible* was never reduced to a simple literal and historical one-eyed Cyclops.

The fact that, in the last few centuries, there has been a tendency to be excessively fussy and preoccupied with a literal approach to the text means that the deeper and sweeter fruit of the text has become concealed. Jordan Peterson, like Northrop Frye, disturb the hard-nosed literalists with their more complex read of the *Bible* and, in that sense, are much more conservative (conserving the classical approach) in their exegesis than the textual literalists (secular or Biblicist) that often oppose or insist such approaches distort how the *Bible* is to be read and applied. A good question might be: who is doing the real distorting?

Peterson's more typological (types in the Hebrew canon— Noah's ark a symbol of the church just as the dove was a symbol of the Holy Spirit) and the tropological (moral, existential, ontological) analysis applied in a more psychological manner has an affinity and convergence with the way both Classical Western thought and Christian exegesis interpreted and applied Greek myth-epics and the *Bible* for soul transformation and character formation. Education is, therefore, in this more classical sense understood that the "techne" information must always be put in the service of self-knowledge (know yourself) and formation through the education of desires ("paideia"). The fact is that Peterson, in his wide ranging use of myth and his turn to the *Bible* as a text of perennial mythic themes, is merely interpreting the text in a way that the historic church and classical thought has always done. There is, of course, more to the layered ways of reading the *Bible* than

Peterson is aware, but he is definitely a portal beyond a more one-dimensional attitude to the text.

Final Reflections

If Jordan Peterson had only limited his interests to lecturing on myth at the University of Toronto, he would have had his detractors but such opposition would never have reached the public and political level it has in the last five years. It was Peterson's confrontational approach to Bill C-16 in 2016 on personal pronouns, cultural Marxism, and postmodernism that drew the ire and attacks from the liberal establishment and progressives. It was also the publications of *12 Rules for Life: An Antidote to Chaos* (2018) and *Beyond Order: 12 More Rules for Life* (2021) that have turned the Left on him and delighted the Right.

The former book, at its best, ponders the need for order and structure in the midst of erratic and ill-disciplined desires and the latter book highlights the dangers of too much order and structure and how it inhibits liberty. Needless to say, the ongoing tightrope walk between liberty and order is a classic one. Sadly so, when many on the progressive left think of Peterson (or excessively react to him) they are dealing with his many public positions on hot button issues in the culture wars. This means they often miss his deeper analysis of myth and the role of myth as a means of maturing in wisdom and insight. This short chapter has, consciously so, dealt with such a doorway into Peterson's thinking and its nuanced application of a reading of the *Bible*.

References

Graves, Robert. 1961. *The Greek Myths*. London: Cassell.
———. 1964. *Hebrew Myths: The Book of Genesis*. New York: McGraw-Hill.
———. 1965. *Mammon and the Black Goddess*. London: Cassell.
———. 1966. *The White Goddess: A Historical Grammar of Poetic Myth*. New York: Farrar, Straus, and Giroux.

Frazer, James George. 1890. *The Golden Bough: A Study in Comparative Religion*. London: Macmillan.

Frye, Northrop. 1980. *Creation and Recreation*. Toronto: University of Toronto Press.

———. 1982. *The Great Code: The Bible and Literature*. Toronto: Academic Press Canada.

———. 1990. *Words with Power*. Markham: Viking.

———. 1991. *The Double Vision*. Toronto: University of Toronto Press.

Jung, Carl G. 1988. *Jung's Seminar of Nietzsche's Zarathustra, 1934–1939*. Princeton: Princeton University Press.

Peterson, Jordan B. 1999. *Maps of Meaning: The Architecture of Belief*. New York: Routledge.

———. 2017. The Psychological Significance of the Biblical Stories. jordanbpeterson.com. <www.jordanbpeterson.com/bible-series>.

———. 2018. *12 Rules for Life: An Antidote to Chaos*. Toronto: Random House Canada.

———. 2021. *Beyond Order: 12 More Rules for Life*. Toronto: Random House Canada.

Part III

The Truth Seeker

[10]
Jordan Peterson's Religious Facts and Values

Stephen R.C. Hicks

Where do we find the meaning of life?

In answering that question, Jordan Peterson is a man with a foot in two worlds. He is a man of science, proficient in the biological bases of psychology and the developments of psychology as an applied science.

At the same time, he is the inheritor of one of the big challenges of the modern world, one that says, bluntly, that there is no relationship between the *fact* orientation in our thinking and the *value* orientation in our thinking. Peterson often seems to agree, saying that we cannot define value in a physicalist scientific framework. To put it crudely and frustratingly: how can a bunch of atoms bouncing around give rise to the highest aspirations of the human spirit?

And that points him back to ancient myths. Since values and meaning are absolutely important to our human identity and the modern scientific project cannot deliver on those, we need to go back to the pre-modern religions to find them.

So Peterson has another foot in the world of religious history and Biblical interpretation, offering a narrative understanding of its myths. Yet Jordan Peterson also frustrates thoughtful people here because his normally clear language seems to become more approximate and metaphorical. Anyone can make up stories, including ancient folk who didn't know much about science, so where are the hard facts to back up those emotionally engaging tales?

Thus the problem is a pair of trade-offs: One approach—the scientific—is factual and rigorous but seems not able to deliver meaningful values, while the other—the religious—is full of heated significance but seemingly without rational grounding.

What to do, then? Peterson argues that Western civilization is built upon ancient Judeo-Christian insights that must somehow be combined with modern, rational-scientific insights. The project then is not to be either a wishful thinking pre-modernist religious person nor a coldly robotic modern scientific person, but to find a synthesis.

Further, to his credit, Peterson adds a modesty about his progress, recognizing that great minds have been grappling with the fact-value-dichotomy problem for centuries, saying in effect that he is trying and it's an ongoing project.

And even further, Peterson is more interestingly complex because he recognizes that the postmodern cynics and outright nihilists are mounting a full assault on both pillars of Western civilization—religion and science. Jordan Peterson is a moralist against the postmodernists, for he believes there are objectively better and worse ways to live:

- **Individuality: The cornerstone of Western morality is "the assumption that every individual is sacred" (1999, p. 261).**

- **Every individual has agency—rather than being merely a pawn of overpowering forces.**

- **Taking responsibility is fundamental—rather than embracing victimhood.**

- **Suffering is built into life, so toughness is essential.**

- **Social life too is complex, so we need honesty and to cultivate listening and openness to alternative views.**

- **Civility and constructive debate must be social fundamentals.**

- **And while we each should strive to improve ourselves and the world, he believes in a strict causal priority: "Set your house in perfect order before you criticize the world" (2018, p. 159).**

Peterson advocates these as genuine and universal values, in contrast to the now-widespread 'It's all subjective' relativism that comes in both casual and hardcore intellectual versions. Consequently, his urgency is to find a workable synthesis before the forces of chaos prevail. That urgency forces us back to the hard questions about where we get value and genuine meaning from:

- **Why the deep assumption that science is factual but value-empty while religion is value-filled but without factual basis?**

- **What is Peterson's alternative?**

- **Does it work?**

- **If it doesn't work and a hard choice has to be made, in his heart of hearts does Peterson come down on the side of religion or science?**

Those questions will structure the rest of this discussion.

The Big Names' Attempted Solutions

How deep are the philosophical waters Peterson is swimming in? The biggest names in intellectual history have thrashed out the major alternatives and bequeathed to us a set of apparently strict options about the source of value and meaning. A quick overview will position Jordan Peterson and us in the flow of ideas.

Two millennia ago, in the context of Greek and Roman cultural dominance, the early Christian Tertullian (c. 155–225 C.E.) asked rhetorically, "What has Athens to do with Jerusalem?" Tertullian was stating the ancient world's big philosophical dualism: Athens represents Greek philosophy, with its tendency to naturalism and rationalism. Jerusalem represents the birthplace of the major Western religions, with their tendency to supernaturalism and non-rational faith. Tertullian's question suggests we face a hard either-or choice.

But whichever option we choose, we run into problems. One set became apparent during the Medieval era, after Rome declined and "Jerusalem" won. Christianity came to dominance, its belief system full of ethical values and meaning and hope in a supernatural world beyond this one. But is it true? Is it rational? What about the natural world?

A thousand years later, "Athens" and "Rome" returned and with them the rise of worldliness, humanism, and science—and the corresponding decline of religion. Faith dissolved and more intellectuals committed to reasoning all the way down to fundamentals and questioning even those.

Hence the early modern world and the great debates of the 1600s and 1700s over Revealed versus Natural Theology. Should we accept on faith certain supernaturalistically revealed truths and resist questioning them, or should we investigate the natural world rationally to find evidence of God's presence in it? The early moderns, increasingly adopting the methods and ethos of science, set Revealed Theology aside and sought proof of the truths of religion using the powers of observation and reason that God endowed us humans with. Each of us, as thinking human beings, should actively seek out and investigate the big *arguments* pro and con about God's existence.

But then the con side won. By the Enlightenment of the 1700s, it became clear that arguing about God is a losing strategy for religion. Four generations of prominent thinkers all reached the same conclusion: the arguments for the existence of God do not prove anything.

David Hume dissected the major arguments and set them aside, arguing that reason not only cannot prove the existence of God but not much of anything, so we should turn to natural feeling as our guide in life. A generation later, Immanuel Kant agreed that reason becomes snarled in conflict if it tries to speak of God or an immortal soul or anything at all about true reality, and so the best we can do is take on faith some fundamental regulative ideas that make sense of our apparent world. A generation later, Arthur Schopenhauer dismissed the arguments for the existence of God's order as a fear-driven imposition upon a seethingly irrational reality. And a generation again later, Søren Kierkegaard agreed that atheism is a consequence of being rational, but only religious commitment can give meaning to life and so one must make an irrational commitment to faith.

The point is that Hume, Kant, Schopenhauer, and Kierkegaard are four intellectual giants, and—while two are atheists and two are theists—all four agree that we cannot prove the existence of God or the truth of religion.

Jordan Peterson agrees: "The 'death of God' in the modern world looks like an accomplished fact" (1999, p. 245). He suggests two reasons for that: "Our constant cross-cultural interchanges and our capacity for critical reason [have] undermined our faith in the traditions of our forebears—perhaps for good reason" (1999, pp. 10–11). Yet we moderns cannot just return to dogmatic faith. We must be willing to recognize when our "maps" fail, and Peterson criticizes those who "will go to almost any length to ensure that their protective cultural 'stories' remain intact" (1999, p. 18).

So again: Where can we get the meaning of life from? Do we have to agree with Dostoevsky's "If God is dead, then everything is permitted," as one of his characters in *The Brothers Karamazov* declared? We cannot live nihilism, but intellectually we seem pushed towards it. If the big brains of philosophy and religion are correct, then religion has failed us because humans need order, principles, purpose—but those cannot come from ungrounded, wishful-thinking stories.

Yet the problem gets worse, because of scientific materialism's simultaneous failure to fill the value void it has created. That is the major weakness of the Enlightenment project. Science might try to replace religion, but science is about facts and facts are merely brute descriptions of what reality is. Peterson accepts the standard negative answer to philosophy's Is-Ought problem: "it is not possible to derive an *ought* from an *is* (this is the 'naturalistic fallacy' of David Hume)" (1999, p. 34). There's a gulf between facts and values. We need values but "science cannot provide that belief" (1999, p. 11).

Thus our modern predicament: we find it hard to believe in supernatural religious sources, and we believe naturalistic science cannot provide values. Consequently, for many of us, "gaping holes remain in our spirits" (1999, p. 245), and neither religion nor science can fill the void.

To his great credit, Peterson is fully cognizant of the problem, and further to his great credit, he is actively wrestling with it and not avoiding it.

Pragmatic Religion?

The next intellectual development thus is religion's *pragmatic* turn by the mid-1800s. Peterson's language is frequently explicitly and often implicitly pragmatic.

Pragmatism says: *By their deeds shall ye know them*. We should not concern ourselves too much with debates over theoretical truth and semantics. The real question is: What difference will it make in *action* and in the *consequences* of those actions? How is an idea to be *operationalized*, and will the operation *work*? To take a workmanlike example, the important question of a tool in my hand is not: *Is this a hammer or a mallet?*—but: *Can I whack something successfully with it?* In the case of religious doctrinal schisms and endless wrangling over definitions and the fine line between orthodoxy and heresy—that's a waste of time, as millennia of futile arguing show. Our pragmatic question is not: *Is religion true?* Rather it is: *Does religion work?*

Thus the rise of functional interpretations of religion, a tradition here that runs through Tocqueville, Nietzsche, Marx, and Freud.

In *Democracy in America*, Alexis de Tocqueville argued that, while unfounded intellectually, religion is practically necessary—especially for active Americans building a new country. Not only are people too busy making a living, religion is hard and confusing:

> Studies of this nature are far above the average capacity of men; and even if the majority of mankind were capable of such pursuits it is evident that the leisure to cultivate them would still be wanting.

If we encourage everyone to think about everything, we're only going to paralyze them with doubt, thus preparing them for servility rather than free living. So we intellectual-leader types should benevolently encourage religious belief among the population, even if we are not believers. While "it must be admitted that, if it [religion] does not save men in another world, it is at least very conducive to their happiness and their greatness in this" (1835, 2.1.5). Religion is not true but socially useful.

A decade later Karl Marx famously argued that religion is made-up—"*Man makes religion*; religion does not make man"—and useful in social-domination power plays. While the rich become so by immiserating the poor masses, religious dicta such as "Theirs is the Kingdom of Heaven" function as a psychic *"opium* of the people" to keep the masses passively accepting of their state. So while Marx disapproved of religion as a malevolently motivated tool of power, he agreed entirely that its truth or falsity is irrelevant and its functionality is critical (1843).

A generation later, Friedrich Nietzsche agreed that religion is false but functional—yet *self-imposed* rather than enforced from outside. We all want to assert our power over the world and others, but most of us are weaklings—and we know it. So out of frustration and envy we construct fantasy worlds to console and give ourselves imaginary revenge over our more powerful betters. Nietzsche invites us to enter into the psychological world of the Judeo-Christians during their formative eras—the Jews as slaves under the Egyptians and the Christians as oppressed under the Romans—and to imagine how that miserable state becomes a workshop for the creation of "slave morality" (1887, Essay 1). "The meek shall inherit the Earth" is a self-delusional consolation. Again, truth or falsity is irrelevant and the issue is usefulness, even if Nietzsche despised the type of person who uses religion.

And again a generation later, Sigmund Freud argued that religion is "so patently infantile, so foreign to reality, that to anyone with a friendly attitude to humanity it is painful to think that the great majority of mortals will never be able to rise above this view of life" (1930, Chapters 1 and 2). When we're infants we need a father-figure to protect, provide, and guide us. But most people never mature enough to dispense with some sort of father figure—"The origin of the religious attitude can be traced back in clear outlines as far as the feeling of infantile helplessness." And since life is so intensely disappointing and frustrating, we need palliatives. Some turn to drink and drugs, while others divert themselves with art or science. But drugs are self-destructive and most people aren't creative or smart enough for art or science, so a simpler option is needed for them. That is exactly the role of religion, which Freud advised for most as a crutch.

All four are religious unbelievers. Yet two (Tocqueville and Freud) *endorse* religion—pragmatically. And two (Marx and Nietzsche) *reject* religion—also pragmatically.

Peterson's Useful Myths

This pragmatism is exactly the territory that Jordan Peterson is working.

Often when asked directly about his religious beliefs—*Do you believe in God?*—Peterson's response is to say: "I act as if God exists." Traditional theists don't like that answer. Nor do traditional atheists. That is because both focus on the question of religion's *truth*. But Peterson is signaling that the important thing is *action*. As a psychologist and as social theorist, his focus is upon religious belief as a personally and socially useful *tool*.

In *Maps of Meaning*, Peterson explains myths as explanations of the world but with normative salience added. Science may say there is no intrinsic goal or *telos* out there in the world. But the myths we respond to are accounts of *our* world and *our* place in it. Myths are not just abstracted descriptions of the world, as science seeks to provide. They're not just theories about the world divorced from action. Rather, they are value-laden and in relation to us. We humans have goals, and we understand the world in relation to our goals—our ambitions, our need to form plans, make commitments, and overcome obstacles. Myths capture this in value-rich narratives. It's the difference between saying the world itself is a drama and saying that we construct a drama of ourselves in the world. Consequently, the right question of a myth is not *Is it true?* but *Is it relevant?* The question is not: *Is the myth factual?* But *Is it workable?*

We might be born into a myth, and we might accept it on faith initially: "Belief has to be grounded in faith" (1999, p. 92). Yet as we become more educated and more mature individuals, we learn that there are many religious myths and dramas out there, including those of the ancients, and that they have been subject to evolutionary forces. So while our individual commitment to any one of them may start as an act of faith, depending on the accidents of one's social birth, our commitments to myths do not remain an act of faith. None of the traditional religions is fully satisfactory, so we as their inheritors in turn should critically assess them (1999, p. 92) and be committed to the ongoing project of improving them. Here intellectual responsibility means adapting the *ethos* of science's method—free investigation and debate—and applying it to religious myths. The ongoing sorting of wheat from chaff and re-mixing of and additions to myths is how we progress.

Note that the construction and reconstruction of myths is about *us* and *our values* in a world that itself has no values. Myths are not scientifically true but are practically essential to us individually and socially: "Narrative description of archetypical behavioral patterns and representational schemas—*myths*—appears as an essential precondition for social construction and subsequent regulation of complexly civilized individual presumption, action, and desire" (1999, 78).

And if we insist upon the *Is it true?* question, then Peterson suggests again that *truth* not quite the right question here. Rather, by their practical fruits shall ye know them. For example: "Traditional societies, predicated on religious notions, have survived—essentially unchanged, in some cases, for tens of thousands of years" (1999, p. 8). That is, their pragmatic survival value is perhaps the better factor to focus upon.

Problems with Pragmatic Religion

How do we properly evaluate pragmatism? Can we ask whether it is true? Or should we use its own criterion self-referentially and ask only whether it works?

In this concluding section I will transition from exposition to critique and raise some challenge questions for pragmatic religious accounts, Peterson's included.

1. How do we determine whether a religion *works*? Peterson sometimes suggests longevity as a criterion: "Traditional societies, predicated on religious notions, have survived—essentially unchanged, in some cases, for tens of thousands of years" (1999, p. 8). Yet longevity alone does not always seem to indicate workability, as lots of useless things can last a long time. Further, questions of truth and goodness persist, as we still find ourselves asking of long-held beliefs and practices whether they're true or good, such as many superstitions and traditions that many now find repugnant. If we push hard on long-term survival as the criterion, that seems to point in the direction of a stagnant conservatism as the ideal, rather than any valorization of innovation and progress. Further, we face a difficult project of choosing between many religious belief systems that have lasted a long time—there are many diverse contenders, and they often contradict each other. And it still seems like it's a reasonable hypothesis to say of any of them that they would have survived *better* if they'd had different beliefs.

All of that points to a criterion of workability outside of long-term survivability, and Peterson indicates his agreement with being open to religious evolution.

2. Yet if we grant that the early religious maps and myths need editing and updating, how do we decide which elements of them to drop or revise? If, for example, we take a religious scripture and decide to produce an updated, good-stuff-only version of it, the standard by which we make editorial choices has to be coming from outside of religious scripture. Here Peterson's evolutionism comes out: Does any given element of scripture *still* have survival value? If we are not faithfully beholden to the text, then we will put each element of it on the block and ask of it whether it works in the actual, current, physical world.

3. A closely related question is about Christianity, the religious tradition that Peterson endorses and from which he draws most of his examples. Yet if we are committed to a pragmatic-workability-of-myths, then why is Christianity special—that is, couldn't Islam or Judaism or Buddhism or Hinduism do just as well in providing a mythic narrative? All of those, arguably, have worked for lots of people for lots of time. The logic of Peterson's pragmatism seems to be that any religion is more or less workable, so any one will get the job done. But if one wants to argue that in fact one does work better, then that's a huge amount of hard comparative work a person must commit to. In the meantime, should we adopt an agnostic pose, or is it that by the time a person is adult, he is already mostly acculturated to a particular religion so one might as well stick with that one? So how do we choose between those options only on *pragmatic* grounds?

4. Religions are mythic narratives with built-in value-richness that serve our psychological and social needs. Does a narrative have to be religious to perform those functions? Movies and literature, for example, do much the same thing, as Peterson certainly recognizes (2018, pp. 324–26), with goal-directed action, plot lines, good-and-bad character types, symbols and tropes, and moral-of-the-story themes. We're all fine with giving functionalist interpretations of what they do for us—they're not true but coherent, meaning-generating, and inspiring narratives. Or we can consider sports, with their constituted rules of order, goal-directed behaviors, inspiring or despised role models, and the many narratives we construct as players and fans about the sporting life.

So does it matter which form or genre of narrative we commit to? Can believing in James Bond the action-hero spy work as well as believing in Muhammad? If a person worships Pelé the soccer star or worships Jesus Christ—same difference? Along with many of our fellow Canadians, could Jordan Peterson and I say that hockey is our religion—complete with social rituals and personal shrines in our homes made up of displays of pennants, jerseys with star players' names on them, and photos of championship teams from the glory days?

If, though, we object to equating religion with movies or sports on the grounds that we know movies aren't real and sports are just made up—so they're not strong enough narratives to satisfy our psychological and social needs fully—then that means that addition to the functional value, we need to believe that it's *really* real for a narrative to work fully. In which case, pragmatism is incomplete.

5. A final comment, returning to Peterson's statement when pressed about whether he really believes: "I act as if God exists." For example, *Be honest and don't lie* will be part of the package of beliefs that we will act upon as if a God has told us and is monitoring our behavior. The *pragmatic* justification of that particular policy is that people who are honest do better psychologically and socially than liars do. Now suppose that claim is empirically supported—we can point out that honest people have better, say, friendships and romantic relationships. But if the *Be honest* belief is now empirically validated, then what more justification do we need? What does "Act as though God told you to be honest" add?

By analogy: a parent may teach a child to eat vegetables, and that may begin in the child's eating behavior as an authority/obedience claim: *I eat as if my mother were watching over me.* But the child grows and learns nutrition science and has plenty of evidence of vegetables' functional value.

So now the more mature person eats vegetables based upon grasping their functional value—and the mother's earlier *dictum* drops out of the justificatory story. Perhaps the former child's mother even has grown old and died. In either case, it would be odd for the now-adult to explain his or her nutritional choices by saying "I eat as if my mom still exists."

Peterson as Pragmatic Aristotelian

Jordan Peterson is a man of science, and I want to suggest that Peterson's views are evolving: from a traditional religion/science duality to a pragmatic account of religion to a kind of Aristotelian pragmatism. That is, the science is slowly prevailing over the religion.

Peterson is a rational realist in *practice*. But he is a pragmatist in *theory*: because devising an epistemological theory of truth is hard, he settles for pragmatic workability. But that workability is ultimately a matter of empirically and rationally assessing facts: What actually works in practice, in the real world?

His evaluation of religious narratives is consistently in evolutionary functional terms: they are a set of myths that work. They work because they capture, sometimes literally and sometimes metaphorically, truths about human action in the world that science cannot express fully and in a way that pre-scientific or non-scientific people can grasp. But their workability is not a matter of timeless absolutes. The real world changes. Even the narratives that have worked for a long while are, in principle, subject to evolutionary revision.

I take seriously his statement that for human beings biological fundamentals are just that—*fundamentals*. Note this strong formulation: we "are *primarily* concerned with the affective and emotional significance of the environment. Along with our animal cousins, we devote ourselves to fundamentals: will this (new) thing eat me? Can I eat it? Will it chase me? Should I chase it? Can I mate with it?" (1999, p. 22). Note that aggression, eating, and sex are *primary* and *fundamental*. That makes *biology* basic. Our big brains do generate *psychological* complexity. Science and religion are *functional* values, creating theories and narrative maps, and their utility is entirely determined by biological conse-quences of action in the material environment.

In philosophical-labelling terms, that pushes Peterson into territory first established by Aristotle. The great biolo-gist-philosopher grounded the good in scientifically identifi-able facts about the natural world: what's good for dolphins and hares and barnacles and any species is their functioning according to their biological (and sometimes psychological) identities. Each species has a natural mode of living, includ-ing humans, who flourish to the extent that they live accord-ing to their natures. Aristotle writes, "we state the function of man to be a certain kind of life, and this to be an activity or actions of the soul implying a rational principle, and the function of a good man to be the good and noble performance of these" (1984). Human beings are *rational* animals, and rationality's purpose is to identify general principles and use them to form our virtues of characters and habits of action. Thus, we cannot flourish in an unprincipled do-whatever-you-feel-like way—and we do not need to appeal to shadowy realms beyond nature to find guidance.

A final question then arises about Jordan Peterson's pub-lic-intellectual advocacy of religion. If the logic of his theo-retical position is that religion is not true but useful, then is publicly promoting it a socially useful fiction? That is, is pragmatic religion a kind of noble lie? Jordan Peterson, as a well-read, highly intelligent psychologist knows it's probably not true, just as Tocqueville and Freud knew it's not true. Is he then following them in urging that even so it's better for the *less-intellectual* masses to believe individually and socially?

I don't know. Yet I suspect the noble-lie interpretation of Peterson is not true, based upon his ruthless honesty in his writings and public appearances. The more likely interpre-tation is that Jordan Peterson is a man of science who prac-tices the virtues of science he preaches. Science—including the science of values—is an evolving discipline, and it is a work in progress for him (as it should be for all of us). So he's calling it as he sees it now: Values and meaning are biologi-cally and pragmatically based, including a functional role for religious myth individually and socially. And that's the truth, as best as he can say *now*.

Bibliography

Aristotle. 1984. Nicomachean Ethics, Book 1. In Jonathan Barnes, ed. *The Complete Works of Aristotle*. Princeton: Princeton University Press.

Champagne, Marc. 2020. *Myth, Meaning, and Antifragile Individualism: On the Ideas of Jordan Peterson*. Exeter: Imprint Academic.

Dostoevsky, Fyodor. 1982. *The Brothers Karamazov*. New York: Farrar, Straus, and Giroux.

Hume, David. 1990. *Dialogues concerning Natural Religion*. New York: Penguin.

Freud, Sigmund. 1960. *Civilization and Its Discontents*. New York: Norton.

Kant, Immanuel. 1963. Second Preface. In *Critique of Pure Reason*. Translated by Norman Kemp Smith. London: Macmillan.

Kierkegaard, Søren. 1994. *Fear and Trembling*. New York: Knopf.

Marx, Karl. 1978. Contribution to the Critique of Hegel's Philosophy of Law. In Robert C. Tucker, ed., *The Marx-Engels Reader*. New York: Norton.

Nietzsche, Friedrich. 1989. *On the Genealogy of Morals*. New York: Vintage.

Peterson, Jordan B. 1999. *Maps of Meaning: The Architecture of Belief*. New York: Routledge.

———. 2018. *12 Rules for Life: An Antidote to Chaos*. Toronto: Random House Canada.

Schopenhauer, Arthur. 1966. *The World as Will and Representation*. Mineola: Dover.

Tertullian. Circa 190–220 C.E. Quid Ergo Athenis et Hierosolymis ["What Has Athens to Do with Jerusalem?"] *De praescriptione haereticorum* [*On the Prescription of Heretics*], Chapter 7.

Tocqueville, Alexis de. 2012. How Religion in the United States Avails Itself of Democratic Tendencies. In *Democracy in America*. Chicago: University of Chicago Press.

Woien, Sandra. 2021. Review of *Myth, Meaning, and Antifragile Individualism: On the Ideas of Jordan Peterson*. *Reason Papers* 42:1, pp. 145–151.

11
We're Science!
We're All about Coulda,
Not Shoulda

MARK GARRON

Sometimes science is fucking wrong and gives us shit we don't need, like sixty-three-year-old women giving birth. Why not come out and go, hey, we made cancer airborne and contagious! We're science! We're all about coulda, not shoulda.

—PATTON OSWALD

In 2017, on Sam Harris's podcast "Waking Up with Sam Harris #62," Harris had a debate with Jordan B. Peterson. These two figures, equally controversial in their views, first met virtually by popular request. Harris is a leading figure in the New Atheism, one of its famous Four Horsemen characterized by a staunch opposition to religion.

Harris believes that not only can there be moral truths as objective facts in the world without religion, but that religion has also done a very bad job at letting us see moral truths. He thinks science can do a better job by carefully studying well-being and how to achieve it. Peterson, as a clinical psychologist, is also interested in well-being. Peterson believes that meaning and responsibility are essential for human well-being but ultimately meaning and responsibility are moral concerns that must come before science.

Followers of both Harris and Peterson expected a clear agreement on the dangers and the problems with what Peterson refers to as a growing postmodernist neo-Marxist ideology—an ideology that is not only hard to define but also takes pride in its lack of definition. Partly because it rejects the very concept of definitions. A main tenet of this amorphous movement is the rejection of the concept of objective truth. Postmodernism describes everything in social construction terms. Since truth is merely a human construct, truth is, therefore, only relative to a paradigm or model. For Peterson, postmodernism presents a threat to well-being by taking away meaning and responsibility leaving people in a state of nihilism. Peterson is concerned that postmodernism will rob us of the right sort of relationship with the truth. Harris, on the other hand, wants a concept of truth that is independent of our relationship to it.

Followers of Harris and Peterson expected a clash on morality, science, and religion. They did not expect them to clash over truth as an epistemic concept. Peterson views truth as constructed like a house. For the edifice to stand it needs to fit together in the right sort of way. Harris on the other hand views truth as the contents of a room regardless of whether the contents build out and supports a useful structure.

Harris is a devout scientific realist, as he believes that truth exists in a radically objective sense. Get rid of all subjects, and truth still exists. Peterson, on the other hand, is a devout pragmatist. While true beliefs exist, a true belief is one that is useful and practical. Yet, subjects also need to exist for there to be beliefs and for those beliefs to be useful. This difference is the foundation for Peterson's claim that what are most true are moral truths.

Harris makes no distinction between the truths that are moral and truths that are scientific—science will be able to discover and describe moral truths. If we scientifically know what well-being is and if we know scientifically what we ought to do to obtain well-being, then we have all that we need for discovering objective moral truth. Science, says Harris, is not just about the 'couldas' but it is also about the 'shouldas'—both equally correspond to a shopping list of what is real. In other words, all truths that are of an 'is' variety are the same as the truths that are of an 'ought' variety. They are true because they correspond with what is real in the right way. This is what makes Harris a moral realist as well as a scientific realist. For him, objective moral truths exist.

Shoulda and Coulda

Sometimes opposites attract. Harris had just such an opposi-
tional relationship with his teacher, the pragmatist, Richard
Rorty. Harris admitted that while an undergraduate at Stanford, "I took every class he taught and just basically did nothing but argue with him about pragmatism" (2017, 32:56).
Pragmatists think of truth, or more specifically true belief, as
a tool to achieve goals. The better a belief helps us achieve
practical goals then the truer it is. Pragmatic truth is not
dependent on a concept of an uninterpreted reality. Truth is
not outside of all schemes and science. So, the house
metaphor is particularly useful as the pragmatist does not
separate out the truth from the overall house it supports. It is
a rather useless truth to know that the room is not on fire
when our concern should be that the house is on fire. Truth is
relative to a scheme. Prior to the podcast, Harris had already
thought long and hard about the various ways of upending
the pragmatic theory of truth using the great pragmatist
Rorty as a foil. Peterson unwittingly walked into and sprung
this dormant trap intended for Rorty. It seemed to have
caught both of them by surprise. However, from the audience's
point of view, Harris seemed to get the better of Peterson.

It's understandable that Rorty's views would generate great
umbrage with Harris. Harris's view of truth is that it exists
out in the world in a radically objective sense; it is a reality
that exists uninterpreted just waiting for science to interpret
it. Rorty described the concept of uninterpreted reality as simply another of the obsequious names of God and by extension,
Harris's commitment to scientific realism as a religious urge
to bow down before a non-human power (Rorty 2007, p. 134).

What ended up happening during the discussion was shocking to fans of Peterson. Harris put Peterson in the position of
defending one of the central pillars of postmodernism: truth is
not mind-independent, not independent of human desires,
goals, and language. This is a mainstay of social constructionism. Harris effectively accuses Peterson of being the same sort
of postmodern social constructionist that Peterson so often rails
against, making Peterson's views subjective and relative. Peterson says no: truth is still objective. It is objective because some
overall schemes like some houses are objectively better constructed than others. This is why they argue over truth.

Shortly after this podcast, Harris expressed disappointment. He thought listeners had come to hear Harris's and Peterson's views on religion and atheism, or the relationship between science and ethics. Instead, two hours were devoted almost entirely to "What is truth?" It seemed as though Harris could not let Rorty and thereby Peterson off the hook. The question of 'What is truth?' is neither new nor easily answered. As Harris acknowledged, the vast majority of their fans found the discussion tedious. However, for those who care about theories of knowledge and belief (epistemology) and for others, theories of reality and existence (metaphysics and ontology) the discussion was not just interesting, but also articulated what was at stake in these two contrasting positions.

Peterson thought it plausible to sidestep their different views on truth altogether, arriving at a consensus regarding religion and atheism and the relationship between science and ethics. To achieve this, they would have to find some common facts or beliefs to build a logically constructed consensus. According to standard pragmatism, "True ideas are those that we can assimilate, validate, corroborate, and verify" (James 2018, p. 97). These are the precise concerns of scientific practice—their disagreement was almost purely metaphysical as there is no practical difference in how science is done per se.

However, as it turned out, Harris was right to be concerned with these two contrasting axiomatic positions. The pragmatist and the scientific realist should be able to carry out the practice of science in roughly the same way; they produce the same results and agreement on scientific claims. As arguments go, the two contrasting concepts of truth failed to produce agreed upon common facts required to win an argument of an ethical or metaphysical kind, as evident in their latter discussions. So what was Harris trying to nail down? It was his belief that the comedian Patton Oswald was wrong. Science is all about the 'shouldas' as well as the 'couldas', in Harris's view.

Harris: Just the Evidence, Ma'am

Harris calls himself a scientific realist (2017, 40:56). However, there is a more subtle commitment to the epistemic theory of evidentialism. Evidentialism is a position regarding epistemic justification; it describes what we should do or what we are obliged to do when it comes to believing. Remember Harris wants science to say something about the 'shouldas' and can be summarized as 'If you want to form a belief then we should follow only the evidence'. Harris shares this commitment to the epistemic theory of evidentialism with a fellow horseman of atheism, Richard Dawkins.

An important caveat is that this ethical obligation only applies to belief. It is a pure epistemic obligation. In this sense, epistemology is nested inside an ethic. Harris cannot dispute that our scientific endeavor is nested, contained or constrained inside our epistemic endeavor. After all what is science if we're not trying to get at the truth and avoid error? The problem is that our desire for true belief is not our only concern. We also want good lives (Harris 2017, 55:43).

It's important to note that there is a certain question-begging bias in Harris's language that needs to be teased out. This is because knowledge implies a justified belief that is true. When Harris uses terms like "worth knowing" or "dangerous to know" that already assumes it has to be true. It is important to substitute 'believe' instead of 'know' because it is the truth of the matter that is in dispute. For the pragmatist and the scientific realist to know something, it implies that what you know is true, or it wouldn't be knowledge.

Harris would say that we want to live good lives, but this raises a big problem. These are ethical and prudential concerns; we ought not to believe a dangerous truth even though it is evidentially true. It can be epistemically rational for someone to form a belief even if they fail to form that belief because it would be bad for them. "We want to know what is worth knowing we don't want to know everything, and we certainly don't want to know truth that will get us all killed or make us all needlessly miserable" (Harris 2017, 55:35). Here Harris is expressing a moral or prudential override a 'prudential shoulda' that somehow trumps the evidence. This comes before we do any science. So how are we supposed to find this scientifically? Peterson translates this into 'We don't want to believe that which will get us killed or needlessly miserable'.

Harris might take prudential shouldas a step further and say 'Well, we value all sorts of things'. We follow all sorts of 'shouldas' that constitute our normative landscape. It is only when we want to get at the truth of some issue that we take a certain belief forming attitude. Getting at the truth is about getting the right sort of justification to believe, and for Harris, that is evidence.

For both Peterson and Harris, our epistemic endeavor needs to meet the criteria of what it takes to believe something. Obviously and necessarily when we say that we believe something we also mean that we believe it to be true. So closely connected is truth to belief that it is hard to separate one from the other. The question then arises how do we come to think something is worth believing? We need reasons. Here again they agree. This seems obvious but what constitutes good reasons? There seems to be two sorts of reasons: incentive and evidence. Harris's answer is a little puzzling, we have all kinds of reasons for wanting to form a belief about all kinds of propositions. For Harris, unlike Peterson the reasons for wanting to form a belief are not epistemic reasons because they are not based purely on evidence. For example, Harris believes that a person ought not to know truths that are too dangerous. Peterson, on the other hand, gives the too dangerous bit epistemic status. Peterson denies that beliefs that are too dangerous can be true and therefore you can't know them because they are not true. For Harris, the reasons for avoiding knowing truths that are too dangerous can't be epistemic.

Fit Neatly into Boxes?

Peterson does not neatly cleave off our epistemic concerns from all our other practical concerns. As Peterson believes, the choice of interest can't help but form part of the parameters from which a person operates (Harris 2017, 1:03:14). This is equally true for scientists. For the pragmatist, truth must have practical consequences. Some pragmatists, such as Peterson, think that how we act reveals what we believe. Truth makes a difference. Since 'useful' is an extremely broad term, Peterson's pragmatism means there are lots of things that we want true beliefs to do for us. Since beliefs are supposed to serve our needs particularly in the way we act in the world, then we should not only consider evidence but also incentives to believe. For Peterson, science gives us lots of 'couldas' but they need to be nested in moral truths that are the 'shouldas'. 'Shouldas' must trump 'couldas'— whether we should "mess around with small pox" or nuclear energy.

Harris is loath to cede this ground. It leaves open the argument that if a religious belief, such as a belief in God, is good for someone or for humans in general then that is a reason to believe, but not evidence to believe. It is a mere incentive and therefore should not count. Harris thinks that the pragmatists are committing a naturalistic fallacy—it is unreasonable to conclude just because something is natural that it is true. This has to be the case if we allow incentive as a reason to believe. There is no reason to believe that the happenstance of evolution has put us in error free contact with reality (Harris 2017, 38:15). Just because a belief is naturally good for us doesn't make it right.

Peterson's position is more amenable to taking epistemic risks. This dance around a mutually agreed definition of truth ultimately has this point in mind. As Harris maintains, "You cannot have a concept of truth that is subordinate to wellbeing" (2017, 56:42). Peterson thinks you can. Harris might say that it could be prudent to believe or not believe something but that has no impact on whether it is true or not (2017, 56:03). Harris's scientific realism is truth-centric and our epistemic practice on its own is supposed to get beliefs to accurately correspond to truth.

This is a big deal. It commits Harris to a dualism between an un-interpreted reality and a scheme that interprets that reality. Peterson, like most pragmatists and empiricists, would deny this duality. There are only the interpretations within a scheme or language. Talking about an uninterpreted reality is nonsense. In the face of dangerous 'truths', the evidentialist says you shouldn't ever be interested in wanting to form a belief about so called dangerous truths. The problem is you really don't know evidentially until after you believe. Peterson denies such truths. The fact that those beliefs are too dangerous is sufficient reason based on incentive not to believe them regardless of what the evidence says.

Micro-Macro Distinction

Harris pointed to three counter-intuitive notions of truth that a pragmatist like Peterson must affirm. First, there are no truths that aren't worth knowing. Second, there are no truths that are too dangerous to know. Third, there are no truths that are in principle impossible to know. "The main take-away is that the truth is the truth regardless of how it affects us. Our concept of the truth-value of any given statement can't be held hostage to its ultimate result for the survival of the species in the end" (Harris 2017, 1:22:19). Harris thinks that statements, or more accurately propositions can be individually evaluated independent of how they fit into a system or web of belief. Therefore, if there are good examples of any of these three sorts of truths, then pragmatism is refuted. In this dialogue all of Harris's examples fit into these three basic categories.

Peterson introduces the micro-macro distinction for a reason. Our belief structure isn't a simple shopping list; rather, evaluation of individual beliefs must be interpreted in respect to this overall belief structure, an overall scheme. Harris argues if individual statements can be evaluated regardless of how they fit into a larger scheme, then there should not be a micro/macro distinction. It's all just micro claims (Harris 2017, 1:26:09). Here is an example he uses: if I think that I could have an even number of hairs on my body I must also hold beliefs about what constitutes a hair, or whether hairs are discrete or continuous (Harris 2017, 1:01:13). I must also have a belief about whether hairs are countable and what are the rules for counting. I must also believe that even number and odd number are mutually exclusive or as Harris says it isn't a non-binary possibility. There must also be lots of beliefs about the rules of logic. While it may be true that from a pragmatic point of view there is no difference in practice for me to have an even or number of hairs, it doesn't mean that I can easily take a stance that there isn't a truth value. All the other beliefs about hairs play a part of my practical life. They are connected in a web of belief.

Peterson thinks beliefs are tools. Tools are designed to do a job. The better they do those jobs, the better they work for us—the better our beliefs do their job then the truer they are. This is a selection mechanism, and this is what makes his pragmatism Darwinian. From Peterson's point of view, the pragmatic approach is minimally objective in so far as there are better and worse theories and therefore better and worse truths. Truths that don't work so well get replaced by truths that work better. A good truth is that the room is not on fire. A better truth is that the fire in the house has not yet reached the room.

Harris is therefore correct to suggest that truth is metaphorically held hostage. It has a gun to its head, should the species die; truth dies too. If we are all dead, then why is the continuation of truth so important to Harris? It is as though Harris would not want to bow down before this sort of truth; a truth that could die with us. This seems like what Rorty called a religious urge.

Why should this come as a surprise? For Peterson, truth is not an inert static relationship. Truth is what happens to an idea. It is verified. It becomes a true idea. For the realist, a truth is a truth regardless of whether it is verified. For the realist, the payoff for true beliefs is knowledge as successful reference. For the pragmatist, the payoff for true beliefs comes from being able to make useful predictions from past experience. Since so much of what is successful reference is indistinguishable from useful practice and prediction it is difficult to make any distinction in how science is done practically. That is the point! The great pragmatic maxim is that there is no difference without a practical difference (Rorty 1999). It is here that Harris and Peterson should agree. In order to evaluate whether any sort of counter-example is able to refute pragmatism, we must first investigate whether there are any practical differences. In many of the examples discussed in the podcast, there were many practical differences lurking under the surface. This means that the disagreement isn't about the coulda propositions but rather about the shoulda propositions. Whether we are talking about our ideas on smallpox or nuclear energy, these ideas sit on the foundation of the scientific method, discarding one probably creeps into our everyday practice.

Harris's check metaphor highlights the different world views very well. Harris claims that for Peterson, we never get to cash 'the truth' check epistemologically (2017, 1:34:19).

This is correct if and only if the truth check is drawn on the currency of reference. For Peterson, the truth check gets cashed in the currency of useful predictions. Useful prediction means it can't merely be only social construction because there is a selection mechanism. This check gets cashed all the time and at the same bank that the scientific realist cashes her check. If we follow Harris's metaphor, when belief and truth stop being useful, such as at the time of our extinction, then the check bounces.

The Harris scientific realist stance takes the posits of the theories of science at face value. These 'posits' have a literal interpretation. If they are true references, then they are definitive—they are true by definition. Recall that postmodernists reject this sort of truth by definition. Postmodernists revel in this very indefinability of their movement. Harris thinks that to be fully objective, truth has a reality fully independent of the mind. Harris thinks that if we don't have this gold standard of objective correspondence then there is no bulwark to stop one from sliding into the worst excess of relativism, postmodernism, and a post-truth world that he accuses his teacher, Rorty, of embracing.

Having 'Scientific' in Your Name Doesn't Make You Scientific

It's easy to make the mistake that 'scientific realism' is more scientific. This isn't the case. Pragmatism is also deeply invested in the scientific project. It comes out of the empiricist cornerstone of what we now think of as the scientific method. Empiricism has a clear idea of why we should do science. Consider what Harris's colleague Dawkins says about reasons for believing in the claims of science. "It works! Planes fly. Cars drive. Computers compute" (2013, 1:10:17). This is a very pragmatic answer. We should believe the claims of science because we have a good incentive to believe the claims of science. Science makes amazing belief tools.

Usefulness can be difficult to pin down. The realist Bertrand Russell argues that "It is so often harder to determine whether a belief is useful than whether it is true" (Russell 1910, p. 121). This seems to be what Harris points out in his example of United States presidents. Knowing the true order of all the US presidents might not be so useful if it gets you killed (2017, 1:16:45). What Peterson must acknowledge is uncertainty and whether uncertainty is a virtue or a vice when it comes to belief. Peterson relies on a selection mechanism for our beliefs. This mechanism weeds out. It replaces less useful beliefs with more useful beliefs. What are favoured are beliefs that will be useful in the future.

This is weird because our expectations of the future shouldn't change the past. Past causes the future not the other way around. If knowing the correct order of US presidents gets you reliably killed, then that means that this future state of affairs will change the past. There is a simple solution to this problem at the micro level. We could just say that the problem isn't with the order of presidents, but rather the thing that is killing you, such as a kidnapper or a tyrant. The true order of the presidents helps you to figure that out. Our practice should be about trying to correct that problem. This doesn't work so well on the macro level. If it turns out that the scientific method as such gets us all killed in the future, then it seems to affect what is true now.

Shouldas before Couldas

What can we all say about truth? Harris and Peterson agree that truth is good, truth is valuable, truth is objective, and truth is worth pursuing. The scientific realist accepts that there are some truths that are not worth pursuing just as Peterson thinks that there are beliefs that are not worth having. Some of these sorts of beliefs are simply bad bets. What are left are true enough beliefs and just as importantly, beliefs that make our total web of beliefs more useful. A truth value of a belief can't just stand alone even though in many cases it might seem that way. This is Peterson's bulwark against postmodernism. On the other hand, according to Harris, there are some truths that may never be believed and there might very well be some truths that could get you killed simply by believing. Therefore, truth's objective ontology or realness can possibly run counter to truth as something worth pursuing.

How else does the idea of truth play in our everyday practice? Consider two people with different and conflicting beliefs without being able to appeal to truth, the interlocutors would only be able to acknowledge their conflicting beliefs as merely interesting. If we posit truth, however, I might believe something and also believe that I could be mistaken. Truth is part of the rules for discussing and changing people's minds. Harris thinks that Peterson, by grafting moral concerns on to his definition of truth, will make it hard to understand what precisely we are appealing to when we claim something is true, He thinks that Peterson is sabotaging the rules of the truth game.

However, this normative concern seems unavoidable. As Peterson points out, "Insufficiently moral people will ask deadly scientific questions" (Harris 2017, 1:26:00). These deadly scientific questions are coulda questions. They are questions like 'can we synthesize deadly viruses?' or 'can we make cancer airborne and contagious?' Peterson thinks that shoulda questions can't come out of asking scientific questions. The moral concerns are in some sense part of the truth house— part of the walls and foundation.

As Karl Popper says in his argument against scientism, "The search for truth presupposes ethics" (Popper 1978, p. 342). Understood in this fashion, Harris's epistemic commitment to truth is nested within a moral commitment. This is the problem. He wants to find ethics; the 'shouldas' in science. As Popper argues, just to get off the ground Harris needs his ethic of belief, his evidentialism. According to Harris's scientific realism, truth cannot be simply a neat and tidy epistemological concept. It has to be at the very least a metaphysical concept as well. Furthermore, in order to be also an ethical concept, it needs to epistemically pull itself up by its own bootstraps. Harris thinks this can be done by the self-evidence of well-being. This means however that there are whole classes of truths that are deeply dependent on well-being.

References

Dawkins, Richard. 2013. In Conversation with Richard Dawkins—Hosted by Stephen Law. <www.youtube.com/watch?v=W28Uo-O231E>.

Harris, Sam. 2017. #62—What Is True? A Conversation with Jordan B. Peterson. January 21st, 2017. <https://samharris.org/podcasts/what-is-true>.

James, William. 2018. *Six Books of Philosophy and Psychology*. B&R Samizdat Express.

Popper, Karl R. 1978. Natural Selection and the Emergence of Mind. *Dialectica*.

Rorty, Richard. 1999. *Truth and Progress*. Cambridge: Cambridge University Press.

———. 2007. *Philosophy as Cultural Politics*. Cambridge: Cambridge University Press.

Russell, Bertrand. 1910. William James's Conception of Truth. *Philosophical Essays*. Cambridge: Cambridge University Press.

[12]
Missing God

Esther O'Reilly

Detroit, Michigan, May 6, 2018: I am sitting with a friend in the Fillmore Theater. In honor of her birthday, we have splurged on good tickets to see an unusual speaker. He's an academic, but he's also a political lightning rod. He's a social scientist, but he's also a student of religion. He's a non-Christian, but he's also a lover of the Bible. He's a thinker, but he's also a preacher.

He takes the stage wearing one of the high-end royal blue suits that have become his stylistic trademark. He has grown out a salt-and-pepper beard (going for "the Old Testament prophet look," he jokes in Q&A). The crowd, a mix of old and young, men and women, couples and singles, puts their hands together for a warm welcome. By now, this is a familiar routine for him. He has already visited numerous cities and received a similar welcome. But he accepts it humbly, as if some part of him still struggles to understand his own success. Then, as the applause settles, he begins to pace and speak.

This particular night's focus is the sixth rule from his hit book *12 Rules for Life*. He warns us that we're going to get a dark lecture, because this is probably the darkest of the rules: "Set your house in perfect order before you criticize the world." The book chapter opens with a glimpse into the mind of one of the Columbine killers—a young man who decided that the human race wasn't worth fighting for, only worth killing. How does any person come to think this way? How

173

can we understand it? What interpretive framework could we impose on it to make sense out of such senseless evil? And how do we chart the path away from it in our societies, in our own hearts?

To find the answer, Peterson tells us we must go back to the beginning. Back to an old book, and an old story of two brothers. As he retells the tale of Cain and Abel, he takes us inside Cain's perspective, exposing the raw nerve of the jealous brother's resentment. When your best offerings have been rejected, your best efforts to earn favor thwarted, well, what do you do? "You take a rock, and you kill your brother."

Just then, I hear a young woman who's been listening with enthusiasm from behind me. She seems either slightly drunk or slightly high. At this moment, she whispers distinctly, "That's what *I* would do."

Rogue Professor

For three hours, we sat quietly under the spell. For three hours, we were haunted by the problem which has haunted Jordan Peterson his whole life long: how to find the meaning of life, now that God is dead, and we have killed him.

Sitting in the crowd, having not only read Peterson's book but binged many of his YouTube lectures, I found that the lecture felt familiar, like listening to a well-loved teacher play variations on a favorite theme. Still, YouTube would not do for the experience of sharing an auditorium, sharing incarnated space with the rogue professor and his sometimes eccentric audience. We knew we were watching a performance, in some sense, but this did not render it any less authentic. Peterson's speech seemed to spring not merely from what he had thought about, but from *who he was*.

As he moved into a discussion of the Holocaust, he told the story of how, like Descartes, he had set out to tear down the whole edifice of his knowledge and rebuild it from the ground up. When he searched for his new foundation stone, for that one certain thing on which he could build everything else, he came up with the purest act of evil he could find: a task set by Nazi guards for the prisoners in their camps, in which the victim was forced to carry a hundred-pound sack of wet salt back and forth, back and forth across the compound. The task had no goal, no point besides inflicting maximal pain, in a maximally pointless way. And here Peterson had found his Absolute: *This is wrong.* From this, he could conclude that there are unquestionably evil acts. From this, he could further conclude that there must be unquestionably good acts. Of this, he was convinced, whether or not he was convinced that there was a God.

But there was the rub. On some level, Peterson still believed the atheist critique of religion was correct. He was still a modern man, and as such, he couldn't be a religious man, at least not in the literal sense. And yet, he was also a clinical psychologist. He understood what happens to people when you take away their faith, their security, their structure for meaning itself.

So what could he give them instead? What could he say today to the young person who had read Richard Dawkins or Christopher Hitchens and felt lost, adrift, wondering if there was any point to anything anymore? Peterson hadn't yet figured that out. But he knew that he had to. It was a matter of life and death.

The Facts of the Matter

Vancouver, June 23, 2018: Sam Harris is a patient man. But even he has his limits. He is sitting on a debate stage with Jordan Peterson, the first time the two have met in person. But even after hours of dialogue, Harris is still unsure exactly who and what he is arguing with. Peterson doesn't sound like the religious apologists who used to be his old sparring partners. Those were the opponents Harris understood, the enemies he knew. He knew how they thought, how they talked, the moves they made. But Peterson isn't in the same ballpark. At moments, he doesn't even seem to be on the same planet. And yet, he has somehow racked up millions of views on his YouTube channel for his lectures on the Bible, a book Harris thought he and his fellow atheist horsemen had successfully relegated to the dustbin of history. So what is the rogue professor's angle? What is his game?

Over the course of four long summer nights, Peterson tried to explain his angle. Biologist Bret Weinstein and British journalist Douglas Murray took turns moderating the dialogues in Canada and the UK respectively. The events didn't feel like your dad's Christian-atheist debates. The old format of opening statements, rebuttals and cross-examination was flung out the window. Even Q & A went out the window as audiences gave up their time and cheered for more action. These extended late-night pub chats were just too interesting to interrupt.

Though they clashed vigorously, Peterson sincerely sought common ground. At times, he consulted his laptop and read out bits of Harris's own book *The Moral Landscape* back to him. In one passage, Harris had written that he wanted to salvage psychological truths from "the rubble" of the world's religions. Well, so did Peterson. But were their salvaging expeditions on the same page? Could they agree that there even *was* treasure in the rubble? Peterson wanted to give Harris the benefit of the doubt, but he suspected Harris's project was more destructive than constructive, particularly when it came to Christianity. The void the New Atheists had left behind them was too deep to be filled by watered-down Buddhism.

So how did Peterson propose to fill it? And where did the Bible come in? To answer this question, Peterson wanted to back up and ask another question: Is the world made up of *matter*, or is it made up of *what matters*? Put another way, is the world a *collection of objects*, or a *forum for action*? If atoms are the fundamental building blocks of the world as we know it, then all knowledge is reducible to empirical observations, and humanity should be able to complete its knowledge-gathering quest via the scientific method. But what if the material is not the most fundamental? What if the most fundamental building blocks of reality aren't discoverable by "objective" means?

David Hume famously argued that one cannot derive an "ought" from an "is." One cannot take raw empirical facts and extract value judgments. Yet we do make value judgments, all the time. But how? What is the interpretive framework that is mediating between us and the numerous facts we encounter every day, so many facts that we cannot possibly internalize and process all of them?

Peterson believes he can name the framework: Story. Story is the abstract made concrete. Story is a proposition acted out in the forum. Story is "Logos," Word, become flesh. Wait, this sounds familiar. Exactly, Peterson says. And this is where, to Sam Harris's confusion and annoyance, the rogue professor insists on Bible-smuggling. The choice we still confront every day is as old as Cain and Abel—the choice between resentment and gratitude, greed and sacrifice, corruption and integrity. Can we measure this choice empirically, with a scientific instrument? No, but we all know that it exists, and the first chapters of the Old Testament have encoded it for us. Thus, Peterson's challenge to the atheists is not just an argument that we *shouldn't* unhitch ourselves from the Bible. It's an argument that we *can't*.

It's a bold argument. But perhaps it is not quite bold *enough*. Peterson wishes to critique the Enlightenment project while still speaking the Enlightenment's language. He wishes to take on David Hume's modern-day successors while accepting Hume's paradigm of facts and values as his starting axiom. But why should he? Why accept that "facts" are always and only the sorts of things that can be measured empirically? Why accept that only statements of empirical fact are "objective," while statements of value are fundamentally "subjective"? This is the challenge for Peterson, the question that demands to be asked: Are there any values which are *also* facts? And if the answer is yes, then what does this mean? To what, or we might ask to Whom, does that lead us?

This was Christian apologist William Lane Craig's suggestion in his one staged encounter with Peterson, discussing the question "Is there meaning to life?" Craig, like Harris a classic modernist, seemed unsure how to read Peterson's sideways approach. Though he attempted to pick out points of connection, the two thinkers struggled to find each other across the divide. Craig neatly and efficiently made his case that without faith in a personal God, all life is ultimately meaningless. Peterson pushed back strongly that people can find meaning regardless of where the universe is "ultimately" heading. He made the analogy to the men and women taking in a celebratory symphony at the fall of the Berlin Wall, who would have simply stared at you if you tapped them on the shoulder and reminded them the symphony was going to end. In an emotional moment, he spoke with feeling about the meaning to be found in nursing a suffering child (as he's done with his own daughter, Mikhaila). A nihilist would say, 'But a million years from now, what does it matter?' Peterson would answer 'It matters because the symphony is playing *now*. The sick child is in your arms *now*.' So how will you act *now*? For Peterson, this is the only question that matters.

For God's Sake

But does Jordan Peterson believe in God? Sam Harris wants to get clear on this, because he's worried there might be some confusion in the audience. He would like to think of Peterson as a rational modern man. In Sam Harris's world, rational modern men simply say "No" when asked if God exists. This should not be hard.

In their first debate in Vancouver, Peterson gives Harris the same answer he's been giving since he started having to answer the question in public: He *acts as if* God exists, which is what really matters. But Harris demands more. He wants to know what Peterson is talking about when he talks about God.

Peterson is glad Harris asked. "God," he says, scrolling through prepared notes on his laptop, "is how we imaginatively and collectively represent the existence of an action of consciousness across time." "God is that which eternally dies and is reborn in the pursuit of higher being and truth." "God is the highest value in the hierarchy of values." "God is the voice of conscience." "God is the source of judgment, mercy, and guilt." "God is the future to which we make sacrifices" (Peterson 2018a).

This goes on for several minutes, until Harris politely cuts in to say he smells an equivocation, here. Where in this list is the God who cares if we masturbate? The God who speaks from a burning bush? The God who can even hear prayer, much less answer it? This is what both Harris and William Lane Craig are talking about when they talk about God. This is the God Harris specifies several nights later in London, kicking off their dialogue with a straw poll to see what percentage of their ten thousand strong audience believes in God. A portion of the crowd cheers affirmatively. This confirms Harris in his concern: that whatever Jordan Peterson's "God" looks like, at the end of the day he's not going to stop *those people* from believing in *their* God. He's going to say they can stay right where they are, immovable, irrational, still clinging to their "shard of the cross." In fact, the more irrational and less astute an individual is, the more Peterson will encourage him to stay where he is, by Peterson's own admission. So, in other words, Harris brutally sums up, "Stupid people need their myths." Peterson protests that "we're all stupid." "But we're not *that* stupid," Harris insists. And the myths were not so harmless. They've left a trail of blood behind them.

But were the anti-myths any less blood-soaked? Peterson thinks not. Naturally, this triggers Harris into rattling off the classic New Atheist talking point that there was no causal connection between the godlessness of the twentieth century's totalitarian regimes and their body count. After all, "There's no doctrine in the mere loss of religion." There's no atheist holy book, no atheist stone tablet etched with the commandment, "Thou shalt build gulags and torture priests in them." There's no temptation for the otherwise "rational person" to commit a crime against humanity.

And yet, as moderator Douglas Murray interjects, in a nod to David Berlinski, there was something the architects and minions of the regimes all shared—the Gestapo and the secret police, the rational men who herded people on trains like cattle, the rational prison guards who lived for the thrill of inflicting maximal pain on the maximally innocent. They all had this in common: They did not believe that God was watching them.

Likewise, as the American journalist Bari Weiss has noted in a recent podcast discussion with Peterson, there was something held in common by the ones who resisted. Sophie Scholl shared something with her Christian student companions in The White Rose, who shared something with the young Christians printing *samizdat* behind the Iron Curtain, who shared something with martyrs like Father Jersey Popiełuszko, tortured and drowned by the KGB for conducting forbidden masses. For all of these heroes and many more, the power to stand up, the power to say "No," came from the same place. They knew whence they had come, who they were, and where, in the end, they were going.

But what manner of God did Sophie Scholl and Father Popiełuszko believe in? What manner of God did Hitler and

Stalin *not* believe in? If you had asked for a list of attributes, they would likely have fit Sam Harris's description a good deal better than Jordan Peterson's. Impoverished as his New Atheist history of everything may be, Harris could fairly be awarded this point over the rogue professor. Indeed, though this was hardly intentional, in his own way he makes the same point C.S. Lewis makes in his fictional *Letters to Malcolm*, writing on the problem with trying to depersonalize God's anger. Lewis's hypothetical young correspondent suggests that we might reframe our experience of this anger as "what inevitably happens to us if we behave inappropriately towards a reality of immense power." A live wire doesn't feel angry when it shocks us, but we know we will be shocked if we brush up against it. But "My dear Malcolm," Lewis writes, "what do you suppose you have gained by substituting the image of a live wire for that of angered majesty? You have shut us all up in despair; for the angry can forgive, and electricity can't" (1964, p. 96).

Harris presses the sharp point home at the end of the first Vancouver debate. He will be more specific than "Do you believe in God?" He will narrow the focus down to a single fixed point: Jesus's resurrection. Did it happen or didn't it? He's heard Peterson say elsewhere that it would take him forty hours to answer the question, but Harris is not in the mood. On this stage, with thousands of eyes watching, he wants a yes or no.

Peterson is uncomfortable with the question. He understands what lies behind it, the status game he is being invited to play. So he hesitates. He demurs. Harris puts it probabilistically: He'll grant the resurrection is *possible*. Anything is *possible*. The question is whether it's *probable*. Peterson, now visibly irritated, protests that for his part he wasn't saying it was. It's just that it would take him forty hours to answer the question. "Well, how's this for an answer," Harris suggests, "Almost certainly not."

The crowd cheers while Peterson sits still, stony-faced. "What's wrong with that?" Harris presses. "It's a fine answer," Peterson says coolly after the applause dies down. It's the stock answer. The reasonable modern man's answer. But "the idea doesn't seem to go away."

"And that's evidence of what, exactly?"

"I don't know."

What's Wrong with the World

Santa Barbara, California, May 4, 2019: Dennis Prager can't say enough good things about Jordan Peterson. But he's saved the best for last. Peterson is brilliant, that's apparent, but he's more than that. "Everybody knows you're bright," Prager enthuses, turning to Peterson directly, "But *I* know you're good" (PragerU 2019, 2:29).

The audience applauds. "I have something to say about that," Peterson says, then pauses as the applause settles, choosing his next words carefully. "See, I don't think it's true."

Then he explains why. He explains that if Prager could have known his younger self, Prager would have seen not a good man, but a tortured man, a man "terrified of how terrible [he] could be." So how did Peterson not become terrible? He tells the audience that he tried to the best of his ability to avoid dark pathways. He tried to keep to the old roads, the roads that seemed to lead out of darkness towards light. None of which made him good. But perhaps there was something in it all which might "approximate good." And so when people ask him, "Do you believe in God?" and he answers "I act as if God exists," this is what he means. In his mind, it's not a dodge. It's the best answer he can come up with, for a question he's still trying to understand.

But what would it mean to say not merely "I act as if," but "I believe"? For Peterson, this is also a terrifying thought. "Who would *dare* say that?" he asks the audience, becoming emotional. If you truly examined your conscience, how could you speak those words and not be crushed by the weight of them? To claim you believed would be to claim that in your soul, in your life, the belief was fully embodied, walked and lived out to the highest and noblest extent. And that, to Peterson, is "an unbearable task."

Yet what if you *could* bear it? What if you really could say those words, and mean them, and live them? Then, "God only knows what you'd be." Peterson says it twice: "God only knows what you'd be if you believed." And so, he concludes, "I try to act like I believe." "But," he adds forcefully, tears flowing, "I'd never claim that I *manage it*."

The contrast with the popular atheist script could not be starker. Here there is no humanist swagger, no self-congratulation, no smug hypothetical after-life confrontations with the Almighty. Rather, there is an honest attempt, however misguided, however lacking in its understanding of the Christian gospel, to wrestle with that most unbearable of all tasks—the task of holiness.

Perhaps the most famous atheistic rant of modern times was composed off-the-cuff by British writer/activist Stephen Fry, in a viral moment from a 2015 Irish radio interview. "Suppose it's all true," asks interviewer Gay Byrne, "and you walk up to the pearly gates, and you are confronted by God. What would Stephen Fry say?" (RTÉ—Ireland's National Public Service Media 2015).

Fry hasn't anticipated this question, but he is only too happy to answer it. Without missing a beat, he launches his hypothetical assault on the "capricious, mean-minded, stupid God" who would create an unjust, painful world like ours, a world where cancer ravages children's bones and parasitic insects drill into their eyes. If the Greek gods were allegedly presiding over all this, that would be one thing. Nobody looks to them as an ideal judge of anyone. But is this the all-good, all-wise, all-loving Creator we're expected to worship, the God we're expected to "spend our life on our knees thanking"? Perish the thought. You see, Fry explains, "Atheism is not just about not believing there is a God, but on the assumption there is one, what *kind* of God is it? It's perfectly apparent that He is monstrous, utterly monstrous, deserves no respect whatsoever. The moment you banish Him, your life becomes simpler, purer, cleaner, more worth living. In my opinion."

Except it's *not* so simple, Jordan Peterson insists. Rage against God all you want, but your rage does not absolve you of your responsibility. All the hard work still lies ahead. Coming from Peterson, this is no cheap platitude. He is a man well-acquainted with grief. The ups and downs of his own suffering have become headline news, as he's seen his wife through a cancer scare, battled crippling anxiety, suffered catastrophically adverse medical reactions, and to this day manages intense chronic pain. As he says directly to Stephen Fry in their 2021 podcast episode, the temptation to resentment in the midst of overwhelming suffering is not a hypothetical for him. It is lived experience. And yet, he has emerged on the other side more convinced than ever that resentment is not the answer. Resentment is the way of corruption, the way of Cain. And just as Cain chose to murder his brother, so we choose daily, in our own lives, by our own malevolence, to create some of the very worst injustices that make the creation groan in pain. This is Peterson's version of the answer G.K. Chesterton is famously said to have given to the *Times* survey question "What's wrong with the world?" As the story goes, he wrote in with a two-word reply: "I am."

It seems paradoxical that such a severe message would have found such a willing audience. Who wants to be told he is what's wrong with the world? Who wants to be told that Cain lurks inside his own heart? Who wants a good doctor to come poking and probing into the darkest corners of his soul, then deliver the bad news that if there were a God, he might have something to answer for? Apparently, many more people than the New Atheists bargained for.

But Peterson anticipates his own critique in conversation with Fry. He anticipates some might say he's dodging Fry's point, making an apology for God. Well, he admits, perhaps he is. "And perhaps there's no God at all," he smiles wryly, "and so what the hell are we talking about?" (Peterson and Fry 2021) But, writing in his sequel *Beyond Order*, Peterson will say this much for the Christian God, in a hat tip to another Chestertonian thought: No other God has been God-forsaken. No other divinity has uttered a cry like the cry of *"Eli, eli, lama sabbachthani."* "Let the revolutionaries choose a creed," Chesterton writes. ". . . let the atheists themselves choose a god. They will find only one divinity who ever uttered their isolation; only one religion in which God seemed for an instant to be an atheist" (1945, p. 257).

And Is It True?

"Banish God, for the moment you banish Him, your life becomes simpler." If Stephen Fry had written his *12 Rules for Life*, no doubt this would be Rule 1. Not that he would make any claim to originality. When his viral rant provoked backlash, he pointed over his shoulder to Bertrand Russell and many other fine minds before him, content to wave their flag into the twenty-first century.

And perhaps there is a sense in which, like their lives, Stephen Fry's life has become simpler. Perhaps it's the same for Sam Harris, or Richard Dawkins. But it's not the same for all who today find themselves wandering in bare ruined choirs, picking aimlessly through the rubble, unsure what they are even looking for now, only sensing inescapably that they still haven't found it, whatever *it* is. They are the "we" in Dennis O'Driscoll's poem "Missing God," when he writes, "Yet, though we rebelled against Him/like adolescents, up-lifted to see/an oppressive father banished—/a bearded her-mit—to the desert,/ we confess to missing Him at times." We may no longer call for His grace before meals. Our fish may multiply and our bread rise without His intercession. Even so, we miss Him—in the wedding conducted by registrar, in the funeral conducted without prayer. We miss Him in the gaunt Crucifixion hanging on a museum wall, eternally judg-ing us for all we have done that we shouldn't, all we haven't done that we should.

And there is Jordan Peterson with us, the rogue profes-sor picking through the rubble himself, himself confounded by the mystery. What does it all mean? Give him forty hours. Give him three years. No, give him a lifetime. He still won't have an answer, or at least not an answer he is satis-fied with. He looks at the hanging God, the empty tomb, and he knows what they represent. He knows the point in time and space they mark, that "the Christians insist" they have to mark, or else. Or else faith is vain. Or else all will be lost, all good things passed away. And his problem, as he tells his good friend Jonathan Pageau through tears, is that he probably believes that. But he doesn't understand his own belief. "It's too hard," he says, "because it's too terrify-ing a reality to fully believe. I don't even know what would happen to you if you fully believed that" (Peterson and Pageau 2021).

"And is it true?" asks John Betjeman in his poem "Christ-mas." "And is it true / This most tremendous tale of all"? For if it is, no other tale, no other joy, no other truth can compare with this: "That God was man in Palestine / And lives today in Bread and Wine."

Bibliography

Betjeman, Sir John. Christmas. All Poetry, accessed July 24th, 2021. <https://allpoetry.com/poem/8493411-Christmas-by-Sir-John-Betjeman>.

Chesterton, G.K. 1945. *Orthodoxy*. New York: Dodd, Mead.

Lewis, C.S. 1963. *Letters to Malcolm*. New York: Harcourt, Brace, Jovanovich.

Peterson, Jordan B. 2018a. AA Harris/Weinstein/Peterson Discussion: Vancouver. <www.youtube.com/watch?v=d-Z9EZE8kpo&>.

———. 2018b. AC Harris/Murray/Peterson Discussion: Dublin. <www.youtube.com/watch?v=ZZI-FwSQRn8&>.

———. 2018c. AD Harris/Murray/Peterson Discussion: London. <www.youtube.com/watch?v=YfdaAGZvYsA&>.

Peterson, Jordan B., and Bari Weiss. 2021. *Jordan B Peterson Podcast*. <www.youtube.com/watch?v=tFTA9MJZ4KY&>.

Peterson, Jordan B., and Jonathan Pageau. 2021. *Jordan B Peterson Podcast*. <www.youtube.com/watch?v=2rAqVmZwqZM&>.

Peterson, Jordan B., and Stephen Fry. 2021. *Jordan B. Peterson Podcast*. <www.youtube.com/watch?v=fFFSKedy9f4&>.

PragerU. 2019. Interview: Jordan Peterson and Dennis Prager at the 2019 PragerU summit. <www.youtube.com/watch?v=L47oJxwp6yg>.

O'Driscoll, Dennis. 2013. Missing God. *The Irish Times* (January 22nd). <www.irishtimes.com/opinion/his-grace-is-no-longer-called-for-before-meals-1.964594>.

ReasonableFaithOrg. 2018. Is There Meaning to Life? William Lane Craig, Rebecca Goldstein, Jordan Peterson. <www.youtube.com/watch?v=xV4oIqnaxlg>.

RTÉ. 2015. Ireland's National Public Service Media. Stephen Fry on God. The Meaning of Life. RTÉ One. <www.youtube.com/watch?v=-suvkwNYSQo>.

[13]
Jordan Peterson on Postmodernism, Truth, and Science

PANU RAATIKAINEN

Jordan Peterson, a Canadian professor of psychology, has quickly risen to fame over the last few years: he has been often eagerly viewed as a leading anti-leftist thinker in the West today and even "one of the great thinkers of our time." *The New York Times* recently labelled him "the most influential public intellectual in the entire Western world right now" (Brooks 2018).

Admirers of Peterson see him as an unwavering defender of rationality and science, freedom of speech, and individual freedom, and a tireless opponent of totalitarianism, postmodernism, and political correctness. Critics accuse him of misogyny and fascism. Although Jordan Peterson is a psychologist by training, much of his output as a public intellectual is essentially philosophical. It is therefore appropriate to evaluate such ideas particularly from the viewpoint of academic philosophy.

"Postmodern neo-Marxism" and Truth

Peterson's central target of criticism is the doctrine he calls "postmodern neo-Marxism." He contends that neo-Marxists now control Western universities, in particular the social science faculties. According to Peterson, the figurehead of postmodernism is the French philosopher Jacques Derrida, and the other key figures are Michel Foucault and Jacques Lacan, also French scholars (all deceased).

As Peterson describes it, postmodernism is set in motion by the idea that there are an innumerable number of possible interpretations for every phenomenon and every text. This, he says, is in itself a correct observation, and it has been made in many contexts. Peterson contends that postmodernism concludes from this that there is no reason to consider any one interpretation to be more valid than any other. The end result, then, is overarching and radical relativism and skepticism (Peterson 2018a; 2018b). According to Peterson's interpretation, postmodernism also advocates radical social constructionism according to which all of reality, even distant galaxies, are mere social constructs. Such a viewpoint is thus in conflict with realism about the external world: it denies the very existence of objective reality as something largely independent of the human mind.

According to Peterson, it is at this point that postmodernism allies with Marxism and brings in the concept of power. The following reasoning then ensues: Since no one interpretation can be elevated above the others as the correct one, it is best to interpret all the options of interpretation as a struggle of different forms of power. There is no external reality: everything is a social construction. There is nothing but power, and conflicts and struggles for power between different groups of people. Power struggles are the only motive for human action (*see* Kraychik 2017).

Indeed, Peterson repeatedly emphasizes that the leading postmodernist thinkers are former Marxists. However, whereas classical Marxism focused on the power struggle between social classes of the bourgeoisie and the proletariat, postmodern neo-Marxism, according to Peterson, recalibrates "class struggle" to include power struggles between arbitrarily defined groups based on sex, race, ethnicity, religion, and sexual orientation. The result is never-ending "identity politics" (*see* Kraychik 2017; Philipp 2017, Sovereign Nations 2018).

Peterson argues that the great error of postmodernism is to infer from the existence of innumerable possible interpretations that there must be innumerable equally *valid* interpretations. In particular, in order to oppose the latter claim and to clarify the concept of validity, Peterson makes a philosophically substantive move: he relies on *the pragmatist the-*

ory of truth. According to his interpretation, a proposition or interpretation is valid if acting on its basis in the world ensures the desired outcome within a specific timeframe. (Peterson refers to the pragmatist philosophers William James and Charles S. Peirce; *see* Peterson 2018a.)

According to Peterson, in reality many things limit significantly the number of *valid* interpretations. First, validity is "constrained by the necessity for iteration." As Peterson (2018a) writes: "Your interpretations have to keep you, at minimum, alive and not suffering too badly today, tomorrow, next week, next month and next year in a context defined by you, your family, your community and the broader systems you are part of." Second, Peterson argues that another limiting factor in interpretations is our own biology: we have evolved to prefer certain types of interpretations to others as a consequence of evolutionary processes.

Will Pragmatism and Biology Really Help?

Peterson's recourse to the pragmatist theory of truth is a step in a very wrong direction. He advocates the pragmatist theory of truth in a quite naive and problematic form that is liable to lead to relativism rather than avoid it. The troubles with such a straightforward view of truth are manifold (see for example David 2004; Raatikainen 2021a): In reality, it can sometimes be more useful or cause less suffering to believe something that is untrue. Believing some theoretical truth can also be practically useless, yet true. Moreover, utility is often relative to the individual, culture, or circumstances. It may be useful for person A to believe p, but useful for person B to believe not-p.

The fact that some interpretations do not work in practice may preclude a few invalid interpretations, but it often leaves far too much room for relativism: numerous mutually inconsistent interpretations may work equally well on a practical level for some limited period of time. They would then all be, according to Peterson's pragmatist conception, equally true. However, this would mean that a contradiction is true, and that is an intolerable conclusion. Identifying truth and utility is thus clearly an unsustainable idea. Even if several competing theories ensured the desired outcome within a specific timeframe, at most one of them can be true.

Our biologically shaped tendencies in reasoning, which Peterson invokes, are also more problematic than he seems to recognize. They certainly limit our interpretations, but many psychological studies—of which one might expect Peterson as a psychologist to be aware—demonstrate that the intuitive "rules of thumb" we routinely use in our mundane reasoning often lead to erroneous conclusions in more complex settings. For example, the studies of Wason, Johnson-Laird, and their collaborators have demonstrated that the great majority of us perform quite badly in a rather simple logical task. Similarly, Tversky, Kahneman, Slovic, and their colleagues have in turn shown with various experiments that people regularly violate basic rules of probabilistic reasoning, when they assess the relative probability of compound events. (For a brief overview, see Stich 1985.) Our biologically evolved reasoning dispositions are thus no guarantee of truth.

Contemporary Philosophy and Radical Postmodernism

Given how much Peterson likes to talk about contemporary philosophy, it is disconcerting to find that in dealing with this vastly broad and multifaceted field, he seems to be drawing (in addition to a seemingly sporadic reading of a few individual philosophers, namely, Nietzsche, Heidegger, Wittgenstein, and Popper) only from one short overview: *Explaining Postmodernism: Skepticism and Socialism from Rousseau to Foucault* by Stephen Hicks (2004). The book is very concise, but in addition it contains, to say the least, some quite controversial interpretations (*see* for instance McManus 2018). It's a pity that a commentator on contemporary philosophy as influential as Peterson has built his analysis on such a scant basis.

Peterson presents Derrida as a leading representative of postmodernism. Now Derrida is well known as a difficult and controversial philosopher, and I am happy to leave the judgment of his enduring significance to philosophy and the possible problems of his thought to history. All the same, Peterson's straightforward interpretations of Derrida seem questionable: Derrida apparently never used the term "post-modernism" to describe his own philosophy, nor did he participate in debates on that theme. Derrida also explicitly denied he would advocate radical relativism, and he refuted that his critical scrutiny of the metaphysical basis of truth was intended to be hostile towards truth and science. It seems that Peterson's "Derrida" is largely a fictional character he has created.

Actual radical postmodernism, such as that of Jean-François Lyotard (1979), certainly deserves to be criticized. Peterson is, of course, quite right to regard radical relativism and steep and over-arching social constructionism as implausible and even potentially harmful. However, his recurring claim that such extreme views dominate Western universities is difficult to believe, and it is arguably largely a "straw man" stood up by Peterson himself. In fact, it is quite implausible that the diverse academic world would be ideologically as homogeneous as Peterson's straightforward description suggests. While some individuals, among millions of academics, may have on some occasions put forward problematic ideas, it is a completely different matter to claim that such views are the prevalent ones. It is actually quite difficult to find thinkers who would really unreservedly advocate the extreme position described by Peterson. In some circles, of course, mere belief in evolution and climate change and respect of everyone's human rights is inherently leftist. In the minds of such people, Marxism no doubt abounds at universities. However, that does not justify the sort of strong characterization that Peterson presents.

Peterson declares that postmodernist philosophy, which is a part of the so-called "continental tradition" of philosophy, dominates Western universities. Thus, in practice, he denies—among other things—the obvious fact that the philosophy departments of many Anglo-American and Nordic universities have long been dominated by the so-called "analytical tradition," which draws heavily on the philosophy of science and logic. Drawing himself on psychoanalysis, Heidegger, and Nietzsche, Peterson is in many ways much closer to the "continental tradition" of philosophy (Nietzsche, Heidegger, and psychoanalysis were also central to Derrida and Foucault), one of the branches of which he attacks, than many more scientifically oriented philosophers who have criticized him.

At least in the case of academic philosophers, we have relatively good data: Via the popular *PhilPapers* database, David Bourget and David Chalmers have conducted a massive *survey* of the views of professional philosophers on thirty central philosophical issues (*see* Bourget and Chalmers 2014). They chose as a special target group all regular faculty members in ninety-nine "leading" departments of philosophy: ninety-two departments in English-speaking countries and seven departments from continental Europe (1,972 philosophers in total). To be sure, the survey did not include questions with terms such as "postmodernism" or "social constructionism," but the following results should give some indication.

Only 1.6% of the target group straightforwardly accepted idealism concerning the external world, while an additional 2.7% said they "leaned towards it." (These answers were more common among theists than atheists.) Some 3.0% leaned toward skepticism, while only 1.8% unconditionally accepted it. No less than 81.6% accepted or leaned towards non-skeptical realism, 75% accepted scientific realism or leaned towards it (that is, realism with respect to the non-observable entities postulated in science), and only 3.3% unreservedly accepted scientific anti-realism. (For the varieties of "realism", *see* for example Raatikainen 2014.) As to knowledge claims, 1.7% leaned toward relativism, and only 1.2% unconditionally accepted it. A new survey was conducted in 2020; its analysis is still in the making, but the preliminary results suggest that there are no significant changes in these numbers. If "postmodern neo-Marxism" with extreme relativism or skepticism and radical social constructionism with its denial of the objective external world were even half as dominant as Peterson suggests they are, surely these numbers would have been very different.

Neo-Marxist Academia: Fact or Fiction?

The picture of "neo-Marxist postmodernists" controlling Western universities that Peterson propagates is in many ways only an updated variant of a conspiracy theory associated with so-called "Cultural Marxism" (*see* for example Jamin 2014, Woods 2019, Busbridge et al. 2020). This theory, which is not without antisemitic aspects, has been popular among the far right and extreme conservatives since the early 1990s.

The narrative goes roughly as follows: When the Communist revolution did not take place in the West, the "Jewish intellectuals" of the so-called Frankfurt School, the "Cultural Marxists," devised a new strategy. So, the story continues, the goal was to destroy the West "from within" by subverting its traditional culture, values, and institutions, and thus break the moral backbone of the West. Marxists have therefore infiltrated the media, educational institutions, and even churches, and they now dominate them. Among other things, feminism, the sexual revolution, and the defense of the rights of sexual and ethnic minorities are all part of Cultural Marxism's cunning plan. The picture suggested is a fantastic conspiracy theory that credits amazing things to a few not-quite-easy-to-understand philosophers. It is, in turn, a modification of the older, openly antisemitic "Cultural Bolshevism" or "Judeo-Bolshevism" conspiracy theory of the Nazis, which obviously has an abhorrent track record. In Peterson's slightly reformed story, classic Marxism, which revolved around the economy, had been so thoroughly discredited by the 1970s that no one could support it publicly. Therefore, communism is no longer spread openly under the direct banner of "communism," but instead under the disguise of "postmodernism" (see for instance Philipp 2017). The Frankfurt school has now been replaced by Derrida and a few other French thinkers, and Peterson's picture has no apparent antisemitic tone; otherwise, the story is quite similar.

It is certainly true that when the social sciences struggled to develop their philosophical self-understanding and looked for alternatives to austere positivism, the philosophy of the social sciences included some "stabbing in the dark," and sometimes, in hindsight, unclear and problematic philosophical theories, including relativist views of varying degrees. However, this was not some novelty brought about by "neo-Marxism" in the 1970s: the groping attempts of the social sciences to position themselves in relation to the natural sciences have continued at least since the nineteenth century. The romanticization and even mystification of the human mind and, consequently, the social sciences have often drawn from the traditions of German idealism and the Counter-Enlightenment, which were more traditionalist and conservative rather than progressive social movements. Relativist views first became popular in connection to such traditions already in the nineteenth century. (For the history of relativism, *see* for example Baghramian 2004, 2010.) To the extent that relativism or social constructionism have actually gained a foothold in the social sciences at universities, this has been just one phase in a long tradition: It is not due to recent leftist indoctrination.

Peterson, Science, and Pseudoscience

Peterson and his admirers like to portray him as an uncompromising defender of rationality and the scientific worldview against postmodernist irrationalism. However, Peterson has, as a matter of fact, shown a tendency towards advocating pseudoscientific ideas.

For example, in August 2018, Peterson shared on Twitter a video titled "Climate Change: What Do Scientists Say?" with his own comment: "Something for the anticapitalist environmentalists to hate." In the video, Richard Lindzen, a notorious climate change denialist who is known to have received money from fossil fuel interests, speaks as the only "scientist" (Herzog 2018). This is not the only time Peterson has downplayed climate change and promoted a denialist message. Peterson seems to be open to pseudo-scientific propaganda if it can be used as a weapon against "the left."

In one of his lectures, Peterson discusses ancient fine art from China and the aboriginals of Australia, among others. He notes that there is ancient art around the world that repeatedly depicts intertwined snake-like figures, and that they are used as healing symbols. Peterson states that he believes these ancient paintings represent the double helix of DNA (*see* Genetically Modified Skeptic, 2018). According to the established history of science, the double helix nature of DNA was not revealed until 1953 by Watson, Crick, Franklin, and Wilkins. The discovery required, among other things, x-rays. When asked about the matter, Peterson explains that "we do not know the limits of observation, especially in certain circumstances." He says he believes that humans have always (for millennia) had "hints" about DNA. Peterson then cites the book *The Cosmic Serpent* by Jeremy Narby as his source (Narby 1998). In the book, Narby contends that already thousands of years ago, Peruvian shamans using hallucinogenic drugs achieved information about DNA that was then encoded into the brains of their offspring as innate information. This is pseudo-scientific hooey so thick that Peterson's appeals to it are utterly embarrassing.

Peterson has also made gestures towards advanced mathematical logic, namely, Gödel's famous incompleteness theorem (*see* Raatikainen 2021b). In his *Maps of Meaning*, he writes:

> A moral system—a system of culture—necessarily shares features in common with other systems. The most fundamental of the shared features of systems was identified by Kurt Gödel. Gödel's Incompleteness Theorem demonstrated that any internally consistent and logical system of propositions must necessarily be predicated upon assumptions that cannot be proved from within the confines of that system. (Peterson 1999, p. 189)

This is baffling. First, Gödel's incompleteness theorem only applies to a certain specific class of formalized *mathematical* theories. It has nothing to do with moral or cultural systems, nor with features shared by such systems. Second, the theorem does not say anything about some assumptions external to the system on which the system should be grounded. It only states that there are sentences in the language of the theory which are neither provable nor refutable in that theory. (For such philosophical misinterpretations of Gödel's theorem, and why they are problematic, *see* Raatikainen 2005, Franzén 2007.) This is a sad example of how Peterson tends to talk confidently about issues of which he clearly does not have even an elementary understanding.

To summarize, whatever Peterson's academic merits in clinical psychology may be, his philosophical output is overly simplistic and in a lot of ways problematic. He does not seem

Panu Raatikainen

to have anything useful to offer philosophical discussions on truth. It is doubtful how well his quick analyses of contemporary Western society and academia in fact correspond to reality. His visible affinity to all sorts of pseudo-science makes him more of an enemy of the scientific worldview than its defender.

References

Baghramian, Maria. 2004. *Relativism*. London: Routledge.
———. 2010. A Brief History of Relativism. In Michael Krausz, ed., *Relativism: A Contemporary Anthology*. New York: Columbia University Press.
Bourget, David, and David J. Chalmers. 2014. What Do Philosophers Believe? *Philosophical Studies* 170.
Brooks, David. 2018. The Jordan Peterson Moment. *The New York Times* (25th January).
Busbridge, Rachel, Benjamin Moffitt, and Joshua Thorburn. 2020. Cultural Marxism: Far-Right Conspiracy Theory in Australia's Culture Wars. *Social Identities* 26.
David, Marian. 2004. Theories of Truth. In Ilkka Niiniluoto, Matti Sintonen, and Jan Woleński, eds., *The Handbook of Epistemology*. Dordrecht: Kluwer.
Franzén, Torkel. 2005. *Gödel's Theorem: An Incomplete Guide to Its Use and Abuse*, Wellesley: A.K. Peters.
Genetically Modified Skeptic. 2018. Jordan Peterson's Most Pseudoscientific Claim Ever. <www.youtube.com/watch?v=iIfLTQAKKfg>.
Herzog, Katie. 2018. Jordan Peterson Pushes Dangerous Myths about Climate Change. *The Stranger* (August 3rd). <www.thestranger.com/slog/2018/08/03/30143461/jordan-peterson-pushes-dangerous-myths-about-climate-change>.
Hicks, Stephen. 2004. *Explaining Postmodernism: Skepticism and Socialism from Rousseau to Foucault*. Tempe: Scholargy.
Jamin, Jérôme. 2014. Cultural Marxism and the Radical Right. In Paul Jackson and Anton Shekhovtsov, eds., *The Post-War Anglo-American Far Right: A Special Relationship of Hate*. Basingstoke: Palgrave.
Kraychik, Robert. 2017. Jordan Peterson Explains Leftism's Core. *The Daily Wire*. <www.dailywire.com/news/jordan-peterson-explains-leftisms-core-robert-kraychik>.

Lyotard, Jean-François. 1979. *La condition postmoderne: rapport sur le savoir*. Paris: Minuit.

McManus, Matt. 2018. A Review of *Explaining Postmodernism* by Stephen Hicks. *Areo*, 17/10/2018. <https://areomagazine.com/2018/10/17/a-review-of-explaining-postmodernism-by-stephen-hicks>.

Narby, Jeremy. 1998. *The Cosmic Serpent: DNA and the Origins of Knowledge*. New York: Jeremy P. Tarcher/Putnam.

Peterson, Jordan B. 1999. *Maps of Meaning: The Architecture of Belief*. New York: Routledge.

———. 2018a. Postmodernism: Definition and Critique (with a Few Comments on its Relationship with Marxism) <www.jordanbpeterson.com/philosophy/postmodernism-definition-and-critique-with-a-few-comments-on-its-relationship-with-marxism>.

———. 2018b. *12 Rules for Life. An Antidote to Chaos*. Toronto: Random House Canada.

Philipp, Joshua. 2017. Jordan Peterson Exposes the Postmodernist Agenda. *Epoch Times*. <www.theepochtimes.com/jordan-peterson-explains-how-communism-came-under-the-guise-of-identity-politics_2259668.html>.

Raatikainen, Panu. 2005. On the Philosophical Relevance of Gödel's Incompleteness Theorems. *Revue Internationale de Philosophie* 59.

———. 2014. Realism: Metaphysical, Semantic, and Scientific. In Kenneth R. Westphal, ed., *Realism, Science, and Pragmatism*. London: Routledge.

———. 2021a. Truth and Theories of Truth. In P. Stalmaszczyk, ed., *The Cambridge Handbook of the Philosophy of Language*. Cambridge University Press.

———. 2021b. Gödel's Incompleteness Theorems. In *The Stanford Encyclopedia of Philosophy*. <https://plato.stanford.edu/archives/spr2021/entries/goedel-incompleteness/>.

Stich, Stephen P. 1985. Could Man Be an Irrational Animal? Some Notes on the Epistemology of Rationality. *Synthese* 64.

Sovereign Nations. 2018. Dr. Jordan B. Peterson: Identity Politics and The Marxist Lie of White Privilege. *Sovereign Nations*. <https://sovereignnations.com/2018/01/30/jordan-peterson-marxist-lie-white-privilege>.

Woods, Andrew. 2019. Cultural Marxism and the Cathedral: Two Alt-Right Perspectives on Critical Theory. In Christine M. Battista and Melissa R. Sande, eds., *Critical Theory and the Humanities in the Age of the Alt-Right*. New York: Springer.

Part IV

The Philosopher

[14]
Are We Made for Happiness?

TRISTAN J. ROGERS

The *New York Times* calls Jordan Peterson "The most influential public intellectual in the Western world right now." Why does Peterson's work appeal to the public? His critics target the perceived political content of his ideas. But Peterson's message is moral, not political. Which is what, exactly?

In his recent books, Peterson plays variations on a theme, with fragments of homespun wisdom such as "Set your house in perfect order before you criticize the world" and "Do not do what you hate" (Peterson 2018, Chapter 6; 2021, Chapter V). Not earth-shattering stuff, but salutary, as our experience of the modern world has become both chaotic *and* monotonous.

Peterson's moral message responds to our existential need for order and psychological need for purpose. While now the purview of self-help and pop psychology—available at airport bookstores everywhere—this is a need philosophy once supplied. Philosophers believed that wisdom consists in care for the soul. Thus, the Greek philosopher Socrates chided his Athenian accusers: "are you not ashamed of your eagerness to possess as much wealth, reputation and honors as possible, while you do not care for nor give thought to wisdom or truth, or the best possible state of your soul?" (Plato 1997, 29e). Could Socrates's diagnosis apply to us? And if it does, what treatment might Peterson's moral philosophy prescribe?

Ancient Greek ethics begins with a search for the good life. The Greeks called the good life *eudaimonia*, usually translated into English as "happiness." Peterson criticizes happiness as an appropriate goal in life for its fleeting quality, a mere feeling. But happiness in the sense of eudaimonia is much more than a feeling. Happiness is having a purpose that makes your life *worthwhile*. The Greek philosophers mostly agreed that happiness requires a virtuous character. So too, Peterson's "rules for life" presuppose the necessity of virtue. Meaning is to be found, as Peterson argues, in adopting responsibility for oneself and others. This is a message we desperately need to hear, as Peterson resurrects the call to wisdom once heralded by ancient Greek virtue ethics.

How Should You Live?

Ethics is the study of value, the study of what *matters*. Is morality independent of your personal feelings and cultural mores? How do you distinguish right from wrong actions? How should you live? Our expectation that these questions have answers assumes that reason can order the chaos of life. Otherwise value would be simply illusory, leaving no means of distinguishing right from wrong, and no guidance for leading a good life.

This duality of chaos and order is central to Peterson's moral philosophy. "Chaos," as Peterson explains, "is the domain of ignorance itself. It's *unexplored territory* . . . Order, by contrast, is *explored territory*" (Peterson 2018, pp. 35–36, emphasis in original). As when you possess a good map, you are in order when you have a good model of your surroundings and can predictably move through it, with the expectation that things will go according to plan. But chaos is the state of being lost in the woods, lacking a map, with danger lurking around every corner. Order is when your knowledge of yourself and the world is good enough to get what you want, chaos when (more than likely) it is not.

The Greek historian Xenophon, who with the philosopher Plato is another source for our knowledge of Socrates, recounts a story—well-known in the ancient world—about the Greek demigod Heracles (Hercules) (Xenophon 1990, pp. 106–09; Annas 2000, Chapter 3). Upon approaching maturity, Heracles faced a choice about the direction of his life. While sitting in a quiet place contemplating the matter, he was visited by two women. The first was naturally beautiful and modestly dressed in white, while the second wore unnatural makeup and a revealing, suggestive manner of dress.

Having rushed up to meet Heracles first, the second woman offers to lead him "by the easiest and pleasantest road . . . without any experience of hardship" (Xenophon 1990, p. 106). Meanwhile, the first woman offers Heracles the path of hardship and responsibility, culminating in "the most beatific happiness" (Xenophon 1990, p. 109). The second woman is called "Happiness" by her friends and "Vice" by her enemies; the first woman is known simply as "Virtue."

Heracles's story presents two paths through chaos and order: the hard way or the easy way. Which should you take? The only honorable choice, it seems, would be to take the hard way, the path offered by Virtue. Yet if we are honest with ourselves, we are also attracted to the life offered by Happiness, especially in a world where "virtue" sounds old-fashioned and pleasures abound. The deeper point of the story, however, is just that ethics requires a choice about the proper path in life, that is, the proper way to mediate between chaos and order. And to make such a choice well, to know truly the paths of Happiness and Virtue, we need philosophy.

But Peterson claims that ethics is nested in something deeper than even philosophy—religion. For Peterson, "Religion concerns itself not with (mere) right and wrong but with good and evil themselves—with the archetypes of right and wrong" (Peterson 2018, p. 102). But personal belief in a supernatural deity is not exactly Peterson's point. Rather, it is that your capacity for genuine ethical choice presumes the existence of ultimate value. As Peterson (1999) argues, the nature of ultimate value is embedded and revealed in the religious and mythological stories we tell, whether we profess belief in God or not. These stories are part of the cultural scaffolding of the society in which you are raised, which, in turn, unconsciously structures your ethical beliefs. Philosophy, as the love of wisdom, then, may need the proverbial fear of God, the fear of transgressing against ultimate value: "The fear of the LORD is the beginning of wisdom" (*King James Version* 1611, Proverbs 9:10).

The Meaning of Happiness

Whatever the metaphysics of ultimate value, what Plato called "The Good," the philosopher Aristotle is a better guide to the practical question of ultimate value. The good, according to Aristotle, is that at which everything aims (Aristotle 2019, 1094a). When I wake up in the morning, I desire to have a good day, which may include subordinate goods, such as a good breakfast. This naturally suggests that some goods are higher than others, where subordinate ends are chosen for the sake of higher ends. A good breakfast is part of a good day, a good day is part of a good week, and so on. Aristotle's observation is that this hierarchy of ends must terminate somewhere, otherwise desire would be pointless. Whatever good is highest, then, will be that which you choose for its own sake and everything else for the sake of it. Ultimate value consists in the highest good you can imagine choosing for yourself.

What could this highest good be? What has ultimate value? Aristotle notes that "As far as its name goes, most people practically agree; for both the many and the cultivated call it happiness" (Aristotle 2019, 1095a18–20). But *eudaimonia*, the Greek word we translate into English as "happiness," is not simply feeling good, or being subjectively content with your life. Being happy, for Aristotle, is living well in some objective sense; it is a life that is truly praiseworthy and worthwhile. It is your life as a whole that is properly described as happy (or not), not moments of pleasure. The reason why I choose the good breakfast that is part of my good day is ultimately because I desire a happy life. Happiness is what Heracles decides upon in his moment of reflection. While Aristotle acknowledges that we disagree about the content of happiness, say, whether it consists in wealth, pleasure, virtue, or some combination thereof, we agree that happiness—whatever it is—has ultimate value.

Aristotle's claim that happiness is the highest good may appear to conflict with Peterson's critique that happiness is *not* an appropriate goal in life. According to Peterson, "the inevitable suffering that life entails can rapidly make a mockery of the idea that happiness is the proper pursuit of the individual" (Peterson 2018, p. xxvii). Happiness is fleeting, and you are fortunate if you have it. But for this very reason, happiness is not a purpose that can order your life. You should, instead, as Peterson urges, strive to live "as if you were someone you are responsible for helping," which means "to consider what would be truly good for you" (Peterson 2018, p. 62). For we do not take care of our children by making them happy; we take care of them by giving them the opportunity for a good life. "I wish your child every happiness" does not mean "I wish your child has a life of pleasant moments," but rather "I wish your child a *good life*" (Russell 2011, p. 38). "Why," then, Peterson asks, "would you think it acceptable to do anything less for yourself?" (Peterson 2018, p. 62).

Peterson's critique rightly targets the modern "feel good" sense of happiness. But it does not undermine Aristotle's claim that happiness is the highest good because it does not apply to happiness in Aristotle's sense of *eudaimonia*. For Aristotle, as we've seen, happiness is about *doing* well, not just feeling good. Further, happiness is something *complete*, worth having for its own sake, not a passing sense of satisfaction. Happiness is also *self-sufficient*, meaning that nothing of value can be added to (or taken away from) it. Finally, the happy life is distinctive to human beings, given our rational nature; it is not just a life of pleasure. Given these criteria, Aristotle thought we could discover the true meaning of happiness as the highest good of human life. What would give your life meaning, order your desires and actions, and be genuinely worthwhile?

The Path through Chaos and Order

The ancient Greek philosophers mostly agreed that you must develop the virtues of character, among them justice, wisdom, courage, and temperance (the "classical" or "cardinal" virtues) (Annas 1993, Chapter 2). For Plato's Socrates, this is because of the *directive* nature of the virtues as goods of the soul. Mere external (or bodily) goods—health, wealth, resources—are not really good. Indeed, they can be positively bad when misused, unless they are directed by a virtuous character (Plato 1997, 30b). For Aristotle, the virtues define what it means to function properly as a human being guided by reason (Aristotle 2019, 1097a15–1098b). You're courageous, for example, when you take the right actions with the right attitude toward things fearful. Finally, the Stoics, who are among the Greek schools of philosophy that flourished after Socrates and into the Roman Period, claim that virtue is the *only* good, since even in dire circumstances, a virtuous path remains open to you (Epictetus 2004, Chapter 1).

The Stoics show the limits of Peterson's critique of happiness. Quoting the great Russian author Aleksandr Solzhenitsyn, Peterson writes, "the 'pitiful ideology' that 'human beings are created for happiness' was an ideology 'done in by the first blow of the work assigner's cudgel'" (Peterson 2018, p. xxvii). But for the Stoics, because happiness is identified with virtue, and virtue is wholly within your control, happiness is available *even to the man in the Gulag*. In this sense, the Stoics conceive of virtue as the exercise of a practical skill (Annas 2011, Chapter 3). Life's circumstances, whether favorable or not, are the materials on which you work, and in doing so, you develop the skill of virtue that will craft a good life out of even poor materials.

If virtue is like a practical skill, how should it be developed? Aristotle recommends that you become just by performing actions characteristic of a just person (Aristotle 2019, 1105a18–20). Virtue is acquired through the careful imitation of others and regular habituation of yourself. This may occur through role-models, whom you admire as virtuous ideals. But, as Peterson stresses, we also have stories. "In stories, we capture observations of the ideal personality . . . Great stories are about characters in action" (Peterson 2021, p. 37). How great, how inspiring, for instance, is Plato's drama of Socrates's trial, imprisonment, and execution? Reading and reflecting on great literature and philosophy is an invitation to imitate visions of the virtuous ideal in your own life.

The skill analogy also makes sense of our moral failures. There is, after all, a vast difference between failing to properly develop a skill, and repudiating the development of skill altogether. The former is characteristic of ordinary moral failures. You strive to be honest and tell the truth, but moral weakness causes the occasional lie. You aim to be temperate, but the extra piece of cake is just too much to resist. But the conscious choice to avoid virtue altogether is the sign of a vicious character that if enabled, leads to something that might properly be described as evil.

We can make the archery metaphor behind the skill analogy explicit to understand moral goodness. Peterson notes that the Greek word translated as "sin" in the New Testament (*hamartia*) "was originally an archery term, and it meant to miss the mark or target" (Peterson 2021, p. 114). Aristotle's doctrine of how to aim properly and hit the target is popularly known as "the golden mean." For Aristotle, you aim properly when you avoid extreme points of excess or deficiency, both in an action itself and its attendant emotions (Aristotle 2019, II.6–9). A generous person, for instance, gives money "to the right person, in the right amount, at the right time, for the right end, and in the right way" (Aristotle 2019, 1109a28–30). To miss the mark of generosity is to give too little—stinginess—or to give too much—profligacy. A generous person also feels good about giving, and generally does so for disinterested reasons. But an ungenerous person, even when giving a large amount, does not feel good about giving, and likely does so for ulterior motives.

Despite Aristotle's practical advice, such matters are not easy to define; there are no strict formulas. Instead, Aristotle recommends that we pay attention to the "particulars," as "the judgment depends on perception" (Aristotle 2019, 1110a23). Virtue is a kind of "seeing" the good in the field of action. It is seeing the proper path through chaos and order. To aim properly, then, in a manner that is most likely to hit the target, is to be virtuous. It is no guarantee of success, of course, since ultimately hitting the target is not fully within your control. A properly fired arrow can be blown off course by a sudden gust of wind. So too with virtue: your greatest efforts will be blown off course by factors not within your control. But even if you get flattened by a hurricane, nobody can take away your virtue.

As Peterson observes, charting the virtuous path through chaos and order is equivalent to the Taoist concept of "The Way" that is represented in the familiar yin and yang symbol (Peterson 2018, p. 43). Virtue is a balance between the known and the unknown; it's the line between chaos and order. Much like the virtuoso, who enters what the psychologist Mihaly Csikszentmihalyi (1990) calls a "flow state," or an athlete "in the zone," striking this balance is uniquely pleasurable. This insight confirms the intuitively plausible idea that happiness, even if not identical with pleasure (in the "feel good" sense), at least involves pleasure. In this sense, pleasure is a kind of emergent property that shines through in virtuous actions (Aristotle 2019, X.4). Peterson treats this as a deep psychological sign that we are on the right path: "The most profound and reliable instinct for meaning—if not perverted by self-deceit and sin (there is no other way to state it)—manifests itself when you are on the path of maximum virtue" (Peterson 2021, p. 135).

Virtue as the Adoption of Responsibility

How can you put virtue into practice and chart a course for happiness? It is, for instance, a standard objection against virtue ethics that its central ethical prescription "do what a virtuous person would characteristically do in the circumstances" is not very instructive. Virtue ethics seems to presume that you already know what a virtuous person is and how such a person would act in a diverse range of circumstances. But of course you rarely have this kind of knowledge, and if you did, you wouldn't need ethics.

How, for instance, is virtue any different from the vague injunction to "do the right thing"? Moral philosophers have generally tried to explain "the right thing" in terms of actions that either produce good outcomes (utilitarianism), or actions of intrinsic moral worth, codified in rules (deontology). Peterson's moral philosophy is interesting because, although he speaks the language of virtue ethics, he lays much emphasis on the utility of rules. Peterson's "rules for life," however, remain fundamentally grounded in the virtues, not abstract moral principles, whether utilitarian, deontological, or otherwise. Consider, for instance, "Tell the truth—or, at least, don't lie" (honesty), "Assume that the person you are listening to might know something you don't" (humility), and "Be grateful in spite of your suffering" (gratitude) (Peterson 2018, Chapters 8–9; 2021, Chapter XII).

These are variants of what the contemporary philosopher Rosalind Hursthouse calls "v-rules," that is, *virtue-rules*: "Do what is honest, do not do what is uncharitable," and so forth (Hursthouse 1999, p. 37). The attraction of virtue-rules is that they make the virtues concrete and practical. Consider another rule: "Notice that opportunity lurks where responsibility has been abdicated" (Peterson 2021, Chapter IV). This rule instructs you to seek virtue in the adoption of responsibility. Who is depending on you? For whom could you make yourself responsible? What is not getting done that you could do? In this sense, the virtues are the proper way to engage with (and expand) your existing social roles and responsibilities. "Do what is grateful" is vague, but "Do what is grateful toward your spouse" summons a concrete idea of how you should treat your spouse. Likewise, Peterson's "Stand up straight with your shoulders back" is a practical injunction to courage: "To stand up straight with your shoulders back is to accept the terrible responsibility of life, with eyes wide open" (Peterson 2018, Chapter 1, p. 27). You simply will not have the strength to develop the virtues if you lack the courage it takes to adopt responsibility for yourself and others.

In addition to your social roles and responsibilities— where ethical reflection begins—there is also the important guidance of the past. Your life is built, in some sense, on traditions handed down through the generations. Just as a musician who does not know the history of his genre is unlikely to be great, so too a citizen unacquainted with the history and traditions of her society is unlikely to lead a good life—or at least will have a much more difficult time doing so. Thus, Peterson's "Do not carelessly denigrate social institutions or creative achievement" is an injunction to respect and revere things of established value (Peterson 2021, Chapter I). Social institutions and the creative achievements of others are indispensable guides to how those who came before you managed to navigate life well. You denigrate them at your great peril.

So, to be virtuous you must master the rules. But tradition is not enough. Eventually, you have to make the tradition your own. The musician Miles Davis was known for saying "there are no wrong notes in jazz." But that's only true for someone, who like Davis, had already mastered the jazz tradition, and indeed, reinvented it several times. Of course there *are* wrong notes for the trumpeter in the high school jazz band. So too for leading a good life. You will not master the virtues on your own. You need the discipline furnished by the rules and institutions of your society.

"Nonetheless," as even Peterson admits, "all states of order, no matter how secure and comfortable, have their flaws" (Peterson 2021, p. xxiv). You must, therefore, remain on the frontiers of your knowledge and character development, with one foot firmly grounded in the wisdom of tradition, and the other on the uncertain, daring path of virtue.

We can now see why Heracles ought to take the path offered by "Virtue," not the path offered by "Happiness" so criticized by Peterson, and why the former leads to "the most beatific happiness." For, "It appears," Peterson writes, "that the meaning that most effectively sustains life is to be found in the adoption of responsibility" (2021, p. 113). And the greater the responsibility, the better. The worth of something is, in some sense, proportional to the difficulty of achieving it. So pick up the heaviest thing you can find and carry it on the path of virtue. In doing so, you may join the likes of Heracles, whose "Twelve Labors" allowed him to atone for the grave sin of slaying his wife and children in a fit of madness. Eventually, Heracles won immortality in the pantheon of the gods. Now that's an ideal of virtue truly worthy of imitation!

References

Annas, Julia. 1993. *The Morality of Happiness*. Oxford: Oxford University Press.

———. 2000. *Ancient Philosophy: A Very Short Introduction*. Oxford: Oxford University Press.

———. 2011. *Intelligent Virtue*. Oxford: Oxford University Press.

Anonymous. 2016 [1611]. *KJV Holy Bible*. Nelson.

Aristotle. 2019. *Nicomachean Ethics*. Indianapolis: Hackett.

Csikszentmihalyi, Mihaly. 1990. *Flow: The Psychology of Optimal Experience*. New York: Harper and Row.

Epictetus. 2004. *Discourses: Books 1 and 2*. Mineola: Dover.

Hursthouse, Rosalind. 1999. *On Virtue Ethics*. Oxford: Oxford University Press.

Peterson, Jordan B. 1999. *Maps of Meaning: The Architecture of Belief*. New York: Routledge.

———. 2018. *12 Rules for Life: An Antidote to Chaos*. Toronto: Random House Canada.

————. 2021. *Beyond Order: 12 More Rules for Life*. New York: Penguin Random House.

Plato. 1997. Apology. In *Plato: Complete Works*. Indianapolis: Hackett.

Russell, Daniel C. 2011. *Happiness for Humans*. Oxford: Oxford University Press.

Xenophon. 1990. *Conversations of Socrates*. London: Penguin.

[15]
How Jordan Peterson Explains Human Behavior

DAVID DENNEN

The philosopher Michael Bratman (2013) has pointed out that we humans have some remarkable capacities: First, we're able to plan out our actions over long stretches of time. Second, we're able to act, not just on our own, but with others to achieve shared goals. And, third, we are, at least some of the time, able to step back from the ongoing rush of experience and make conscious decisions about how to act. As adults, we're all familiar with these capacities. But where do they come from? How do they actually work? These questions are not so easy to answer.

What Is Reality?

First of all, action always happens *somewhere*. Action is in and of the world. As living, desiring creatures, we are thrown into the world where we must act toward the satisfaction of our desires. But the world, ultimately, Jordan Peterson argues, is an unknowable, unfathomable "sea of complexity" (2013, p. 17). To act, we must simplify the world into a set of more or less useful objects. But the ultimate complexity of the world never really disappears.

All the objects in our world are systems of relations that can be viewed at many different "levels of resolution." Consider your coffee mug. Most immediately it is a tool for conveying coffee (or other liquids) into your body. But it is many other things besides. It is an object that has existed and will exist for a certain number of years, days, minutes. It was made by a certain person or company. It has a certain weight, a certain diameter, a certain height. It has a certain level of heat and shock resistance. It contains a certain quantity of quartz and feldspar. It has a certain level of toxicity to human beings (hopefully very low). All these properties, and more, put this simple object into complex relations with other objects and events in the universe. We ignore or are unable to see many of these properties and relations. But they are there and sometimes they matter: One day we heat the mug too long in the microwave oven and it cracks; one day we discover that one of the substances of which the mug is made is in fact highly toxic to humans. Anomaly—something unexpected—is then introduced into our world. A broken mug is not the most threatening kind of anomaly one can imagine. Any mature adult should be able to process such an event and get on with his or her day. But discovering that we have for years been drinking out of a toxic cup may indeed make our world a darker, more threatening, more uncertain place.

Reality, then, is a "forum for action" made up of objects that are *meaningful* to us (Peterson 1999). They are mean-ingful because they have implications for our action: they help us or hinder us in our efforts to satisfy our desires. Because this environment of objects is full of hidden complexity—maybe promising, maybe threatening—behavior can be understood as the "management of complexity" (Peterson and Flanders 2002; Peterson 2013).

How Individuals Manage Complexity

Say you are trying to cross a busy street without pedestrian signals. There is a very large number of things that you *could* pay attention to, but how do you know *what* to pay attention to? For example, there is the position of the sun in the sky and the shape of the clouds; the texture of the concrete between your feet; details of the vehicles, such as their makes and models, license plate numbers, colors; your own bodily sensations, such as the feel of your clothing, the rate of your heartbeat, feelings of hunger or satiation; and on and on. We know, however, that most or all of this is irrelevant. How do we know?

The key here is *motivation*. We have inherited a certain number of basic motivations (for food, for companionship, and so forth), as living creatures belonging to a certain species. But we have also picked up many more over the course of our individual developments as members of particular societies. Motivation, Peterson argues, "provides the most stable of the psychological strategies" for survival. It brings order to the world by creating objects and values. It creates what Peterson calls "determinate microworlds of experience" (2000, 2013). When we are motivated to cross the busy street, our perception is narrowed to include only what we have learned matters for this task: the vehicles, their relative distances to us, their relative speeds. At the same time, a set of actions is brought into play: directed head and eye movements as we look for vehicles and toward our destination; leg movements involved in locomotion. And emotions: we may feel frustrated if there are no gaps in traffic sufficient for us; scared if a car narrowly misses or honks its horn at us; relieved when we make it across safely. To be motivated, then, is to have one's perceptions biased in a particular way (biased *toward* some aspects of reality and *against* others) and to be primed to act and feel in a particular way. Peterson (2013, p. 22) calls this condition a *motivation, action, and perception (MAP) schema*. Our MAP schemas create the little worlds we inhabit, filled as they are with a small number of objects and properties important at the moment to whatever goal we are trying to accomplish.

Just as they create a known little world of experience, they create the possibility for the unknown. To be manageable, a microworld must exclude quite a lot. So imagine you are getting ready to cross the street. After watching the traffic attentively and with a certain growing impatience, a gap finally opens up that appears to be sufficient for you to pass safely. You decide to go for it. But just as you step off the curb, there is a shout from nearby: "Hey, you!"

An *anomaly* has just been introduced into your world. You stop in your tracks. Your body turns toward the sound as your eyes widen, your heart rate increases, your muscles tense. This is *anxiety*, our natural response to the unknown. You begin to *explore* the anomaly: Who is speaking? What do they want? Your eyes focus: It's a police officer! Your anxiety rises. "Hey," he says, "there's a pedestrian underpass fifty meters that way. Please use it." "Oh," you reply meekly, heart rate slowing, muscles relaxing. "Okay, thank you." You begin to walk in the direction indicated.

With your attention focused on crossing the street, you had failed to notice someone approaching you—and a thousand other things besides.

A Digression on the Brain

This is, in a nutshell, how Peterson understands human action. We build a simplified picture of the world that is usually good enough to get us from a less than satisfactory present (being on *this* side of the street) to a future we think will be better (being on the *other* side of the street). But since our microworld excludes almost everything, we're always vulnerable to the anomalous.

It ought to be briefly mentioned that our MAP schemas have a neurophysiological existence as well (Hirsh et al. 2012; Peterson 2013). While certain brain regions (the hypothalamus, the dorsolateral prefrontal cortex) construct and impose MAP schemas on our experience, another set of brain areas (labeled as the septo-hippocampal comparator system) compares the neural version of the MAP schema with signals from our eyes, ears, and other sense organs. If there is a mismatch between desire and perception—an anomaly—a part of this system takes over. One line of research Peterson draws from has called this the "orienting reaction" (Vinogradova 2001); another has called it the "behavioral inhibition system" (Gray and McNaughton 2003). In any case, this subsystem sends signals and starts the release of hormones that "inhibit" brain areas responsible for ongoing action and "disinhibit" brain areas responsible for anxiety and attentiveness.

How Groups Manage Complexity

Our MAP schemas simplify the world, but they do not necessarily lead to a simple world. This is because we have multiple motivations—multiple MAP schemas—working within us simultaneously, on different time-scales: We need to finish that report for next week and spend time with our kids and get dinner ready and think about what we'll say at that meeting tomorrow and worry about whether our partner is really invested in this relationship and think about how we're going to manage our retirement . . .

How do we organize all this? There is an *intrapersonal* and an *interpersonal* side to this issue. The intrapersonal problem is that we can only really do one thing at a time. How do we decide which thing should be done at which time? Then there is the interpersonal issue: Other people (our spouses, children, friends, coworkers, etc.) are involved in our MAP schemas (our plans), but they also have their own. And *their* MAP schemas may or may not be compatible with *ours* on any given occasion—as when you need help in the microworld of getting-dinner-ready but your spouse is lost in the microworld of watching-the-football-game. We'll focus on the interpersonal issue, because it is through learning how to organize plans socially that we learn how to organize our individual plans.

As adults we organize ourselves into *dominance hierarchies*. Though some have argued that hierarchies make people more aggressive, it is more likely, as Peterson argues, that dominance hierarchies are nature's way of keeping aggression under control. By following the rules of social hierarchies, one gains access to the resources provided by those hierarchies such as status, mates, and food (Peterson 2013, p. 25).

A well-functioning dominance hierarchy is, in fact, "a form of extended co-operation" in which competition can take place in such a way that aggression is carefully controlled. It's controlled because, first of all, we feel empathy to those we consider to be kin or "on our team." And it's controlled because the other members of a hierarchy are self-interested: Most of them would lose out if their hierarchy devolved into a war of all against all; they have an interest in working together to stamp out flares of violence (Peterson 2013, pp. 25–26).

Dominance hierarchies are important not just for controlling violence; they are how we solve many other social problems. Hierarchies exist because some people are better at solving particular problems than others. Such problems can be anything from building community infrastructure to allocating scarce resources to educating children to providing community entertainment. Whether you want to be an electrician or an elementary school teacher or a superstar basketball player, you are seeking a place within a hierarchy. This involves co-operating and competing with others to solve social problems. It means adopting a shared MAP schema into which your more personal plans become nested.

Learning How to Co-operate and Compete

Drawing from the work of developmental psychologists like Jean Piaget, Peterson provides a rich picture of how children learn to participate in hierarchies and build MAP schemas. Briefly, it's like this. Young children first have to experiment to attain their goals. Through trial and error, the children gradually build up little MAP schemas that are successful in, say, getting food or attention. These are imitated and practiced until they become automatic. As children develop, they also begin to observe and imitate those around them (Peterson and Flanders 2005, pp. 141–42). On a neuro-physiological level, this is enabled by the mirror neuron system (Peterson 2013, pp. 28–29).

At this time, play is an especially important activity for developing social action schemas. The first stage is rough-and-tumble play. Rough-and-tumble play is how children learn to adjust themselves to others, to find the boundaries of what is acceptable to another person. Too aloof or too aggressive and the other kids won't want to play with you.

As children get older, play becomes more abstract and dramatic. They start to inhabit "fictional" worlds in which their motivations, emotions, and perceptions can be mutually organized over broader spans of space and time (Peterson and Flanders 2005, p. 138). Imagine the complex space-time co-ordination involved in a "simple" game such as hide-and-seek. In such games, contact is broken up over large (for a child) distances and stretches of time, but held together by an agreed-upon narrative structure.

Through play, then, children learn to regulate or "govern" their behavior vis-a-vis others, "to understand and to embody" each other's motivational and emotional states, and "to work cooperatively toward a common goal." All this prepares children for the eventual adoption of functional roles in the broader society (Peterson and Flanders 2005, p. 138). The more advanced forms of play are, after all, a complex mix of competition and cooperation, just like society's adult institutions. Look at it this way: Children want to perform their roles well in relation to each other and win the game (if it is the sort of game with a winner). But this can only happen—there can only be a winner—if a common frame or story is accepted by all the individual players (Peterson and Flanders 2005, p. 143). Only by co-operating can one experience the thrill of competition.

Life Is But a (Meta)Game

Peterson has argued in many places that there is a best way to play: *"The best player is he who is invited to play the most games*. Sacrificing a future invitation for present victory is a counterproductive long-term strategy."* By extension there is a best way to participate in a social dominance hierarchy, because "life is a sequence of games" played within and by means of such hierarchies (Peterson 2013, p. 28; also see Peterson 2018, pp. 101–03). And by even further extension there is a best way to *be*, across all dimensions. Peterson speaks of this as "living properly" (2018, p. xxxix).

Lessons on how best to *be*—how to live properly—are deposited in myths, which distill situations and ways of acting in them down to their essences (1999, p. 75). Myths are "road maps to being"—stories "not about how to play the game, but about how to play the metagame, the game of games" (Peterson 2013, p. 41).

The primary myth, for Peterson, is the hero myth. This is because hero myths are about confronting the fundamental chaos of the world when society's dominance hierarchies are no longer serving the good of society but using society to serve themselves. The hero sees with the eye that transcends dominance hierarchies (Peterson 2018, pp. 216–17), sees "the glimmers of redemptive chaos shining through the damaged structure of our current schemas" (Peterson 2013, p. 42). The hero breaks apart and reformulates these schemas, creating the world anew and revitalizing society (Peterson 2013, p. 41). In myth, this is symbolized as "paradise, encounter with chaos, fall, and redemption" (Peterson 1999). In MAP-schematic, reality-producing terms, we can see this as "world-construction, anomaly-introduction, world dissolution, world-reconstruction" (Peterson 2000).

Free Will, or Something Close Enough

We've seen something of how actions get organized over time, individually and socially. Much of what we do occurs "automatically," without our consciously thinking about it. But we also—or so it seems—consciously deliberate about at least some of our actions. How is it that we are able to "put our thumbs on the causal scales of the universe" in this way? How is it that we have something that might be called freedom of will?

Consider a skilled pianist performing from notation. Such a performance is a kind of MAP schema, with its own goal (playing a piece of music well), objects of perception (instrument, notation, audience, and their relevant properties), and actions (especially eye, hand, and foot movements).

The performance unfolds as a series of what Peterson in one essay calls "macros," by analogy to the software tool (Shariff and Peterson 2005). We can think of these as the smallest units of the MAP schema, where the schema "grounds out" in actual muscle movement. When the pianist looks at the notation, it calls up patterns of finger movements—macros—that have become automatic through practice. As the pianist looks ahead in the notation these macros are initiated and seem to "just happen." Once a macro begins—say, the performance of a musical phrase—it cannot normally be changed.

Well, at least those parts of it that will occur less than about half a second in the future can't be changed. We cannot "think" sufficiently fast enough to consciously alter such actions (though they might be altered by automatic reflexes as when, for example, we are suddenly frightened). There is a limit on how fast nerve impulses can travel around in the human body. However, if a phrase unfolds over a period of several seconds, or if the performer is looking far ahead in the notation, she can decide to "do it differently this time." She may be paying attention to the audience reaction or her own mood, etc., and decide that the next section of music needs more dynamic contrast, or heavier rubato. Then an alternate set of macros is deployed. If this is not truly "free will" it is, as Shariff and Peterson say, "close enough."

In other words, we can deliberate about our actions, but only if they lie far enough in the future. Because of this we learn to perceive "in the future," and our predictions of the future infuse our experience of the present (Shariff and Peterson 2005, p. 206).

Managing the Complexity of Reality

We set out trying to answer how we can organize our actions over time as individuals and groups, and how we can "step back from the psychic flow" (Bratman 2013, p. 47) and decide our own actions. For Peterson, the ultimate answers are to be found in the biological and cultural evolution of our species. But as individuals we pick much of this up through socialization—especially through the increasingly complex forms of imitation and play in which we engage from childhood on. We learn how to inhabit "determinate micro-worlds of experience" set by our motivations and consisting of meaningful objects of perception and effective patterns of action.

Humans need to be able to function both individually and as members of groups. As we learn how to inhabit social narratives made up of hierarchically organized plans and roles, we also learn how to build our own MAP schemas, our own self-narratives. MAP schemas ultimately filter down into the particular muscle movements that get us (ideally) closer to our goals. Again, through experience and experiment, we learn the extent to which these movements can be changed. We learn to perceive-in-the-future such that one set of muscle-patterns can be substituted for another if conditions change. In these ways we are able to manage—at least for a time—the intrinsic complexity of reality.

And this, at least in broad strokes, is how Peterson explains human behavior.

References

Bratman, Michael E. 2013. The Fecundity of Planning Agency. In David Shoemaker, ed., *Oxford Studies in Agency and Responsibility Volume 1*. Oxford: Oxford University Press.

Gray, Jeffrey A., and Neil McNaughton. 2003. *The Neuropsychology of Anxiety: An Enquiry into the Function of the Septal-Hippocampal System*. 2nd edition. Oxford: Oxford University Press.

Hirsh, Jacob B., Raymond A. Mar, and Jordan B. Peterson. 2012. Psychological Entropy: A Framework for Understanding Uncertainty-Related Anxiety. *Psychological Review* 119:2. <https://doi.org/10.1037/a0026767>.

Peterson, Jordan B. 1999. *Maps of Meaning: The Architecture of Belief*. New York: Routledge.

———. 2000. The Pragmatics of Meaning. *Semioticon* <https://semioticon.com/frontline/jordan_b.htm>.

———. 2013. Three Forms of Meaning and the Management of Complexity. In K.D. Markman, T. Proulx, and M.J. Lindberg, eds., *The Psychology of Meaning*. Washington: American Psychological Association. <https://doi.org/10.1037/14040-002>.

———. 2018. *12 Rules for Life: An Antidote to Chaos*. Toronto: Random House Canada.

Peterson, Jordan B., and Joseph L. Flanders. 2002. Complexity Management Theory: Motivation for Ideological Rigidity and Social Conflict. *Cortex* 38:3 <https://doi.org/10.1016/S0010-9452(08)70680-4>.

———. 2005. Play and the Regulation of Aggression. In R.E. Tremblay, W.W. Hartup, and J. Archer, eds., *Developmental Origins of Aggression*. New York: Guilford Press.

Shariff, Azim F., and Jordan B. Peterson. 2005. Anticipatory Consciousness, Libet's Veto and a Close-Enough Theory of Free Will. In R. D. Ellis and N. Newton, eds., *Consciousness and Emotion: Agency, Conscious Choice, and Selective Perception*. Amsterdam: John Benjamins. <https://doi.org/10.1075/ceb.1.12sha>.

Vinogradova, Olga S. 2001. Hippocampus as Comparator: Role of the Two Input and Two Output Systems of the Hippocampus in Selection and Registration of Information. *Hippocampus* 11:5) <https://doi.org/10.1002/hipo.1073>.

[16]
Could Jordan Peterson Be a Stoic?

SANDRA WOIEN

Once upon a time, when theism dominated the hearts and minds of a much larger population than it does today, Stoicism was a forgotten philosophy. After Christianity and then Islam became ascendant, there was no room and no need for another strict moral system. Yet, with the modern rise of atheism and the absence of a code for people to live their lives by, Stoicism has entered its renaissance. Nowadays many popular books and podcasts such as *The Daily Stoic* focus on this ancient philosophy.

Following suit, I started to teach a class on Stoicism because I sympathize with the need of newer generations to find a philosophy of life. Now enters Jordan Peterson. Like clockwork, I am asked every class if I know who Jordan Peterson is, and if so, whether I think he could be classified as a Stoic.

The clear answer is an underwhelming no. Peterson has never mentioned Stoicism as any form of influence, so this inclines most people who are somewhat knowledgeable about the two to dismiss the question in haste. Yet, if we slow down and probe just a bit, this query uncovers some broad similarities. Both are concerned with how we ought to live and impart practical wisdom about how to live well, and both Peterson's popularity and the renewed interest in Stoicism reveal that something is missing in people's lives. While there is more to being a Stoic than focusing on how we should live and imparting helpful advice, if we dig deeper, what will we find? Let's see. A good place to start is at Stoicism's origins.

Ancient Stoicism and Its Rivals

Stoicism is one of the Hellenistic schools of philosophy. Following the ancient period with notable philosophers such as Socrates, Plato, and Aristotle, the Hellenistic period, marked by the victories of Alexander the Great and the spread of Greek culture, gave rise to a variety of schools. In addition to the Stoics, other notable schools included the Cynics and the Epicureans. Unlike modern philosophical movements, such as analytic philosophy with an overemphasis on the analysis of concepts, these schools had a practical emphasis since they were focused on how we ought to live, although, being philosophical rivals, they had different visions of what living well entailed.

Stoicism was founded in the third century B.C. by Zeno of Citium, after he was shipwrecked in Athens. Zeno was influenced by the teachings of the Cynics. Like his teachers, Zeno thought we ought to live virtuously according to nature, but through his teachings, the latter Stoics would come to understand the maxim—live according to nature—differently than the Cynics did. It didn't entail shunning social conventions or public life. In this way, Stoicism differed from Epicureanism too—its most significant contemporaneous rival.

Epicureanism, based on the teachings of its founder Epicurus, differed from Stoicism more fundamentally. The Epicureans not only maintained that the good life consisted of happiness, a life of tranquil and reliable pleasures, and the absence of pain, but also maintained that the pursuit of happiness ought to be sought outside of public life. Stoicism's name comes from the location where Zeno taught, at the *Stoa Poikile*, the Painted Porch, in the Athenian Agora, the heart of public life. In contrast, Epicurus's school, like Plato's Academy, was housed outside of Athens. They preferred withdrawing completely from public life; withdrawal, Epicurus taught, was most conducive to cultivating pleasure and avoiding pain and other types of mental disturbance.

The terms associated with all three of these Hellenistic schools have mutated into simplistic caricatures. Being a

Stoic does not mean being unaffected by the various emotions any more than being an Epicurean means being partial to the better things in life such as delicious food and drink, or being a Cynic means embracing a distrustful and critical attitude toward life. When I talk about being a Stoic, I am referring to a person who upholds the central tenets of Stoicism, so what are these?

There are two approaches to answer this question. First, there is the ancient Stoic conception that sees Stoicism as a complete philosophy. This view was popularized by Cleanthes, Zeno's successor, and while there were a few ancient detractors, it, more or less, became the official Stoic doctrine throughout the Hellenistic period.

Ancient Stoicism was divided into three parts or subjects: logic, ethics, and physics. Logic essentially covered everything about reason and human discourse. Ethics was the study of topics related to living well, and physics explored how the world works. No part took priority. All three were essential and interconnected, as exemplified in some common Stoic similes.

Some Stoics, for example, compared their philosophy to an egg. Logic was the shell; ethics was the egg white, and physics was the yolk. Others compared their philosophy to a living animal with logic as the bones, ethics as the flesh, and physics as the soul (Inwood 2018). Since Ancient Stoicism was a complete worldview, certain fundamental beliefs flowed from it. In terms of logic, humans were rational animals. In terms of ethics, virtue was the only good, and in terms of physics, the universe exhibited a type of interconnectedness and divine purpose. The Stoics believed in fate, causation, and materialism.

Second, there is modern Stoicism. Modern Stoicism, at minimum, attempts to elevate ethics over the other two parts, or it attempts to divorce, as much as possible, ethics from logic and physics, especially the way they were originally understood. Brad Inwood refers to this approach as Minimal Stoicism (2018). Since both approaches agree that virtue is the only good and that we ought to live according to nature, let's take this as our starting point in deriving the minimum characteristics to be called a Stoic.

Minimal Stoicism

First and foremost, there is the Stoic theory of value that tells us what things are intrinsically and instrumentally good and bad, and while theories of value can be quite complex and pluralistic, the Stoics had a straightforward approach—the only intrinsic good is virtue, the only intrinsic bad (evil) is vice. That's it! Thus, all good and bad is within a person's control. As Epictetus wrote in his *Discourses:*

> For who is there among us at this present time who cannot give a systematic account of what is good and bad? That some things are good, others bad, and others again indifferent; that the virtues and what partakes in the virtues are good, while things of the opposite nature are bad, and that wealth, health, and reputation are indifferent. (2.9.15)

The Stoics classified anything other than virtue or vice as an indifferent. However, they did make a delineation among the indifferents—that of preferred and dispreferred. They believed it is within our nature to pursue preferred indifferents such as health and wealth, so they had a type of instrumental value. The dispreferred indifferents, however, such as defamation and physical pain were negative, so it was in our nature to avoid them. Yet, no amount of instrumental value could outweigh intrinsic value, rendering preferred indifferents incommensurate with virtue.

Their theory of value informed their vision of the good life that gives us a recipe, if you will, on how to live well and to flourish. Like any recipe, different ingredients may be added or subtracted, but the end product will be judged or measured by some metric. A good life comes in different degrees— a given life may be judged more worthy of being lived or better than another life due to the high degree of the presence of certain goods. Again, the Stoics had a simple recipe— virtue is the only ingredient needed. It was the only metric needed to measure the quality of someone's life, and the more virtue, the better the life.

Thus, their overall vision of the good life was teleological or goal oriented: the goal was to become a virtuous person. About this, Inwood writes, "Whereas we might ask 'why should I be virtuous?' that question wouldn't make sense in the teleological framework of ancient ethics. Their version of the question, 'Why should I be excellent?' would seem pointless" (2018, p. 69). While virtue is the only thing good for a person and thereby the only thing toward which she should aim, for the Stoics, virtue came in four fundamental forms: wisdom, courage, temperance, and justice.

The Greeks used the term *arete* for virtue, but the term is more basically translated as excellence. Since virtue is inextricably bound to excellence, it is telling who the Stoics viewed as their sages or moral exemplars: Socrates and Hercules (Heracles to the Greeks). Both chose the path of virtue and adversity, rather than the path of happiness and ease. Throughout the *Enchiridion*, Epictetus praises Socrates, and ends with a Socratic quote: "If so it pleases the Gods, so let it be; Anytus and Melitus are able indeed to kill me, but they cannot harm me" (2004, p. 22). Socrates was a Stoic hero because he lived and died virtuously, and like the Stoics themselves, he believed that virtue was the only good. As a result, no evil could befall a good person, for the only evil, vice, was self-inflicted.

Hercules, likewise, was a hero about whom the Stoic, Seneca, wrote plays, and whose choices were extolled. Xenophon, one of Socrates's students, recounts a story told by Socrates about Hercules. Hercules found himself on a forked road. Wondering what way to go, he was approached by two goddesses. One wanted him to go down her path. It was short, and it promised ease and sensual pleasure. When Hercules asked her name, she replied that her friends call her Happiness while her foes call her Vice. The other goddess approached and wanted him to choose her path. It was long and difficult, and it promised adversity and hard work. He didn't have to ask her name, however. He immediately recognized her as Virtue. Hercules, as legend goes, chose Virtue's path (Xenophon 1990).

Since Stoicism inextricably connects good, bad, and human flourishing to virtue (or lack of), it is part of the eudaimonistic tradition that started with Socrates. Yet, saying that someone is a Stoic simply because she believes that virtue is the only good or that the good life consists of the pursuit and achievement of virtue is insufficient. The Aristotelians and the Cynics also maintained that the pursuit of virtue was the fundamental feature of living well. In addition to maintaining that virtue was the only good, what set Stoicism apart as its own philosophical school was what it meant by living according to nature.

The Stoics, as early as Cleanthes, endorsed the behest to live in accordance with nature. This is where the biggest disagreement comes between the ancient and modern approach to Stoicism. Living according to nature, in terms of Ancient Stoicism, smuggles in all kinds of metaphysical claims such as fatalism, non-atomism, the universe exhibiting divine purpose, and so forth, but since similarities need to be found between the two approaches, it is fair to say that a commitment to a naturalistic approach to ethics is necessary for a person to be called a Stoic, even nowadays. Naturalism, generally described, is a commitment to using facts about the natural world to guide us in how we ought to live. In describing such an approach, Lawrence Becker notes, "It constructs normative propositions from facts about existing values, preferences, projects, commitments, and conventions" (2018, p. 12).

In addition to taking a naturalistic approach to ethics, when the Stoics talk about following nature, at minimum, they are talking about following our human nature, and some aspects of our human nature are inescapable. Take the four fundamental virtues: wisdom, courage, temperance, and justice. These virtues, the Stoics believed, were rooted in our human nature, and are achievable by any person in any condition. Moreover, humans, by nature, are rational, social animals. Even though we are interconnected, the Stoics endorsed individuality and personal agency, for exercising individual agency was the only way to achieve virtue and to flourish.

Following this general line of thought, unlike both of its rival schools, the Stoics did not shun social conventions, as did the Cynics, nor did they withdraw from public life, as did the Epicureans. They believed that living naturally and virtuously entailed that people are socially embedded and therefore should be active in public life. They also stressed human rationality and the importance of reason. As Becker discusses in his attempt to reconceptualize the Stoic behest to "follow nature," Stoics are committed to "follow the facts" And Inwood writes, "philosophical theorizing and debate, along with engaged problem solving, are essential to the ultimate goal of making human life better" (2018, p. 26).

Sketch of Peterson's Ethics

Two caveats are in order. Peterson has produced copious amounts of work through his lectures, videos, and writings. I will primarily draw from his published books, mainly his last two, as their fundamental gist is giving moral advice. Moreover, while Peterson has explored metaethical issues in his conversations with Sam Harris, metaethics is different from normative ethics—the focus of the latter is what has value and how we should act. In order to ascertain whether Peterson is a Stoic, we need to analyze two central issues in normative ethics: his theory of value—what things are intrinsically good and bad, and his theory of the good life— what things are intrinsically good for humans. Thus, what follows is somewhat of a derivative exercise in extracting a sketch of Peterson's ethical positions in order to do a suitable comparison.

Peterson's primary concern is with meaning, and more specifically, how humans create meaning, making his account both descriptive and prescriptive. In his first book, *Maps of Meaning*, he laid out a tripartite, but interconnected, account of meaning. First, what is? Second, what should be? Third, how should we act? (1999, p. 13). His description of these three areas is *"What is the nature* (meaning, the significance) *of current being?, to what* (desirable) *end should that state be moving?*, and finally, *what are the processes by which the present state might be transformed into that which is desired?* (1999, p. 16). First, we must look at the current states of affairs. Then, drawing from that, we need to formulate some desired future, as an aim. Finally, we need to act in such a way to obtain that aim. Hence, Peterson's account of meaning is oriented toward achieving, or trying to achieve, some goal. Narratives, along with myths, work to hold together his account of meaning, and maps are meant as guides that not only show us our desired destination, but how to get there.

Since we need to choose some valuable goal at which to aim, we might now ask: what should we aim at? Peterson

responds, "aim at the highest good (you) can possibly manage" (2021, p. 133). So, what is this highest good? Peterson's
answer is the betterment of Being. He writes:

> And if there is something that is *not good,* then there is something
> that *is good.* If the worst sin is the torment of others, merely for the
> sake of the suffering produced—then the good is whatever is dia-
> metrically opposed to that. The good is whatever stops such things
> from happening. It was from this that I drew my fundamental moral
> conclusions. Aim up. Pay attention. Fix what you can…And, above
> all, don't lie . . . Consider then that the alleviation of unnecessary
> pain and suffering is a good. Make that an axiom: to the best of
> my ability, I will act in a manner that leads to the alleviation of
> unnecessary pain and suffering. You have now placed at the pin-
> nacle of your moral hierarchy a set of presuppositions and actions
> aimed at the betterment of Being. (2018, p. 198)

For Peterson, Being refers to a conscious creature's subjective experiences along with the totality of human experiences (2018, p. xxxi). Since the ultimate goal is to improve
the quality of our lives, he has a fundamental axiom upon
which to construct his value hierarchy. And once we have a
value structure aimed at the highest good—that of improving the experiences of conscious creatures—then we can find
a type of deep meaning that is life-sustaining.

Next, we need to know how we should act. Pursuing such
a lofty goal is bound to be difficult, so we need some type of
fortitude to continue, when the going gets rough. This is
where responsibility becomes key. He writes:

> What is the antidote to the suffering and malevolence of life? The
> highest possible goal. What is the prerequisite to pursuit of the
> highest possible goal? Willingness to adopt the maximum degree
> of responsibility . . . Your life becomes meaningful in precise pro-
> portion to the depths of the responsibility you are willing to shoul-
> der. (2021, p. 134)

With a destination in mind and armed with responsibility,
we still need direction, a more detailed map to help us navigate well. For Peterson, maps may be incomplete or inaccurate, and if they are, we are led astray. Now, enters the
importance of practical wisdom in the form of his 12 rules

series. His rules are meant as a set of prescriptions to successfully navigate uncharted territory and the path between the excesses of chaos and order in order to reach our destination. To serve as guides, his rules are fairly general, so that they can apply in many situations in which we find ourselves. "Stand up straight with your shoulders back," "Tell the truth—or at least, don't lie," "Be grateful in spite of your suffering." This is akin to saying: you are responsible for your posture. You are responsible for telling the truth. You are responsible for feeling grateful. And, if you take this responsibility, it will help you lead a flourishing and meaningful life.

Then, there is his conception of the good life. Since the betterment of Being is his paramount value, he is fundamentally concerned with human flourishing. Yet, he is definitely not a hedonist, as the Epicureans were, as he does not think pleasure is the only good. In fact, he seems the complete opposite. For him, suffering is an unavoidable aspect of life, and people should not pursue happiness. In this sense, he fully endorses the paradox of hedonism – that the best way to become happy is by not pursuing happiness! Yet, he doesn't appear to believe that virtue is the only good for humans either, as the Stoics did. His conception of the good life, like his value theory, is pluralistic. He writes, "Many things make life worth living: love, play, courage, gratitude, work, friendship, truth, grace, hope, virtue, and responsibility. But beauty is among the greatest of these" (2021, 226). In another passage, he talks about Abraham's challenge—where at a late age, Abraham followed the call of God and embarked on a difficult path fulfilling God's commands. About choosing the path of difficulty, he writes, "this is where the life that is worth living is to be eternally found" (2021, p. 138).

Fundamental Divergences

While both Stoicism and Peterson are essentially teleological in that they are directed toward achieving some goal and broadly eudaimonistic in that they are both concerned with achieving human flourishing, their ends are different. For the Stoics, the end goal was to become an excellent person—to attain virtue and live according to nature. For Peterson, the goal is to improve the totality of our individual and collective experiences, and the byproduct is the creation of meaning.

Moreover, the Stoics gave a monistic account of value. Everything other than virtue or vice was either a preferred or dispreferred indifferent. Thus, for anyone to be fairly called a Stoic, at minimum, he would have to maintain that virtue is the only good. Peterson does not maintain this, nor does he share the Stoic conception of the good life. Again, the Stoics thought only one thing was good for humans: virtue. This is the only property that can improve a person's quality of life. Peterson, on the other hand, endorses a pluralistic account of the good life; many things can improve the quality of a person's life. Even though Peterson cannot be classified as a Stoic, his value system shares some fundamental parallels, which is striking, considering that the Stoics had no direct influence on its development.

Three Significant Parallels

Even though Peterson does not maintain that virtue is the only good, he does tangentially stress the importance of virtue. Unlike many contemporary thinkers, Peterson, through his study of Jung and human psychology, clearly sees the dark side of human nature and what can happen if we allow vice free reign. Yet, like the Stoics, he thinks we have personal agency that bestows us with the ability and responsibility to take care of our characters. If we aim correctly, we can not only better ourselves but improve the world.

Peterson is in the pragmatist tradition in terms of beliefs, and broadly construed, pragmatists view beliefs as dispositions to act a certain way. For instance, if you hold that belief that you should act courageously, you are more likely to act courageously. Likewise, others are more likely to judge you as courageous when they see your actions revealing your beliefs. You thereby become courageous by habitually acting in a courageous manner. The Stoics had a similar conception of virtue. Virtue, similarly, can be looked at as a behavioral disposition to do the right thing, and the more of the virtues we have, the more we can act rightly in any circumstance we find ourselves. The Stoics' cardinal virtues were: wisdom, courage, temperance, and justice, and these four virtues manifest throughout his rules. Telling the truth and precision in speech embody the virtue of wisdom. Standing up straight and not hiding things in the fog embody courage. Cleaning your room and working hard on one thing embody temperance. Not comparing yourself to others and not carelessly denigrating social institutions embody justice.

Since wisdom is a cardinal virtue, the Stoics believed in telling the truth. As Marcus Aurelius exhorted, "If it's not true, don't say it" (12.17), or "Say only what is true, without holding back" (12.29). Likewise, for Peterson, the rule "Tell the truth—or at least, don't lie" is one of the highest values, and his actions align. More than any other contemporary public intellectual, Peterson stands for freedom to speak truthfully. His catapult into the public arena was driven by his intransigent stance on legislation that he believed would compel him to say things he believed to be untrue. In a recent interview, he was asked whether that decision made him happy.

His reply was telling. He said that when he was in his mid-twenties that he made a decision to tell the truth for the sake of telling the truth, and that this decision was a type of adventure. Yet, like most adventures, this has not always brought him happiness. "It has been stressful beyond comprehension . . . being pilloried in public is part of that" (2021b, 1:20). Yet, it wasn't a mistake. "Whatever happens as a consequence of telling the truth is the best thing that can happen" (2:08) He goes on to make it clear that actions cannot be assessed based on their consequences. Instead, his justification rested on the axiom that telling the truth is intrinsically good regardless of the consequences; it is the best thing a person can do despite a multitude of other realistic alternatives (Peterson 2021b). In this interview, he fully embodied the spirit of Stoicism: that virtue is its own reward, and should be pursued regardless of the consequences.

Another striking parallel is his appreciation of the Stoic idea of living according to nature. The Stoics firmly maintained that nature bestows us with certain inclinations that we must follow to live well. In a similar spirit, Peterson asserts that "Human nature is not infinitely malleable."

(1999, p. 11). More pointedly, about Peterson, Marc Champagne writes, "social reforms cannot disregard millennia of biological adaptation" (2020, p. 48). Just like other conscious beings, humans can no more escape our history than we can transcend our biology.

For this, Peterson has both been praised, as in his Hail Lobster parody (his reaction to being associated with a Marvel supervillain, Red Skull) and of course, lambasted for maintaining that biological adaptations gave rise to evolutionary hierarchies that go as far back as lobsters. Drawing from selective scientific research, Peterson made the case that we should stand up straight and act confidently. By doing so, we, like our (very) distant relatives such as lobsters, can improve our position in the world along with our subjective experiences living in it. For males, this is an especially prudent tactic since it may lead to greater reproductive success.

Although evolution was not in the Stoic purview, they did maintain that the natural world was ordered according to a *scala naturae*. The highest rung in this hierarchy was reserved for their gods and sages who possessed perfect reason; humans, animals, plants, and inorganic objects followed in descending order. While they believed, like Peterson and the Christian moral tradition, that humans are inherently equal, there is nothing in Stoicism that maintains that everyone must have equal access to resources, whether in the form of power or mating partners. They unequivocally taught non-attachment to preferred indifferents such as wealth and power as these things have no intrinsic value. As a result, we should not care if we possess them or not, nor should we care if we lose them. The good life was available to all humans because we only need our personal agency and reason, the avenues leading to virtue, to achieve it. In this sense, Stoicism is essentially a conservative philosophy. It is not about transforming the world to meet our conception of how things *should be*. Instead, it is fundamentally about living well and achieving tranquility despite how things *are*.

Another similarity involves the importance of rationality and human agency, along with the ability to change. These ideas permeate extant Stoic writings. Take Epictetus's *Enchiridion*. It starts with his famous dichotomy of control that reminds us to only concern ourselves with what we can control (in his opinion, only our beliefs and actions), but goes on to read in a similar vein to Peterson's 12 Rules series. The *Enchiridion* is loaded with advice from how to conduct ourselves at banquets, a metaphor for life, and the proper way to respond to negative criticism, to speaking precisely, yet sparingly. Marcus Aurelius's *Meditations* reads much the same way. As a personal journal, it is replete with practical wisdom from refraining from complaining, procrastinating, and blaming to profound reminders such as the impermanence of life. Peterson, like the Stoics, grasps that the only domain truly under our reign is our own beliefs and actions. Such framing allows us to see, and hopefully to banish, the evil lurking within each of us.

Peterson is trained as a psychologist, and some of the Stoics were psychologists of the ancient world who later influenced modern psychologists like Albert Ellis and Aaron Beck. They, like Peterson, accept that suffering, while a natural part of life, can be mitigated, and that there are techniques to do so. Drawing from her toolbox, a Stoic employs a variety of techniques to suffer less. These range from negative visualization—intentionally meditating on the loss of some preferred indifferent to inure us against its possible loss—to what is commonly called the view from above—a technique that allows her to see the bigger picture and frame life's challenges well. Since good and evil are inextricably tied to human character and the only things within our control are our own beliefs and actions, they were staunchly against blaming others or outside forces. Both Peterson and the Stoics force us to ask. how many problems would be solved if each of us became a better person? Only after this has been answered can we truly understand what problems ought to be tackled on a social level.

Stoicism, like Jordan Peterson's rules, is a philosophy for every person. Its famous practitioners in the ancient world literally ranged from a slave, like Epictetus who was later freed, to an emperor, like Marcus Aurelius, the most powerful man in the world while alive. Despite some similarities, Jordan Peterson is not a Stoic. Yet, their similarities are not simply superficial. Once we delve deeper, Peterson's value system does share some notable parallels with Stoicism, making the question—Could Jordan Peterson be a Stoic?—

when taken seriously, a truly fruitful one. Now, as to the issue of whether Stoicism or Peterson offers the best path to the good life, I will let the reader decide. Unlike Hercules's dilemma, neither of these paths promise ease. Both will take hard work and discipline.

As Tolstoy noted, "A good life is given only to those who make efforts to achieve it"—something on which both the Stoics and Peterson would definitely agree.

References

Aurelius, Marcus. 2003. *Meditations*. New York: Modern Library.

Becker, Lawrence C. 2018. *A New Stoicism,* Revised Edition. Princeton: Princeton University Press.

Champagne, Marc. 2020. *Myth, Meaning, and Antifragile Individualism: On the Ideas of Jordan Peterson*. Exeter: Imprint Academic.

Epictetus. 2004. *Enchiridion*. Mineola: Dover.

———. 2014. *Discourses, Fragments, Handbook*. Oxford: Oxford University Press.

Inwood, Brad. 2018. *Stoicism: A Very Short Introduction*. Oxford: Oxford University Press.

Peterson, Jordan B. 1999. *Maps of Meaning: The Architecture of Belief*. New York: Routledge.

———. 2018. *12 Rules for Life: An Antidote to Chaos*. Toronto: Random House.

———. 2021a. *Beyond Order: 12 More Rules for Life*. Toronto: Random House.

———. 2021b. *Jordan Peterson Tells Tucker: Truth in Speech Is of Divine Significance*. <www.youtube.com/watch?v=rarY7pR03ns>.

Xenophon. 1990. *Conversations of Socrates*. London: Penguin.

[17]
The Musical Mediation of Order and Chaos

DAVID COTTER

The act(s) and art(s) of musical performance have been studied and theorized in myriad ways. Approaches to exploring musical performance and its intrinsic relationships with analysis, creativity, expression, gesture, interaction, interpretation, pedagogy, physiology, and psychology (to name but a few) have proliferated in recent decades. There has been much activity within the academy, notably as a product of the rise of the field of musical performance studies, and artistic research more generally.

Many universities currently provide tuition, and facilitate research, within numerous musical sub-disciplines. Take the University of Cambridge. It has recently led courses involving 'Aesthetics of Music', 'Composition', 'Ethnomusicology', 'Music Analysis', 'Music and Science', 'Music as Text', 'Music History', 'Music Psychology', 'Music Skills', 'Musicology and its Debates', 'Notation and Source Studies', 'Pop, Politics and Protest', 'Problems in the Philosophy of Music', and 'Techniques of Performance Studies'. However, despite this breadth of enquiry (with many musical fields often considered as interdisciplinary, multidisciplinary, or transdisciplinary), there is one notable absence: 'Music and Mythology'. As Jordan Peterson laments, "we have lost the mythic universe of the pre-experimental mind" for "the mythological perspective has been overthrown by the empirical; or so it appears" (Peterson 1999, pp. 5–6).

There is an argument to be made that a 'return to the mythic' within musicological contexts may be propitious. According to one recent study concerned with collaborative creativity, "there are still comparatively few detailed accounts of the actual processes at play" during interactions between musicians (Clarke and Doffman 2017, p. 116). I believe musical performance, especially live musical co-performance (that is, any instance where two or more musicians are collaborating in 'real-time'), to be an extraordinary manifestation of the mediation between order and chaos. Equipping music researchers and, most importantly, musicians with an enhanced understanding of their multifarious practices in terms of order and chaos may result in musical performances which are increasingly creative and more meaningful: "The mythic imagination is concerned with the world in the manner of the phenomenologist, who seeks to discover the nature of subjective reality, instead of concerning himself with description of the objective world" (Peterson 1999, p. 13).

Order and Chaos

Peterson has spoken and written, both at great length, about the importance of order and chaos and how these eternal elements pervade our lives. *12 Rules for Life* (2018) provided "an antidote to chaos" whilst *Beyond Order* (2021) focused on how an "excess of order leads to a lack of curiosity and creative vitality." However, it is within Peterson's magnum opus, *Maps of Meaning* (1999), that order and chaos are most magnificently explored.

Profound meaning can be found on the path that divides these two fundamental principles of reality, and as an understatement, Peterson's teachings have helped millions of people around the world to better balance order and chaos in their own lives. Often using second-person tense in a universalizing way, Peterson synthesizes meaningful connections between conservatism, constructivism, education, existentialism, humanism, liberalism, Marxism, metaphysics, mythology, (neuro)psychology, phenomenology, politics, postmodernism, and religion, before distilling complex theories into simple stories with immediate utility for artists, athletes, children, educators, lawyers, and parents alike.

Peterson states that music has intrinsic meaning, and thus, I believe musicians have much to benefit from investigating his thinking. What do we really mean when we say that performers are 'in sync' or 'on fire'? During such instances of heightened affect, it is the eternal forces of order and chaos that are being negotiated.

'Order' and 'chaos' have many synonyms within divergent spheres of thought (for example, and most commonly, the 'known' and the 'unknown'). Peterson goes to great lengths in order to integrate and orchestrate these:

> The *unknown* is unexplored territory, nature, the unconscious, dionysian [sic] force, the *id*, the Great Mother goddess, the queen, the matrix, the matriarch, the container, the object to be fertilized, the source of all things, the strange, the unconscious, the sensual, the foreigner, the place of return and rest, the maw of the earth, the belly of the beast, the dragon, the evil stepmother, the deep, the fecund, the pregnant, the valley, the cleft, the cave, hell, death and the grave, the moon (ruler of the night and the mysterious dark), uncontrollable emotion, matter and the earth. (Peterson 1999, p. 103)

Anyone who has ever performed, either alone or in tandem, has encountered the chaos of the unknown. Imagine you are a twelve-year-old flutist about to play in front of your school. The uniform you wear on a daily basis, and usually give no thought to, suddenly feels like an inevitable trip-hazard. The comforting smiles of friends are now lost within a sea of unfamiliar foe. Placed in front of the piano, lacking eye contact with your accompanist, you have no idea when to begin. Who usually starts? No idea. This all seemed so simple before.

They decide to take the initiative, and now you are already behind. The loose key on your instrument that you should have fixed months ago now threatens to sever. Cold blasts from the air conditioning flatten your instrument, and with each new musical phrase the distance between you and your accompanist opens up further. The curious eyes of the students in the front row are now uninterested. They want to be outside enjoying their lunch break, and you, yes you, are stopping them. As for those you believe to still be watching, their stares are waiting for you to fail. No, they are willing you to fail. Schadenfreude. The school bell buzzes. Any sense of flow is obliterated. Commotion breaks out at the back. Your focus is gone. That difficult ending is now upon you, and you are reminded of your lack of preparation like a slap in the face. Bright red, hands sticky with sweat, instrument out-of-tune, and with fingers flailing hopefully yet helplessly, the piano pronounces the final chords before you stumble over the musical finishing line a few moments later. Silence ensues.

Now, let us consider the opposite:

> The *known* is explored territory, culture, Apollinian control, superego, the conscience, the rational, the kind, the patriarch, the wise old man and the tyrant, the giant, the ogre, the cyclops, order and authority and the crushing weight of tradition, dogma, the day sky, the countryman, the island, the heights, the ancestral spirits and the activity of the dead. (Peterson 1999, p. 104)

Musicians, especially classical musicians, especially professional classical musicians, attempt to manifest order at all levels of their musical lives. Imagine you are a guitarist about to make your debut at the Royal Albert Hall. The technique that you possess is a product of at least two hundred years of dutiful pedagogy, developed by the best who have ever lived, and passed down accordingly. Your instrument is made of the finest Brazilian rosewood, was built by expert luthiers in Spain, and has been in your loving possession for over a decade. Each and every note of the music you are about to play has been annotated, carefully considered, and practiced, alongside, and in accordance with, the valuable opinions of many of the world's most eminent musicians. New strings, thoughtfully attached a week ago, are perfectly settled and tuned to the nearest tenth of a hertz. Your suit is tailor made, with cufflinks tidily out of the way. You stride on stage purposefully, with polished shoes and smile. Chair and footstool have been raised to your specific requirements, and perfectly placed in relation to your expecting audience. Introductions have been memorized verbatim, and not just one, but two encores are at the ready. With the customary bow out of the way, you sit, shape your hands, align them with your instrument, breathe, breathe again, pause, and then pluck the first chord, beautifully, some may say perfectly, cutting any tension, and removing all apprehension. With your opening gesture still resonating around the room, what happens next?

Two questions arise. Firstly, despite such masterful and meticulous preparation, is it even possible that your performance, the whole concert in fact, will proceed without chaos, without the unexpected occurring? Secondly, and assuming the former is even possible, would anyone in their right mind enjoy such an occasion? Let us imagine: musical interpretations exactly mirroring those of the masters who have graced the hallowed halls before; musical interpretations that are executed exactly 'as planned' without a single thought for the mood of the performer, the feel and reception of the audience, the nature of the venue, or the evolving nature of the event itself; musical interpretations that are repeated, with mind-numbing exactitude, night after night, regardless of audience, background noise, lighting, location, performance space, programming, temperature, or time.

Instead, musicians operating creatively, innovatively, and meaningfully, must carefully preserve, reject, and propel their respective performance paradigms. They must become 'knowers' and straddle the fundamental duality between order and chaos, with "one foot firmly planted in order and security, and the other in chaos, possibility, growth and adventure" (Peterson 2018, p. 43).

> The *knower* is the creative explorer, the ego, the I, the eye, the phallus, the plow, the subject, consciousness, the illuminated or *enlightened* one, the trickster, the fool, the hero, the coward; spirit (as opposed to matter, as opposed to dogma); the sun, son of the unknown and the known (son of the Great Mother and the Great Father). (Peterson 1999, pp. 103–04)

Tao

It is possible for twenty-first-century musicians to enhance the processes and products of their creative exploration by considering artistic practices through the lens of Taoism—the ancient Chinese philosophical and spiritual tradition of living in harmony with the Tao (that is, 'meaning' or the 'way'). After all, the image of the Taijitu (the black and white yin and yang symbol) is culturally ubiquitous today, adapted within various flags and other contemporary images, pervasive, and almost ever-present.

> [The Taijitu] utilizes the image of a circle to represent totality; the paisleys that make up that circle are opposed but balanced. The image is rendered additionally sophisticated by the presence of the white circle in the black paisley, and vice versa. Too much chaos breeds desire for order. Yin may therefore serve as mother to Yang. Conversely, too much order breeds the desire for novelty, as antidote to stultifying predictability. In this manner, Yang serves as father to Yin. (Peterson 1999, p. 339)

The universe is composed of order and chaos, with these two elements as permanent constituents of human experience. As Peterson often explores in great depth and breadth, such elements (in various guises) permeate many of the world's major philosophies and religions. Furthermore, they were also pertinent to those figures who had the most profound effect upon him: notably Carl Jung (1875–1961) and Erich Neumann (1905–1960). The interplay between order and chaos is fundamental to how many people conceive of the world and their existence within it. Indeed, it is so pervasive that "it is to this 'metaphorical' universe that our nervous system appears to have adapted" (Peterson 1999, p. 23). Order and chaos are to be found within the macro and the micro; on various levels of resolution. Establishing harmony between order and chaos is equally necessary for the composer aiming to predicate their personal musical language on an existing stylistic landscape whilst also venturing forwards into the unknown (consider the Baroque, Classical, Romantic, and subsequent periods, their lineage, and how traditions are both preserved and rejected), and for the performer aiming to manifest interpretations of intrinsic novelty and value.

Collaboration

In recent years, and as an active professional musician (primarily a guitarist), I have collaborated with cellists, choirs, clarinetists, composers, contemporary collectives, flutists, guitarists, guitar orchestras, harpists, live electronics operators, percussionists, pianists, recorder players, singers, and violinists. Each and every instance provided opportunities for the mutual appropriation and co-construction of performance approaches, techniques, and ideas, but the 'cultural distance' between me and my collaborators would affect the manifestation of chaos and/or order within our artistic endeavours. For example, my collaborations with other guitarists often involved us performing repertoire conceived for the 'guitar duo' instrumentarium, perhaps even sharing the same material score, both using the same instrumental techniques, and coordinating with one another (aesthetically, sonically, temporally, visually, etc.) with relative ease. Whilst such endeavors evidently manifested order, opportunities to step into the unknown and make significant contributions to our artistic domain which led to radical change were obviously rare.

Collaborating with contemporary music collectives has been an entirely different affair. In one specific ensemble which I led, members used chairs, coins, jumpers, string, and toothbrushes (alongside 'traditional' instruments) to create interesting musical soundscapes. Performing at contemporary music festivals, unexplored territory surrounded me, tangible curiosity would fill the room, and opportunities for the mutual appropriation of performance approaches, techniques, and ideas were abundant, maybe even limitless. Yet, opportunities to establish order were now more limited. It could be fairly stated that curating a meaningful musical performance (especially one which would appease a non-specialist audience seeking aesthetic, harmonic, and/or textural synthesis) was sometimes quite a challenge.

Latent

As a quasi-case study, I will explore my on-going collaboration with the academic, composer, guitarist, and Associate Professor of Music at Staffordshire University in the UK, Marc Estibeiro, and in particular, the development and subsequent performances of our composition *Latent* (Estibeiro 2021). At all levels of resolution, the constituent elements of order and chaos have powerfully permeated our collaboration.

Having met whilst both studying at the University of Durham in the UK, our respective yet complementary interests were developed within the contemporary music festivals DurhamKLANG and NoiseFloor, and our friendship and academic relationship was strengthened though the International Guitar Research Centre. However, it wasn't until the chaos of the international coronavirus pandemic provoked lockdowns in the UK that we officially began collaborating. On 13th January 2021, Marc initiated an invitation to work together on a composition and performance. At this early stage, although unspecified, both of us were equally driven 'to do something with the guitar that had not been done before'. In time, and through intensive virtual discussion and experimentation, the collaboration came to center around designing a bespoke digital environment for guitar performance which encouraged us to embrace latency. More frequently referred to as 'lag', latency is the time difference between input and output which, when large, can cause problems for users endeavoring to share audio and/or video 'online'.

Chaos and order were ever-present. Nationwide lockdowns meant a relative cessation of in-person musical activity, but also stimulated our project. Shared musical interests provided us with common ground, whilst our different areas of expertise offered multitudinous learning opportunities. For example, Marc could be classed as an expert computer coder, whilst I was a relative novice. Various software and technologies (Facebook Messenger, Google Drive, OBS, SonoBus, SuperCollider, Zoom, etc.) aided our remote collaboration, but we still lacked access to recording equipment and performance spaces of a higher quality. During the 'composition phase', Marc devised musical gestures which were mostly a product of experimentation with his instrument, whilst mine, generally shorter, were both responses to Marc's compositional idiom, and influenced by the 'guitaristic' musical gestures of the Cuban composer Leo Brouwer (1939–present) amongst others. At every level of resolution, there was a tension between known and unknown territories.

Marc's primary domain of activity was writing the code for the live electronics, whilst I was tasked with creating the musical score. Aesthetically, I was influenced by Peterson's painting/sculpture *The Meaning of Music* (1989), alongside the graphic scores of numerous composers including Brian Ferneyhough (1943–present), George Crumb (1929–present), and Karlheinz Stockhausen (1928–2007). The musical score for *Latent* measures 1m X 1m and can be viewed, alongside full performance directions, on my personal website (Cotter 2021). For the musical score, the Taijitu is used both as an infrastructure for our compositional material and as an environment for the guitarists to navigate themselves around during performance: player one controls yin (the black paisley, and the musical material it holds) whilst player two controls yang (the white paisley, with its respective musical material). During performance, the guitarists improvise in and around numerous musical fragments. The white circle within the black paisley, and *vice versa*, both contain a single note of E (to be played on the lowest string, with its ubiquitous sound and connotations). Players return to this gesture every sixty seconds, reinforcing the structural integrity of the piece. Furthermore, the pre-composed musical material within yin has been tested to corroborate and 'resonate' with the pre-composed musical material within yang. However, the indeterminate nature of the score means that performers are able to sequence the order of musical gestures *ad libitum* so that each and every performance may be structured differently. Therefore, a performance of *Latent* is not a 'free improvisation' whereby players can 'do whatever they wish', but rather a musical exploration of the tension between certainty and uncertainty. Textual directions to 'pursue what is meaningful' and/or 'pursue what is expedient' (directly inspired by Peterson) are eminently open to interpretation, and unambiguously compel the performer to immediately consider the emergent order and chaos.

The non-time-critical score of *Latent* allows, and indeed encourages, interaction between the guitarists and the electronics (a semi-autonomous SuperCollider patch) in 'real time'. This is antithetical to the prevalent practice (especially during 'lockdowns') of musicians pre-recording individual parts of ensemble pieces before multiple audio and video files are subsequently compiled by an 'editor'. *Latent* affords each player relatively unrestricted opportunities to significantly mediate expressive musical parameters (dynamics, pitch, tempo, timbre, etc.) in accordance with their live electronics, the decisions of their co-performer, their co-performer's live electronics, and the nature of the performance environment as a whole. Studying the omnidirectional feedback loops which exist between co-performers has been enlightening. The 'unknown' nature of how one's co-performer may act in 'real time', the multitude of decisions they could make, and the embryonic potential these carry, is something musicians should not shy away from, but embrace. Indeterminate stimuli place us in conflict, but always allow meaning to emerge anew. In recent years, numerous academicians (such as musicologists Daniel Leech-Wilkinson and Mine Doğantan-Dack) have beseeched their students to challenge existing paradigms by pursuing novel modes of performance. It is the present author's opinion that identifying elements of 'order', mapping opportunities for 'chaos', and mediating appropriately between them in 'real time' may lead to more meaningful musical experiences, for both performers and audiences.

Fire

Peterson laments that "We have lost our fear of fire" as "Fire, insofar as we can control it, has been rendered predictable, nonthreatening—even familiar and comforting" (Peterson 1999, p. 101). Audiences revel when musicians are 'on fire'. Thus, I present the following framework as having enormous utility for musicians looking to elevate their creative practices. The cognitive psychologist and cultural-historical theorist Vera John-Steiner developed a 'four stages of collaboration' model (John-Steiner 2000) which, as I propose, can be considered through the lens of 'order and chaos' with unequivocal precision. Previously, the model has been used in various contexts, such as to map the "macro artistic trajectory" of a piano-duo partnership (Viney and Grinberg 2014, p. 157). Here, I give examples of how John-Steiner's scheme of collaborative patterns can also be used to illustrate the elements and interplay of order and chaos during 'live' musical performance.

PATTERNS	Roles	Values	Working Methods
Distributed	Informal and Voluntary	Similar Interests	Spontaneous and Responsive
Complementary	Clear Division of Labour	Overlapping Values	Discipline-Based Approaches
Family	Fluidity of Roles	Common Vision and Trust	Dynamic Integration of Expertise
Integrative	Braided Roles	Visionary Commitment	Transformative Co-construction

Table 1. 'Four Stages of Collaboration' (adapted from John-Steiner 2000, p. 197)

'Distributed collaboration' can be used to illustrate the excess of chaos: two musicians, beginners, with relatively similar interests, decide to play together on the spur of the moment. A brief exchange takes place regarding who should 'take the first part' and who will be 'left with the second'. Little thought, if any, is given to tempo, and other matters of interpretation. Chaotic moments of surprise continually threaten critical instability. Meaningful synthesis is missing. There is limited order, and the potential for chaos to cease all activity is ever-present.

'Complementary collaboration' can be used to illustrate the excess of order: two musicians, keen amateurs, plan to explore some contemporary duo repertoire together. The player with faster fingers, slightly better technique, and perhaps a more developed sense of musicianship, assumes responsibility of the more difficult part. The other agrees that their specific skillset is more suited to the somewhat-ancillary rhythmic accompaniment. Both players polish their respective parts and the result is musically pleasing. A couple of laid-back 'show and tell' performances subsequently take place within a local music group. The repertoire is repeated on a couple of occasions, in a similar manner each time. Audiences applaud, but inspiration is absent.

'Family collaboration' can be used to illustrate the path to meaningful performance: two musicians, professionals, perform a suite of pieces. Their performance is characterized by cueing, gesturing, signaling, and turn-taking. Sometimes, player one will direct player two with sharp intakes of breath and arresting glances. At other points, player two 'takes centre stage', increasing the size and frequency of their bodily movements, arresting the audience's attention and causing player one to reconsider their 'authority'. There is relative stability and internal consistency, yet the performance is also dynamic and interesting. Perhaps, although unbeknownst to the audience, a novel and personally-meaningful interpretation of the suite is taking shape.

'Integrative collaboration' can be used to illustrate Tao: two musicians, highly eminent creators, come together. Both have a consummate understanding of the repertoire, themselves, and each other. Neither has dominion. Both are constantly attuned to each other, and their audience. Watertight technique and meticulous preparation offer a firm footing in order, and thus allow them to invite chaos. Influenced by the almost tangible responses of the audience, player one begins interpreting the music in a somewhat unfamiliar manner, extensively mediating musical parameters in accordance with the ever-evolving approaches of their co-performer, and employing innovative expressive devices which had not been planned, perhaps simply devised 'on the spot'. The music manifests new meanings as a novel performance approach is 'transformatively co-constructed' (John-Steiner 2000, p. 197) in 'real time'. Embodying visionary commitment to both the music and their craft, other performers in attendance are inspired to continue ordering their musical lives, but introduce more chaos in future.

Coda

Peterson encourages his audiences to balance the two fundamental principles of reality, order and chaos, in all aspects of their lives, and musicians have much to gain from listening to this message of vital importance. As Peterson intimates, "adherence to the Eastern way (Tao)—extant on the border between chaos (*yin*) and order (*yang*)—ensures that the 'cosmos' will continue to endure" (Peterson 1999, p. 185). Classical musicians operating in the twenty-first century, against a backdrop of rapid social and technological changes, and responding to the recurrent doomsday call that 'classical music is dying', would therefore do well to interrogate the order and chaos of their artistry, not least as the endurance of their very profession or avocation may be at stake: "We live at a critical time for classical music" (Scruton 2018, Introduction).

Excesses of musical authoritarianism or nihilism do not breed meaningful creativity, and whilst there is little substitute for the mastery of explored territory, accepting that "the infinite human capacity for error means that encounter with the unknown is inevitable" (Peterson 1999, p. 47) is freeing. Essentially, humans are biologically programmed to respond appropriately to the unknown, at first with attention redirection, then with emotional progression from fear to curiosity, and finally, and where the fun truly starts, with a compulsion for exploration. Artists might ask themselves whether they are "living in *Tao*, on the razor's edge, on the straight and narrow path, on the proper road, in meaning" (Peterson 1999, p. 104). With one foot firmly planted in order, active exploration of chaos with the other allows us to transcend our innate limitations, rather than simply remaining subject to them, and it is when the infinitely unpredictable emerges that creativity may arise.

Bibliography

Clarke, Eric, and Mark Doffman, eds. 2017. *Distributed Creativity: Collaboration and Improvisation in Contemporary Music*. New York: Oxford University Press.

Cotter, David. n.d. 'David Thomas Cotter'. Accessed 14th August 2021. <www.davidthomascotter.com>.

Estibeiro, Marc. n.d. Marc Estibeiro. Accessed 14th August 2021 <www.marcestibeiro.com>.

John-Steiner, Vera. 2000. *Creative Collaboration*. Oxford: Oxford University Press.

Peterson, Jordan B. 1989. *The Meaning of Music*. Painting/Sculpture.

———. 1999. *Maps of Meaning: The Architecture of Belief*. New York: Routledge.

————. 2018. *12 Rules for Life: An Antidote to Chaos*. London: Allen Lane.

————. 2021. *Beyond Order: 12 More Rules for Life*. London: Allen Lane.

Scruton, Roger. 2018. *Music as an Art*. London: Bloomsbury Continuum.

Viney, Liam, and Anna Grinberg. 2014. Collaboration In Duo Piano Performance: Piano Spheres. In Margaret Barrett, ed., *Collaborative Creative Thought and Practice in Music*. SEMPRE Studies in the Psychology of Music. Farnham: Ashgate.

[18]
On Peterson's Truth

Teemu Tauriainen

Above all, the search after truth and its eager pursuit are peculiar to man.

—Cicero, "On Duties," p. 15

Jordan Peterson's remarks on the nature of truth are voluminous. He devotes whole lectures and book chapters to its analysis. Despite this, widespread confusion persists on the details of Peterson's distinctive understanding of truth. One reason for this is that Peterson's treatment of truth is scattered and unsystematic. Another reason is that the scholarly work on Peterson's truth is lacking. In this chapter, I will clarify Peterson's views by deploying powerful instruments of analysis from contemporary philosophy.

Based on this clarification, Peterson's truth proves nowhere near as ludicrous as critics make it seem, for it accommodates a long and healthy tradition of theorizing labeled *anti-realism*. The core thesis of this approach is that truth is an inherently mind-dependent notion, so that nothing in the world is true or false without cognitive agents. Peterson deploys this general standpoint and develops it further to include distinctively human-bound commitments, such as the Nietzschean paradigm, according to which truth exists to serve life, and the Darwinian-pragmatist approach, according to which truth is that which is useful to believe and thus aids survival across time.

Much of Peterson's thinking relies on his understanding of truth. From his works, we find frequent remarks on the importance of speaking the truth, and numerous statements on the value of truth as a perquisite for human flourishing. Take the eighth chapter of Peterson's bestseller *12 Rules for Life* titled "Tell the truth—or, at least, don't lie" where he writes:

> To tell the truth is to bring the most habitable reality into Being. Truth builds edifices that can stand a thousand years. Truth feeds and clothes the poor, and makes nations wealthy and safe. Truth reduces the terrible complexity of a man to the simplicity of his word, so that he can become a partner, rather than an enemy. Truth makes the past truly past, and makes the best use of the future's possibilities. Truth is the ultimate, inexhaustible natural resource. It's the light in the darkness. See the truth. Tell the truth. (p. 230)

While repeatedly emphasizing the immense value that truth bears for our lives, more often than not, Peterson *assumes* a notion of truth rather than offering an explicit definition. This is understandable. The abstract and exceedingly complex nature of truth makes it a challenging subject of analysis. Philosophers have theorized about its nature from the pre-Socratics to the present-day with no consensus in sight. Far from it, for views about the nature of truth show notorious variety in the history of western thought, amounting to mutually exclusive definitions of various kinds.

Some see truth as a fully objective matter, representing things 'as they are' independent of minds, and others equate it with what science has at any given time proven to be the case. Further complicating matters, definitions of truth are notoriously enmeshed with paradoxes. Perhaps the most well-known example is the liar's paradox, demonstrated by the famous Cretan two and a half millennia ago, who claimed that all Cretans are liars, thereby causing confusion on whether he himself was telling the truth.

Complicating matters more, the inevitable challenges with defining truth are in plain contrast with the foundational role it has for our lives. True beliefs enable navigation in the world, and they ground our beliefs to that which is real, in contrast to mere illusion or wishful thinking. Finally, the fundamentality of truth is indicated by its intuitiveness and at least seeming clarity. Children learn the meaning of the word 'true' at an early age, and we do not think that there is any confusion involved with the term, for example, when obliging people to tell the truth and nothing but the truth in our courtrooms.

It is because of such inevitable challenges with defining truth that Peterson is wary of offering an explicit definition of it. This wariness should not be confused with a view about the defectiveness or redundancy of truth. As has become increasingly clear in the political atmosphere of recent years, real threat lies in the decay of appreciation towards truth. When presidents of global superpowers make materially false claims, and when bald-faced lies and deception are tolerated from our leaders, the Petersonian thesis that we should speak the truth, or at least not lie, is plainly contradicted on a grandiose scale. But Peterson is no stranger to defending truth from those who seek to corrode it, for his status as a public intellectual was largely sparked by his opposition to the relativism about truth associated with post-modernist thinking. The threat that Peterson diagnosed from relativism is serious and real, well in line with the interpretation of Hannah Arendt, who diagnosed similar issues with the decay of truth in relation to totalitarian regimes:

> The ideal subject of totalitarian rule is not the convinced Nazi or the convinced Communist, but people for whom the distinction between fact and fiction (i.e., the reality of experience) and the distinction between true and false (i.e., the standards of thought) no longer exist. (1951, p. 474)

Without a robust notion of truth, societies become exposed to the control of tyrants, who are first to criticize the notion, bearing the wish that it can be fabricated or molded to aid their means. As the old tale goes, describing virtue as a shield and truth as a sword, the people in power understand that when resistance is expected, the crowds better be disarmed. It is this task, of exploring, recovering, and defending a robust notion of truth that Peterson commits to both explicitly and implicitly in substantive sections of his work, and it is the task of the remainder of this paper to clarify his project.

The Nature of Truth

Philosophers and laymen alike have been interested in the nature of truth throughout the history of Western thought. This tendency was adequately summarized by Cicero in antiquity, according to whom humans are by nature truth-oriented beings. But past general interest, not much has been agreed upon regarding the nature of truth. One central disagreement that cuts across the history of Western philosophy is whether truth is dependent or independent of human concerns, such as our knowledge about it. One manifestation of this disagreement is the old dilemma that asks whether sound is made by a tree falling in a forest when no one is around.

More sophisticated iteration of the same problem asks whether there is a truth concerning the even or uneven number of planets in the universe, even if there is in principle no way for us to know about it. While we are inclined to answer that yes, truth exists about this matter, questions about truth seem to emerge only in the context of minds, and speaking about truth past what can be known seems redundant and unworthwhile. The frustration involved with these types of questions is evident in the age-old debate about the existence of God. Whether or not he does indeed exist, there seems to be no way for us to know about it from our limited human perspective, so concluding judgements are better left unmade. It is a matter of faith, and not of knowledge, what position we choose to deploy. In this sense, there seems to be little use for a transcendent, fully objective notion of truth that stands disconnected from our ability to know about it.

Interestingly enough, much of the confusion and criticism regarding Peterson's truth directly relates to the question of whether truth is a mind-dependent or mind-independent notion. It is precisely here that Peterson's famous debate with Sam Harris got stuck on the topic of truth. Conflict emerged when Harris diagnosed a disagreement between him and Peterson, refusing to continue discussion before a mutual understanding about the nature of truth was achieved. But keeping in mind the unavoidable challenges with defining truth and it's widely disagreed upon nature, this strategy rests on a superfluous requirement. Surely, we need not agree on details about truth's nature before discussion becomes meaningful. But the worry that Harris bears is not completely meritless. As noted, the possession of a robust notion of truth is a precondition for serious-minded discussion and debate. To illustrate, take the specific phenomena of disagreement that is oftentimes the motivating force behind our debates.

When disagreeing on an important topic, such as climate change or the utility of vaccinations, we do not view these disagreements as satisfactory conclusions. Rather, we make considerable efforts to resolve them by figuring out the *truth*. The worry is that if we operate with incompatible notions of truth, discussion itself becomes meaningless, for we are aiming at different goals. Thus, there must rest some agreement upon the nature of truth that facilitates the possibility of rational discourse in the first place. But I do not think that Harris and Peterson disagree on this point. Surely, they both agree that in one way or another truth describes things as they are, and that truth is that which is in general correct to believe. It is not obvious, however, why this basic intuition is not enough to facilitate meaningful discussion and debate.

But what sparked the conflict between Harris and Peterson might have been a misdiagnosis in the first place. According to Harris, the central point of disagreement between him and Peterson is whether truth is *objective*. Objectivity here means that truth is a mind-independent matter, so that truth is independent of human concerns, even our ability to know about it. For Harris, every belief that is subject to truth is necessarily true or false, independent of anyone's beliefs about it, full stop. For Peterson, beliefs can be true or false, or true enough, depending on their ability to help achieve our goals. In this sense, the fundamentals of truth are those that guide action, and truth must be studied in relation to achieving success in our practices. Objectivity is of secondary interest. To illustrate this difference, take a map of the New York subway system. In an objective, mind-independent sense, this map fails to be a true representation, for it is a wholly inaccurate misrepresentation of its geometrical structure. It lacks dimension and is crudely simplifying. But in the non-objective, mind-dependent sense, the map is very much a true description, more so than an objective representation would be, for it enables us to navigate the system with great success. Of course, in other situations where you have motives other than navigation, the objective representation could serve your means better. But this is precisely the point that Peterson makes. Truth must be studied in relation to achieving success in our practices. Presumably, this is the context where the phenomena of truth emerged in the first place, as a pre-theoretical understanding of what we should believe to bring the best possible reality into being.

Thus, one crucial point of disagreement between Harris and Peterson is that while the former commits strictly to the minimal intuition that truth's nature is exhausted by its objectivity as demonstrated by the relatively recent theoretical definitions, the latter holds that this is not the case, for more is entailed in the notion, such as the moral constitution of being useful to believe. But what critics have failed to appreciate is that Peterson only objects to the negative claim that *nothing else* is involved with truth than objectivity. Since Peterson has no qualms with the objective aspects of truth as such, closer analysis proves illuminating.

Truth's Human-bound or Unbound Nature

As it happens, the views of truth that Harris and Peterson commit to run in line with a broader and much older philosophical debate between *realist* and *anti-realist* approaches to truth. According to the former, truth is a fully objective matter, representing how things are independent of minds, and independent of any human concerns. For example, there is a truth about the even or uneven number of planets in the universe, independent of our ability to know about it, full stop. Harris persists in maintaining that this minimal intuition captures the essence of truth. There are static truths about the world, known or unknown, and valuable or nonvaluable to believe.

But if this were the case, why not just replace the concept of truth with objectivity? For Peterson, objectivity alone does not exhaust the nature of truth, falling short by downplaying the significance of its historical constitution and complexity and the significance it has for our lives. Following the Nietzschean paradigm, because truth is intimately tied to human-concerns as an instrument of serving life, beliefs can be not only true or false, but true enough in relation to their ability to help achieve our aspirations. Indeed, the law of bivalence, the idea that there are *only* two truth-values (true and false) is a hallmark commitment of realist theories, while widely rejected by the anti-realists. For the latter, beliefs can be not only true or false, but more or less true, true enough, or unknown. To illustrate this further, let's assume that Smith has been systematically unfaithful to his wife. Both beliefs that Smith possibly cheated on his wife, and that he has systematically done so are equally true in the realist sense. But surely, when asked about the faithfulness of Smith, one of these truths is truer than the other. The realist might oppose that here we fail to make a distinction between truth and accuracy. Both beliefs are true, yet one is also accurate. But whether or not truth can be so disconnected from other concepts is debatable, as shown in the distinct views promoted by Harris and Peterson.

While Harris presents his realist approach to truth as the standard view, Peterson is surely not alone in opposing it by committing to a form of anti-realism. As Donald Davidson, perhaps the most prominent theorist of truth of the latter part of the twentieth century adequately summarizes: "Nothing in the world, no object or event, would be true or false if there were not thinking creatures." (1990, p. 279). But this intuition about the mind-dependency of truth is much older, already suggested by Aristotle, according to whom the existence of humans grounds the truth that humans exist but not the other way around. There are truths about things only insofar as there are humans, or thinking creatures, to uphold them. Peterson's approach is well in line with this general intuition. Whether and to what extent this applies to Harris is debatable, for as noted, he commits to the thesis that truth is fully independent of minds. For Peterson, we have a concept of truth now because it has proven useful to have before, and this ability to aid human aspirations ought to be taken as an essential feature of truth.

One consequence of Peterson's approach is that questions about the transcendent, mind-independent or fully objective nature of truth become not only of secondary interest, but somewhat questionable in the first place. Because humans are finite creatures with limited cognitive capabilities, there seems to be no way for us to step beyond the limits of our understanding to evaluate the full objectivity of our claims. But according to the realists, truth *is* independent of our knowledge bearing frameworks, resting outside of them as idealized object. How can we make such a claim immanently from the inherently limited human-perspective? One issue with these types of transcendental arguments is present in the never-ending debate about whether the will is truly free from causal influence. There seems to be no way for us to know, for knowing would imply stepping beyond the limits of our understanding. There's no such Archimedean view-point from which the full objectivity of our claims can be evaluated, from which we can determinately explain how thoughts emerge, or whether we possess a 'correct' under-standing of truth past what is accessible to us in midst of our practices.

It's more common, however, to understand objectivity in a looser sense as that which is *indicative* of truth, rather than a description of the 'whole truth'. But if understood in this sense, then the criticism that Peterson's view of truth fails to accommodate the basic objectivist intuition is misplaced, for there is a way to account for it just as well, if not better to the realist approaches that render truth an unreachable abstraction that is disconnected from our concrete practices.

Truth as an Instrument to Serve Life

Some have argued that Peterson's commitment to a Darwin-ian-pragmatist form of anti-realism runs in conflict with the basic intuition that truth is objective. One way to understand the Darwinian-pragmatist approach to truth is to see it as arising from the Nietzschean paradigm, according to which truth exists to serve life. By providing pragmatic utility and thus aiding survival across time, speaking and believing the truth amounts to the increase of human flourishing. Regard-ing truth's nature, the key realization is that both of these approaches are manifestations of anti-realism regarding the notion. Truth is an inherently mind-dependent notion, and its nature derives from the role it has for our practices.

Some see this as a problematic conclusion, claiming that it contradicts the basic intuition that truth is objective and independent of any human concerns. Simply put, if truth is that which is useful to believe, it cannot be simultaneously independent of anyone's beliefs about it. The subsequent worry is that if truth indeed is dependent on human concerns, this renders it relative. If truth depends on what is useful to believe, yet what at any given time is useful to whom depends on various factors, then truth becomes relative to the circumstance in which utility is being evaluated. Finally, there seem to be truths that are in no way valuable to believe, like the trillionth decimal of π, and falsehoods that provide immense practical utility, such as occasional ungrounded self-confidence. Thus, by committing to his distinctively human-centric form of anti-realism, Peterson subjects his notion of truth to pressing and well-grounded critique.

But the criticism that Peterson's understanding of truth runs in conflict with the basic objectivist intuition is misplaced, for he is free to argue that objectivity is simply one aspect of truth that humans have constructed, and which has proven useful to possess, especially for our scientific understanding of the world. Because Peterson does not commit to the negative thesis that nothing else than this or that is entailed in truth, he is free to include various aspects under his notion, some being objective and others non-objective. This is only intuitive, for surely sometimes truth depends on mind-independent states of affairs, and other times on our human ways of thinking about the world. There are truths about medium sized physical entities such as stones and chairs, and there are truths about ethics and law such as what is permitted or prohibited to do. In this sense, Peterson simply acknowledges the breadth that truth displays in our cognitive lives, so that there is no limit to the aspects it can manifest in the constraints of the Nietzschean paradigm of serving life. All aspects of truth, even the ones that predicate objectivity, arise from the general need for such concepts, the existence of which is justified by their ability to aid our aspirations.

What has been described above is an equally tenable conclusion to the disconnected view of truth as a transcendent, fully objective and mind-independent notion that some critics uphold. In their view, because of the near infinite progress of science, *nothing* we ever discover is true in the fully objective sense. Simply put, everyone is always more or less wrong when measured up against an idealized notion of the 'whole truth'. But what use is there for such a disconnected concept? The human predicament is that we are limited creatures and as such, our cognitive capabilities can never match up with the full complexity of the world. Despite this, it is extremely useful for us to hold that some things *are* true, even if not eternally so. What science has proven to be the case now is true, for all we know, and we use these truths as instruments for fueling further discussions, debate, and the subsequent progress that follows. Again, no higher tribunal of truth than success in our practices.

Nesting Argument

What has been described above is Peterson's (2018, p. 144) fundamental *nesting argument* that critics have failed to appreciate, resulting in confusion and misinterpretations of his views. Because of truth's historically constructed nature, the concept overall is much older and broader than simple objective truth, which is a fairly recent theoretical invention. This historical grounding should be respected when studying truth's nature and it is here that the intimate link between truth and our practices is grounded in. For example, in Old English, the term 'true' means that a person or an object like an axe is trustworthy and adheres to standards. But the idea that there is a connection between truth and the good is much older, already discoverable from the works of Plato, who states in the *Republic* that:

> So that what gives truth to the things known [beliefs] and the power to know to the knower is the form of the good. And though it is the cause of knowledge and truth, it is also an object of knowledge. Both knowledge and truth are beautiful things, but the [form of the] good is other and more beautiful than they. In the visible realm, light and sight are rightly considered sunlike, but it is wrong to think that they are the sun [the form of the good], so here it is right to think of knowledge and truth as goodlike but wrong to think that either of them is the good—for the good is yet more prized. (508e)

Thus, according to one prominent view, truth has inherent moral constitution as that which is good to believe, for its nature derives from the *form of the good*, which is the highest ideal, shared by all particular things that are in one way or another good.

But of course, for the concept of truth to be useful in our time, the historical aspects alone, such as the idea of truth as that which is good to believe, do not suffice, for they are potentially blind to the problems that we face here and now. Because of this, we want a concept of truth that respects its origins, but which is also useful in solving the problems that manifest in our time. Indeed, from this project of in one hand preserving the virtues of the old concept, and in the other developing it so that it better serves us now, we get to a result where the objectivity of truth need not be discarded. Objectivity can simply be treated as one of the newer aspects of Truth unqualified that is especially useful for those paths of inquiry that direct themselves towards mind-independent facets of the world. Even the notions of full objectivity or the whole truth can be accounted for by Peterson's anti-realist approach by treating them as useful *features* or *instruments* of our scientific understanding of the world. The usefulness of these ideas is evident, for example, in situations when something we hold to be true turns out false. We do not say that our beliefs became false. Rather, we say that they were false all along, and that we were simply mistaken in relation to the truth. But to emphasize, the existence of this feature is grounded in our need for it, and the utility it provides for our understanding of the world. In no way need the notions of truth or objectivity be understood as something mind-independent or transcendent. Further, in no way should objectivity be treated as the primary aspect of truth. What should be prioritized is the moral constitution of truth as that which is correct, useful or good to believe. Indeed, the priority of the moral constitution is evident when realizing that we would not have the ideas of truth, objectivity or the whole truth in the first place, were it not for their usefulness and the utility they provide for aiding our aspirations. Thus, if we admit that truth is an inherently human-bound notion, there to serve our aspirations like all other concepts, then the objectivity of truth can be preserved without a threat of a disconnect. Objectivity too, as a useful ideal, exists to serve.

But Peterson's conception of truth is not devoid of problems. Because of its immense breadth, giving a clear, exhaustive, and non-contradictory definition of truth in the Petersonian sense becomes virtually impossible. I think Peterson is well aware of this consequence. However, the issue here might be misdiagnosed, for it is not obvious that such a definition can be offered in the first place. Truth is both a fundamental and exceedingly broad concept, displaying inconsistencies and paradoxes throughout, so there is no guarantee it can ever be defined in a manner that is exhaustive and non-contradictory. Simply put, the assumption that all concepts can be so defined might be where the problem lies. Further, by committing to a form of pragmatism, Peterson positions to oppose this type of theory-first approach that could see the indefinability issues as a sign of truth's defectiveness. Indeed, it is pragmatism that saves truth from claims of redundancy in the first place, for our current inability to achieve an exhaustive definition of truth is no argument for its abandonment. The immense utility that truth provides for both daily life and our more theoretical aspirations is of utmost importance, and whether or not the concept can be exhaustively defined is of secondary interest. Supposedly we operate with a concept of truth even before our ability to speak about it, let alone try defining it. All this is very much in line with a philosophical theory called *primitivism*, according to which truth is such a fundamental notion that no exhaustive definition of it can even be achieved.

Talking Past Each Other

One thing to note is that the conflict between Peterson and Harris is partially caused by them speaking past each other. Contrary to widespread interpretation, the problem point is not so much about whether truth is objective or not. Rather, the disagreement is more about which aspects of truth are fundamental and should be prioritized. The point of Harris and other realists is that the objectivity and throughout mind-independentness of truth must not be compromised. Peterson, on the other hand, emphasizes the broader importance of truth, even at the cost of downplaying the significance of its objectivity. But surely there are approaches to truth that lie in between the minimal objectivist view and the exceedingly broad approach inspired by the Nietzschean paradigm. For example, we could endorse a type of goldilocks principle where not too little nor too much is included in our understanding of truth.

It might be that while Harris and other realists risk error by taking the too little side, constraining truth to the extent that it does not adequately cover all the ways in which it manifests in our lives, Peterson risks falling on the too much side, potentially confusing the truth with independent questions about what is useful, valuable, or accurate to believe. Nonetheless, an important lesson from all of this is that both Harris and Peterson clearly see the topic of truth as having great importance, to the extent that they are willing to commit considerable effort to resolving disagreements about its nature. As I noted the beginning of this chapter, this attitude is much needed in our time, when truth is once more the target of widespread skepticism and criticism in both academic and less formal debates.[1]

References

Arendt, Hannah. 1951. *The Origins of Totalitarianism*. Berlin: Schocken.

Cicero, Marcus Tullius. 1913. *De Officiis* [On Duties]. London: Heinemann.

Davidson, Donald 1990. The Structure and Content of Truth. *The Journal of Philosophy* 87.

Harris, Sam. 2017. Speaking of 'Truth' with Jordan Peterson. <https://samharris.org/speaking-of-truth-with-jordan-b-peterson/>.

---

[1] This chapter is dedicated to a close friend and talented scholar Jukka Kortelainen who unfortunately passed away while it was being written. It was Jukka who first introduced me to Peterson's thinking, and he is one of the few friends with whom I had the pleasure of discussing Peterson's ideas. Were it not for Jukka's influence, this chapter would never have been written. I hope it does justice to honoring his memory.

Peterson, Jordan B. 2018. *12 Rules for Life: An Antidote to Chaos.* Toronto: Random House Canada.

———. *Beyond Order: 12 More Rules for Life.* Toronto: Random House Canada.

Plato. 1997. *Complete Works.* Indianapolis: Hackett.

Bibliography

Adorno, Theodor W. 2019. *Night Music: Essays on Music, 1928–1962*. Seagull.

Adorno, Theodor W., Else Frenkel-Brunswik, Daniel J. Levinson, and R. Nevitt Sandford. 2019 [1950]. *The Authoritarian Personality*. Verso.

Aitkenhead, Decca. 2021. Jordan Peterson on His Depression, Drug Dependency, and Russian Rehab Hell. *The Times* (January 30th).

Al-Andalusi, Abdullah. 2019. Should Muslims be Left-wing or Right-Wing? Why Muslims Don't Need Dr Jordan Peterson. abdullahalandalusi.com blog post (July 16th).

Alchian, Armen A., and Harold Demsetz. 1972. Production, Information Costs, and Economic Organization. *American Economic Review* 62:5 (December).

Alnabulsi, Hani, John Drury, Vivian L. Vignoles, Sander Oogink. 2020. Understanding the Impact of the Hajj: Explaining Experiences of Self change at a Religious Mass Gathering. *European Journal of Social Psychology* 50:2.

Annas, Julia. 1993. *The Morality of Happiness*. Oxford University Press.

———. 2001. *Ancient Philosophy: A Very Short Introduction*. Oxford University Press.

———. 2011. *Intelligent Virtue*. Oxford University Press.

Anonymous. 2016 [1611]. *KJV Holy Bible*. Nelson.

Arendt, Hannah. 1973 [1951]. *The Origins of Totalitarianism*. Harcourt, Brace.

Aristotle. 1984. Nicomachean Ethics Book 1. In Jonathan Barnes, ed. *The Complete Works of Aristotle*. Princeton University Press.

———. 2019. *Nicomachean Ethics*. Hackett.

Aurelius, Marcus. 2003. *Meditations*. Modern Library.

Baghramian, Maria. 2004. *Relativism*. Routledge.

———. 2010. A Brief History of Relativism. In Michael Krausz, ed., *Relativism: A Contemporary Anthology*. Columbia University Press.

Bartky, Sandra. 1990. *Femininity and Domination: Studies in the Phenomenology of Oppression*. Routledge.

Becker, Lawrence C. 2018. *A New Stoicism,* Revised Edition. Princeton University Press.

Berenbaum, Sheri A. 2018. Beyond Pink and Blue: The Complexity of Early Androgen Effects on Gender Development. *Child Development Perspectives* 12:1 <https://doi.org/10.1111/cdep.12261>.

Bertrand, Marianne, Claudia Goldin, and Lawrence F. Katz. 2010. Dynamics of the Gender Gap for Young Professionals in the Financial and Corporate Sectors. *American Economic Journal: Applied Economics* 2:3 <https://doi.org/10.1257/app.2.3.228>.

Betjeman, Sir John. Christmas. <https://allpoetry.com/poem/8493411-Christmas-by-Sir-John-Betjeman>.

Billington, James H. 2017 [1980]. *Fire in the Minds of Men: Origins of the Revolutionary Faith*. Routledge.

Bite-Sized Philosophy. 2017. Jordan Peterson: Why Postmodernists Reject Logic and Evidence. <www.youtube.com/watch?v=CTBOU77czpY&t=139s>.

Böhm-Bawerk, Eugen von. 1959 [1884]. *Capital and Interest*. Libertarian Press.

———. 2007 [1896] *Karl Marx and the Close of His System*. Mises Institute.

Bourget, David, and David J. Chalmers. 2014. What Do Philosophers Believe? *Philosophical Studies* 170.

Bratman, Michael E. 2013. The Fecundity of Planning Agency. In David Shoemaker, ed., *Oxford Studies in Agency and Responsibility Volume 1*. Oxford University Press.

Brooks, David. 2018. The Jordan Peterson Moment. *The New York Times*. <www.nytimes.com/2018/01/25/opinion/jordan-peterson-moment.html>.

Bryant, Ben. 2018. Why Do Young Men Worship Professor Jordan Peterson? <www.bbc.co.uk/bbcthree/article/f1d7fed0-4ddf-4a8a-94b9-ea05f913cdd2>.

Budig, Michelle J., and Paula England. 2001. The Wage Penalty for Motherhood. *American Sociological Review* 66:2 <https://doi.org/10.2307/2657415>.

Burgis, Ben, Conrad Hamilton, Matthew McManus, and Marion Trejo. 2020. *Myth and Mayhem: A Leftist Critique of Jordan Peterson*. Zero.

Burton, Tara. 2020. Jordan Peterson's Perfectly Petersonian Health Scare. *Religion News Service*. <https://religionnews.com/2020/02/18/jordan-petersons-perfectly-petersonian-health-scare>.

Busbridge, Rachel, Benjamin Moffitt, and Joshua Thorburn. 2020. Cultural Marxism: Far-Right Conspiracy Theory in Australia's Culture Wars. *Social Identities* 26.

Butler, Judith. 1997. *The Psychic Life of Power: Theories in Subjection*. Stanford University Press.

———. 2006. *Gender Trouble: Feminism and the Subversion of Identity*. Routledge.

Cummings, Whitney. 2017. *The Female Brain*. IFC Films.

Callinicos, Alex. 1991: *Against Postmodernism: A Marxist Critique*. Polity.

Campbell, Joseph. 1988. *The Power of Myth*. Doubleday.

———. 2008 [1949]. *The Hero with a Thousand Faces*. New World Library.

Carrier, Richard. 2017. *The Scientist in the Early Roman Empire*. Pitchstone.

Carroll, Glenn R., and David J. Teece, 1999. *Firms, Markets, and Hierarchies: The Transaction Cost Economic Perspective*. Oxford University Press.

CBC News. 2016. Heated Debate on Gender Pronouns and Free Speech in Toronto. <https://www.youtube.com/watch?v=SiijS_9hPkM>.

Champagne, Marc. 2015. Don't Be an Ass: Rational Choice and its Limits. *Reason Papers* 37:1.

———. 2016. Diagrams of the Past: How Timelines Can Aid the Growth of Historical Knowledge. *Cognitive Semiotics* 9:1.

———. 2019. Consciousness and the Philosophy of Signs: A New Précis. *American Journal of Semiotics* 35:3–4.

———. 2020. *Myth, Meaning, and Antifragile Individualism: On the Ideas of Jordan Peterson*. Imprint Academic.

———. Forthcoming. Putting Aside One's Natural Attitude—and Smartphone—to See What Matters More Clearly. In Mohammad Shafiei and Ahti-Veikko Pietarinen, eds., *Phenomenology and Phaneroscopy*. Springer.

Cheng, Nien. 1995. *Life and Death in Shanghai*. HarperCollins.

Chesterton, G.K. 1945. *Orthodoxy*. Dodd, Mead.

Chomsky, Noam. 1995. Noam Chomsky on Postmodernism. <http://bactra.org/chomsky-on-postmodernism.html>.

Cicero, Marcus Tullius. 1913. *De Officiis* [On Duties]. Heinemann.

Clarke, Eric, and Mark Doffman, eds. 2017. *Distributed Creativity: Collaboration and Improvisation in Contemporary Music*. Oxford University Press.

Coase, Ronald H. 1937. The Nature of the Firm. *Economica* NS IV. Reprinted in Coase 1988.

———. 1988. *The Firm, the Market, and the Law*. University of Chicago Press.

Coase, Ronald H., and N. Wang. 2012. *How China Became Capitalist*. Palgrave Macmillan.

Coburn, Jo. 2018. Conversation with Ayesha Hazarika and Jordan Peterson. Daily Politics. <https://bbc.co.uk/programmes/b0b3kq88>.

Costa, Paul T., Antonio Terracciano, and Robert R. McRae. 2001. Gender Differences in Personality Traits across Cultures: Robust and Surprising Findings. *Journal of Personality and Social Psychology* 81:2 <https://doi.org/10.1037/0022-3514.81.2.322>.

Cotter, David. n.d. David Thomas Cotter. <www.davidthomascotter.com>.

Courtois, Stéphane, et. al. 1999. *The Black Book of Communism: Crimes, Terror, Repression*. Harvard University Press.

Crossan, John Dominic. 2012. *The Power of Parable: How Fiction by Jesus Became Fiction about Jesus*. HarperCollins.

Csikszentmihalyi, Mihaly. 1990. *Flow: The Psychology of Optimal Experience*. Harper and Row.

Dart, Ron, ed. 2020. *Myth and Meaning in Jordan Peterson: A Christian Perspective*. Lexham.

David, Marian. 2004. Theories of Truth. In Ilkka Niiniluoto, Matti Sintonen, and Jan Woleński, eds., *The Handbook of Epistemology*. Kluwer.

Davidson, Donald 1990. The Structure and Content of Truth. *Journal of Philosophy* 87.

Dawkins, Richard. 2013. In Conversation with Richard Dawkins—Hosted by Stephen Law. <www.youtube.com/watch?v=W28Uo-O231E>.

Dennett, Daniel C. 1995. *Darwin's Dangerous Idea: Evolution and the Meaning of Life*. Simon and Schuster.

Detmer, David. 2003. *Challenging Postmodernism: Philosophy and the Politics of Truth*. Prometheus.

DeWitt, Jerry. 2013. *Hope after Faith: An Ex-Pastor's Journey from Belief to Atheism*. Da Capo.

Dewrell, Heath D. 2017. *Child Sacrifice in Ancient Israel*. Penn State University Press.

Diener, Ed, and Shigehiro Oishi. 2000. Money and Happiness: Income and Subjective Well-Being across Nations. In Diener and Suh 2000.

Diener, Ed, and Eunkook M. Suh, eds. 2000. *Culture and Subjective Well-being*. MIT Press.

Dostoevsky, Fyodor. 1982. *The Brothers Karamazov*. Farrar, Straus, and Giroux.

———. 1994. *Notes from Underground*. Vintage.

———. 1995. *Demons*. Random House.

Eagleton, Terry. 1996. *The Illusions of Postmodernism*. Blackwell.

Eliade, Mircea. 1998 [1963]. *Myth and Reality*. Waveland.

———. 2005 [1954]. *The Myth of the Eternal Return: Cosmos and History*. Princeton University Press.

Engels, Frederick. 1987 [1878]. Anti-Dühring: Herr Eugen Dühring's Revolution in Science. In *Karl Marx Frederick Engels Collected Works*, Volume 25. International.

———. 1989 [1880]. Socialism, Utopian and Scientific. In *Karl Marx Frederick Engels Collected Works*, Volume 24. International.

Epictetus. 2004a. *Discourses: Books 1 and 2*. Mineola: Dover.

———. 2004b. *Enchiridion*. Mineola: Dover.

———. 2014. *Discourses, Fragments, Handbook*. Oxford: Oxford University Press.

Estibeiro, Marc, n.d. Marc Estibeiro. <www.marcestibiero.com>.

Estupinyà, Pere. 2013. *S=EX²: La Ciencia del Sexo*. Debate.

Everett, Dan. 2009. *Don't Sleep, There are Snakes: Life and Language in the Amazonian Jungle*. Random House.

Feldman, Simon. 2015. *Against Authenticity: Why You Shouldn't Be Yourself*. Lexington.

Ferrara, Alessandro. 1998. *Reflective Authenticity*. London: Routledge.

Feyerabend, Paul K. 2001. *Conquest of Abundance: A Tale of Abstraction versus the Richness of Being*. University of Chicago Press.

Fine, Cordelia. 2010. *Delusions of Gender: How Our Minds, Society, and Neurosexism Create Difference*. Norton.

Franzén, Torkel. 2005. *Gödel's Theorem: An Incomplete Guide to Its Use and Abuse*. Peters.

Frazer, James George. 1890. *The Golden Bough: A Study in Comparative Religion*. Macmillan.

Freud, Sigmund. 1960. *Civilization and Its Discontents*. Norton.

Fry, Stephen, Jordan B. Peterson, Michael Eric Dyson, and Michelle Goldberg. 2018. *Political Correctness Gone Mad?* Oneworld.

Frye, Northrop. 1980. *Creation and Recreation*. University of Toronto Press.

———. 1982. *The Great Code: The Bible and Literature*. Academic Press Canada.

———. 1990. *Words with Power*. Viking.

———. 1991. *The Double Vision.* University of Toronto Press.

Genetically Modified Skeptic. 2018. Jordan Peterson's Most Pseudoscientific Claim Ever. <www.youtube.com/watch?v=iIfLTQAKKfg>.

Gopnik, Alison. 2009. *The Philosophical Baby: What Children's Minds Tell Us about Truth, Love, and the Meaning of Life.* Farrar, Straus, and Giroux.

Gopnik, Alison, and Andrew N. Meltzoff. 1997. *Words, Thoughts, and Theories.* MIT Press.

Gopnik, Alison, Andrew N. Meltzoff, and Patricia K. Kuhl. 1999. *The Scientist in the Crib: Minds, Brains, and How Children Learn.* Morrow.

Gordon, David. 1986. *Critics of Marxism.* Transaction.

———. 1991 [1990]. *Resurrecting Marx: The Analytical Marxists on Freedom, Exploitation, and Justice.* Routledge.

———. 2020. Wicksteed on Surplus Value. *Mises Wire.* Mises Institute <https://mises.org/wire/wicksteed-surplus-value>.

Graves, Robert. 1961. *The Greek Myths.* Cassell.

———. 1964. *Hebrew Myths: The Book of Genesis.* McGraw-Hill.

———. 1965. *Mammon and the Black Goddess.* Cassell.

———. 1966. *The White Goddess: A Historical Grammar of Poetic Myth.* Farrar, Straus, and Giroux.

Gray, Jeffrey A., and Neil McNaughton. 2003. *The Neuropsychology of Anxiety: An Enquiry into the Function of the Septal-Hippocampal System.* Second edition. Oxford University Press.

Haidt, Jonathan. 2006. *The Happiness Hypothesis: Finding Modern Truth in Ancient Wisdom.* Basic Books.

Hallpike, C.R. 1986. *The Principles of Social Evolution.* Oxford University Press.

Harris, Sam. 2017a. #62—What Is True? A Conversation with Jordan B. Peterson. <https://samharris.org/podcasts/what-is-true>.

———. 2017b. Speaking of 'Truth' with Jordan Peterson. <https://samharris.org/speaking-of-truth-with-jordan-b-peterson/>.

———. 2020. A Pandemic of Incompetence: A Conversation with Nicholas Christakis. <https://samharris.org/podcasts/222-pandemic-incompetence>.

Hayek, F.A., ed. 1935. *Collectivist Economic Planning.* Routledge.

———. 1948. *Individualism and Economic Order.* University of Chicago Press.

———. 2017 [1944]. *The Road to Serfdom.* University of Chicago Press.

Held, David. 1980. *Introduction to Critical Theory*. University of California Press.

Herzog, Katie. 2018. Jordan Peterson Pushes Dangerous Myths about Climate Change. *The Stranger* (August 3rd). <www.thestranger.com/slog/2018/08/03/30143461/jordan-peterson-pushes-dangerous-myths-about-climate-change>.

Hicks, Stephen R.C. 2004. *Explaining Postmodernism: Skepticism and Socialism from Rousseau to Foucault*. Scholargy.

Hirsh, Jacob B., Raymond A. Mar, and Jordan B. Peterson. 2012. Psychological Entropy: A Framework for Understanding Uncertainty-Related Anxiety. *Psychological Review* 119:2. <https://doi.org/10.1037/a0026767>.

Holt, Hayley. 2019. Jordan Peterson Says Young Men Attend His Talks to Turn Their Lives Around. 1 NEWS <https://youtu.be/VICsw43SOV8>.

Horkheimer, Max. 1972a. *Critical Theory: Selected Essays*. Herder and Herder.

Horkheimer, Max, and Theodor W. Adorno. 1972b [1944]. *Dialectic of Enlightenment*. Herder and Herder.

Hume, David. 1985 [1739]. *A Treatise of Human Nature: Being an Attempt to Introduce the Experimental Method of Reasoning into Moral Subjects*. Penguin.

———. 1990 [1779]. *Dialogues concerning Natural Religion*. Penguin.

Hunt, Richard N. 1974. *The Political Ideas of Marx and Engels I: Marxism and Totalitarian Democracy 1818–1850*. University of Pittsburgh Press.

———. 1984. *The Political Ideas of Marx and Engels II: Classical Marxism 1850–1895*. University of Pittsburgh Press.

Hursthouse, Rosalind. 1999. *On Virtue Ethics*. Oxford University Press.

Inwood, Brad. 2018. *Stoicism: A Very Short Introduction*. Oxford: Oxford University Press.

Jadva, Vasanti, Melissa Hines, and Susan Golombok. 2010. Infants' Preferences for Toys, Colors, and Shapes: Sex Differences and Similarities. *Archives of Sexual Behavior* 39:6 <https://doi.org/10.1007/s10508-010-9618-z>.

James, William. 2018. *Six Books of Philosophy and Psychology*. B&R Samizdat Express.

Jamin, Jérôme. 2014. Cultural Marxism and the Radical Right. In Paul Jackson and Anton Shekhovtsov, eds., *The Post-War Anglo-American Far Right: A Special Relationship of Hate*. Palgrave.

John-Steiner, Vera. 2000. *Creative Collaboration*. Oxford University Press.

Jones, Tony. 2019. Jordan Peterson Destroys Q&A. Australian
 Broadcasting Corporation.
 <https://abc.net.au/qanda/2019-25-02/10811138>.
JRE Clips. 2017. Jordan Peterson on Cleaning Your Room. *The
 Joe Rogan Experience.*
 <https://www.youtube.com/watch?v=Z8_gUmt0k8o>.
Jung, Carl G. 1988. *Jung's Seminar of Nietzsche's Zarathustra,
 1934–1939.* Princeton University Press.
———. 2003 [1912]. *Psychology of the Unconscious.* Dover.
Kaczor, Christopher, and Matthew R. Petrusek. 2021. *Jordan
 Peterson, God, and Christianity: The Search for a Meaningful
 Life.* Word on Fire.
Kant, Immanuel. 1963. *Critique of Pure Reason.* MacMillan.
Kierkegaard, Søren. 1994. *Fear and Trembling.* Knopf.
Kotkin, Stephen. 2017. *Stalin: Waiting for Hitler, 1929–1941.* Penguin.
Kraychik, Robert. 2017. Jordan Peterson Explains Leftism's Core.
 The Daily Wire. <www.dailywire.com/news/jordan-peterson-
 explains-leftisms-core-robert-kraychik>.
Kreimer, Roxana. 2020a. Is It Sexist to Recognize that Men and
 Women Are Not Identical? A Critical Evaluation of Neuro-
 feminist Rhetoric. *Disputatio: Philosophical Research
 Bulletin* 9:13 <https://doi.org/10.5281/zenodo.3567201>.
———. 2020b. *Verdades Para Crédulas.*
 <https://youtu.be/qenahT2N3I>.
Lacewing, Michael. 2016. Can Non-Theists Appropriately Feel
 Existential Gratitude? *Religious Studies* 52:2.
Lewis, C.S. 1963. *Letters to Malcolm.* New York: Harcourt, Brace.
———. 1989. *The Screwtape Letters: Letters from a Senior to a
 Junior Devil.* Collins.
Lewis, Helen. 2018. Jordan Peterson: There Was Plenty of
 Motivation to Take Me Out. It Just Didn't Work.
 <https://youtu.be/yZYQpge1W5s>.
Lightman, Alan. 2007. *The Role of the Public Intellectual.*
 <https://web.mit.edu/comm-
 forum/legacy/papers/lightman.html>.
Lindberg, David C. 2007 [1992]. *The Beginnings of Western
 Science: The European Scientific Tradition in Philosophical,
 Religious, and Institutional Context, Prehistory to 1450.*
 Second edition. University of Chicago Press.
Lindsay, James. 2020. The Truth about Critical Methods.
 <www.youtube.com/watch?v=rSHL-
 rSMIrohttps://www.youtube.com/watch?v=rSHL-rSMIro>.
———. 2020. Woke Utopia: The End of the West and a New Cult.
 <www.youtube.com/watch?v=dE8p-mcFdNg>.
Lynskey, Dorian. 2018. How Dangerous Is Jordan B Peterson, the
 Rightwing Professor Who 'Hit a Hornet's Nest'? *The*

Guardian. <www.theguardian.com/science/2018/feb/07/how-dangerous-is-jordan-b-peterson-the-rightwing-professor-who-hit-a-hornets-nest>.

Lyotard, Jean-François. 1979. *La condition postmoderne: rapport sur le savoir*. Minuit.

Manning, E.C. 1967. *Political Realignment: A Challenge to Thoughtful Canadians*. McClelland and Stewart.

Marcuse, Herbert. 1971. *An Essay on Liberation*. Beacon Press.

———. 1983. *From Luther to Popper*. Schocken.

———. 1989. *Counterrevolution and Revolt*. Beacon Press.

———. 2007. *The Essential Marcuse: Selected Writings of Philosopher and Social Critic Herbert Marcuse*. Beacon Press.

Marks, Jonathan 2017. *We Don't Need No Stinking Thought Leaders.* <www.insidehighered.com/views/2017/07/11/why-academics-should-strive-be-public-intellectuals-not-thought-leaders-essay>.

Marx, Karl. 1970 [1876]. *Capital: A Critical Analysis of Capitalist Production*. Volume I. Progress.

———. 1972 [1894] *Capital: A Critique of Political Economy*. Volume III. Progress.

———. 1978. Contribution to the Critique of Hegel's Philosophy of Law. In Robert C. Tucker, ed., *The Marx-Engels Reader*. Norton.

———. 1979 [1852] The Eighteenth Brumaire of Louis Bonaparte. *In Karl Marx Frederick Engels Collected Works,* Volume 11. International.

———. 1989 [1873]. Critique of the Gotha Programme. In *Karl Marx Frederick Engels Collected Works,* Volume 24. International.

Marx, Karl, and Friedrich Engels. 1976 [1848]. Manifesto of the Communist Party. In *Karl Marx Frederick Engels Collected Works*, Volume 6. International.

McAfee, Noëlle. 2018. Feminist Philosophy. *Stanford Encyclopedia of Philosophy*. Stanford University.

McElvoy, Anne. 2018. Jordan Peterson on Gender, Patriarchy, and the Slide Towards Tyranny. Intelligence Squared. <https://youtu.be/7QRQjrsFnR4>.

McGregor, Steven. 2018. Jordan Peterson's Third Way. *The New Criterion* 37:1 (September).

McInnes, Neil. 1972. *The Western Marxists*. Library Press.

McManus, Matt. 2018. A Review of *Explaining Postmodernism* by Stephen Hicks. *Areo.* <https://areomagazine.com/2018/10/17/a-review-of-explaining-postmodernism-by-stephen-hicks>.

Michels, Robert. 1966 [1911]. *Political Parties: A Sociological Study of the Oligarchical Tendencies of Modern Democracy*. Collier Macmillan.

Mises, Ludwig Edler von. 1920. Die Wirtschaftsrechnung im sozialistischen Gemeinwesen. *Archiv für Sozialwissenschaften und Sozialpolitk* 47:1 (April).

———. 1935. Economic Calculation in the Socialist Commonwealth. Translation of Mises 1920. In Hayek 1935.

———. 1966 [1949]. *Human Action: A Treatise on Economics*. Regnery.

———. 2007 [1957]. *Theory and History: An Interpretation of Social and Economic Evolution*. Ludwig von Mises Institute.

———. 2015 [1944]. *Omnipotent Government: The Rise of the Total State and Total War*. Ludwig von Mises Institute.

Misra, Joya, Michelle J. Budig, and Stephanie Moller. 2007. Reconciliation Policies and the Effects of Motherhood on Employment, Earnings, and Poverty. *Journal of Comparative Policy Analysis: Research and Practice* 9:2. <https://doi.org/10.1080/13876980701311588>.

Narby, Jeremy. 1998. *The Cosmic Serpent: DNA and the Origins of Knowledge*. Tarcher/Putnam.

Neher, Andrew. 1996. Jung's Theory of Archetypes: A Critique. *Journal of Humanistic Psychology* 36:2.

Neumann, Erich. 1994. *The Fear of the Feminine: And Other Essays on Feminine Psychology*. Princeton University Press.

———. 2014. *The Origins and History of Consciousness*. Princeton University Press.

Nietzsche, Friedrich. 1989. *On the Genealogy of Morals*. Vintage.

———. 1990. *Twilight of the Idols / The Anti-Christ*. Penguin.

———. 2003. *Beyond Good and Evil: Prelude to a Philosophy of the Future*. Penguin.

O'Driscoll, Dennis. 2013. Missing God. *The Irish Times* (January 22nd). <www.irishtimes.com/opinion/his-grace-is-no-longer-called-for-before-meals-1.964594>.

Orwell, George. 1937. *The Road to Wigan Pier*. London: Gollancz.

———. 2021. *Nineteen Eighty-Four*. Penguin.

Paikin, Steve, Justin Trottier, Kathy Shaidle, Gretta Vosper, Jordan B. Peterson, and Rob Buckman. 2009. Advertising Atheism. *The Agenda with Steve Paikin*, TVO television program, aired February 19th.

Peterson, Jordan B. 1999. *Maps of Meaning: The Architecture of Belief*. New York: Routledge.

———. 2000. The Pragmatics of Meaning. *Semioticon* <https://semioticon.com/frontline/jordan_b.htm>.

———. 2013. Three Forms of Meaning and the Management of Complexity. In K.D. Markman, T. Proulx, and M.J. Lindberg, eds., *The Psychology of Meaning*. American Psychological Association. <https://doi.org/10.1037/14040-002>.

———. 2017a. Biblical Series I: Introduction to the Idea of God. Lecture given at Toronto's Isabel Bader Theatre, May 16th.

———. 2017b. Biblical Series II: Genesis 1: Chaos and Order. Lecture given at Toronto's Isabel Bader Theatre, May 23rd.

———. 2017c. The Great Sacrifice: Abraham and Isaac. <https://www.youtube.com/watch?v=yUP40gwht0&t=2772s>.

———. 2017d. Cain and Abel. <www.youtube.com/watch?v=vMJnpwwpytg>.

———. 2017e. The Psychological Significance of the Biblical Stories. jordanbpeterson.com. <www.jordanbpeterson.com/bible-series>.

———. 2017f. Identity Politics and the Marxist Lie of White Privilege. <www.youtube.com/watch?v=8u3aTURVEC8&t=1561s>.

———. 2017g. Existentialism: Nietzsche, Dostoevsky, and Kierkegaard. <https://m.youtube.com/watch?v=4qZ3EsrKPsc&t=4734s>.

———. 2018a. *12 Rules for Life: An Antidote to Chaos*. Random House Canada.

———. 2018b. Postmodernism: Definition and Critique (with a Few Comments on its Relationship with Marxism) <www.jordanbpeterson.com/philosophy/postmodernism-definition-and-critique-with-a-few-comments-on-its-relationship-with-marxism>.

———. 2018c. AA Harris/Weinstein/Peterson Discussion: Vancouver. <www.youtube.com/watch?v=d-Z9EZE8kpo&>.

———. 2018d. AC Harris/Murray/Peterson Discussion: Dublin. <www.youtube.com/watch?v=ZZI-FwSQRn8&>.

———. 2018e. AD Harris/Murray/Peterson Discussion: London. <www.youtube.com/watch?v=YfdaAGZvYsA&>.

———. 2018f. The Master and His Emissary: Conversation with Dr. Iain McGilchrist. February 17th <www.youtube.com/watch?v=xtf4FDlpPZ8>.

———. 2021a. *Beyond Order: 12 More Rules for Life*. Random House Canada.

———. 2021b. *Jordan Peterson Tells Tucker: Truth in Speech Is of Divine Significance*. <www.youtube.com/watch?v=rarY7pR03ns>.

Peterson, Jordan B., and Joseph L. Flanders. 2002. Complexity Management Theory: Motivation for Ideological Rigidity and Social Conflict. *Cortex* 38:3 <https://doi.org/10.1016/S0010-9452(08)70680-4>.

———. 2005. Play and the Regulation of Aggression. In R.E. Tremblay, W.W. Hartup, and J. Archer, eds., *Developmental Origins of Aggression*. New York: Guilford Press.

Peterson, Jordan B., and Jonathan Pageau. 2021. *Jordan B Peterson Podcast.*
<www.youtube.com/watch?v=2rAqVmZwqZM&>.
Peterson, Jordan B., and Stephen Fry. 2021. *Jordan B. Peterson Podcast.* <www.youtube.com/watch?v=fFFSKedy9f4&>.
Peterson, Jordan B., and Bari Weiss. 2021. *Jordan B Peterson Podcast.* <www.youtube.com/watch?v=tFTA9MJZ4KY&>.
Peterson, Jordan B., and Slavoj Žižek. 2019. Slavoj Žižek Debates Jordan Peterson.
<www.youtube.com/watch?v=qsHJ3LvUWTs&t=1790s>.
Peterson, Mikhaila, Mark Manson, and Jordan B. Peterson. 2021. Responsibility. *The Mikhaila Peterson Podcast* <www.youtube.com/watch?v=dGDF2tTq6xw&t=1315s>.
Philipp, Joshua. 2017. Jordan Peterson Exposes the Postmodernist Agenda. *Epoch Times.* <www.theepochtimes.com/jordan-peterson-explains-how-communism-came-under-the-guise-of-identity-politics_2259668.html>.
Pinker, Steven. 2002. *The Blank Slate: The Modern Denial of Human Nature.* Viking.
Plato. 1997. Apology. In *Plato: Complete Works.* Hackett.
Plato. 1997. *Complete Works.* Hackett.
Pluckrose, Helen, and James Lindsay. 2020. *Cynical Theories: How Activist Scholarship Made Everything about Race, Gender, and Identity—and Why This Harms Everybody.* Pitchstone.
Popper, Karl R. 1961. *The Poverty of Historicism.* Harper and Row.
———. 1978. Natural Selection and the Emergence of Mind. *Dialectica.*
———. 1979 [1972]. *Objective Knowledge: An Evolutionary Approach.* Routledge.
———. 1983. *Realism and the Aim of Science.* Rowman and Littlefield.
———. 2002 [1935]. *The Logic of Scientific Discovery.* Routledge.
———. 2020 [1945]. *The Open Society and Its Enemies.* Two volumes. Princeton University Press.
PragerU. 2019. Interview: Jordan Peterson and Dennis Prager at the 2019 PragerU summit.
<www.youtube.com/watch?v=L47oJxwp6yg>.
Principe, Lawrence M. 2011. Learning about Alchemy with Larry Principe.
<https://www.youtube.com/watch?v=MbCol-h_ql0>.
———. 2013. *The Secrets of Alchemy.* University of Chicago Press.
Proser, Jim. 2020. *Savage Messiah: How Dr. Jordan Peterson Is Saving Western Civilization.* St. Martin's Press.

Raatikainen, Panu. 2005. On the Philosophical Relevance of Gödel's Incompleteness Theorems. *Revue Internationale de Philosophie* 59.

———. 2014. Realism: Metaphysical, Semantic, and Scientific. In Kenneth R. Westphal, ed., *Realism, Science, and Pragmatism*. Routledge.

———. 2021a. Truth and Theories of Truth. In P. Stalmaszczyk, ed., *The Cambridge Handbook of the Philosophy of Language*. Cambridge University Press.

———. 2021b. Gödel's Incompleteness Theorems. In *The Stanford Encyclopedia of Philosophy*. <https://plato.stanford.edu/archives/spr2021/entries/goedel-incompleteness/>.

ReasonableFaithOrg. 2018. Is There Meaning to Life? William Lane Craig, Rebecca Goldstein, Jordan Peterson. <www.youtube.com/watch?v=xV4oIqnaxlg>.

Reiner, William G., and John P. Gearhart. 2004. Discordant Sexual Identity in Some Genetic Males with Cloacal Exstrophy Assigned to Female Sex at Birth. *New England Journal of Medicine* 350:4 <https://doi.org/10.1056/NEJMoa022236>.

Rizvi, Sajjad H. 2012. 'Only the Imam Knows Best': The Maktab-e Tafkīk's Attack on the Legitimacy of Philosophy in Iran. *Journal of the Royal Asiatic Society* 22:3–4.

Rogan, Joe. 2017. Jordan Peterson and Brett Weinstein. *Joe Rogan Experience*. <https://youtu.be/6G59zsjM2UI>.

Rohr, Richard. 2018. Parts of a Whole. Daily Meditations. August 16th. <https://cac.org/category/daily-meditations/2018/08/page/2>.

Rorty, Richard. 1999. *Truth and Progress*. Cambridge: Cambridge University Press.

———. 2007. *Philosophy as Cultural Politics*. Cambridge: Cambridge University Press.

RTÉ. 2015. Ireland's National Public Service Media. Stephen Fry on God. The Meaning of Life. RTÉ One. <www.youtube.com/watch?v=-suvkwNYSQo>.

Russell, Bertrand. 1910. William James's Conception of Truth. In Russell, *Philosophical Essays*. Cambridge University Press.

———. 1972 [1945]. *A History of Western Philosophy*. Simon and Schuster.

Russell, Daniel C. 2011. *Happiness for Humans*. Oxford University Press.

Russo, Lucio. 2004 [1996]. *The Forgotten Revolution: How Science Was Born in 300 BC and Why It Had to Be Reborn*. Springer.

Saad, Gad. 2020. *The Parasitic Mind: How Infectious Ideas Are Killing Common Sense*. Regnery.

———. 2021. My Chat with Jordan Peterson.
<www.youtube.com/watch?v=9KF2cwcADtU>.

Saslow, Laura R., Robb Willer, Matthew Feinberg, Paul K. Piff, Katharine Clark, Dacher Keltner, and Sarina R. Saturn. 2013. My Brother's Keeper? Compassion Predicts Generosity More Among Less Religious Individuals. *Social Psychological and Personality Science* 4:1.

Schopenhauer, Arthur. 1966. *The World as Will and Representation*. Dover.

Scott, Michael. 2015. Yuval Noah Harari on the Myths We Need to Survive. Royal Geographical Society: Intelligence Squared. <https://youtu.be/UTcgioiHM0U>.

Scruton, Roger. 2018. *Music as an Art*. Bloomsbury Continuum.

Shariff, Azim F., and Jordan B. Peterson. 2005. Anticipatory Consciousness, Libet's Veto and a Close-Enough Theory of Free Will. In R.D. Ellis and N. Newton, eds., *Consciousness and Emotion: Agency, Conscious Choice, and Selective Perception*. Benjamins. <https://doi.org/10.1075/ceb.1.12sha>.

Singer, Peter. 1999. *A Darwinian Left: Politics, Evolution, and Co-operation*. Yale University Press.

Skavlan, Fredrik. 2018. Full Interview with Jordan B. Peterson. Skavlan. SVT/TV2. <https://youtu.be/_iudkPi4_sY>.

Slattery, Dennis Patrick. 2021. *The Way of Myth: Stories' Subtle Wisdom*. Mandorla.

Sokal, Alan, and Jean Bricmont. 1999. *Intellectual Impostures: Post-Modern Philosophers' Abuse of Science*. Profile.

Solzhenitsyn, Aleksandr. 2018. *The Gulag Archipelago*. With a foreword by Jordan B. Peterson. Random House.

Sommers, Christina Hoff, and Danielle Crittenden. 2020. The Jordan Peterson You Don't Know. *The Femsplainers Podcast* <https://youtu.be/O4IBh-MgvFc>.

Sovereign Nations. 2018. Dr. Jordan B. Peterson: Identity Politics and The Marxist Lie of White Privilege. *Sovereign Nations*. <https://sovereignnations.com/2018/01/30/jordan-peterson-marxist-lie-white-privilege>.

Steele, David Ramsay. 1992. *From Marx to Mises: Post-Capitalist Society and the Challenge of Economic Calculation*. Open Court.

———. 2005. Life, Liberty, and the Treadmill. *Liberty* 19:2. Reprinted in Steele 2019.

———. 2017. *Orwell Your Orwell: A Worldview on the Slab*. St. Augustine's Press.

———. 2019. *The Mystery of Fascism: David Ramsay Steele's Greatest Hits*. St. Augustine's Press.

Stein, Murray. 1998. *Jung's Map of the Soul*. Open Court.

Stich, Stephen P. 1985. Could Man Be an Irrational Animal? Some Notes on the Epistemology of Rationality. *Synthese* 64.

Stoet, Gijsbert, and David C. Geary. 2018. The Gender-Equality Paradox in Science, Technology, Engineering, and Mathematics Education. *Psychological Science* 29:4. <https://doi.org/10.1177/0956797617741719>.

Su, Rong, James Rounds, and Patrick Ian Armstrong. 2009. Men and Things, Women and People: A Meta-Analysis of Sex Differences in Interests. Psychological Bulletin 135:6 <https://doi.org/10.1037/a0017364>.

Taylor, Charles. 1992. *The Ethics of Authenticity*. Harvard University Press.

Temple, Robert. 1986. *The Genius of China: 3,000 Years of Science, Discovery, and Invention*. Simon and Schuster.

Tertullian. Circa 190–220 C.E. Quid Ergo Athenis et Hierosolymis ["What Has Athens to Do with Jerusalem?"] *De praescriptione haereticorum [On the Prescription of Heretics]*, Chapter 7.

Tocqueville, Alexis de. 2012. How Religion in the United States Avails Itself of Democratic Tendencies. In *Democracy in America*. University of Chicago Press.

Tupy, Marian L. 2017. 100 Years of Communism: Death and Deprivation. *Cato Institute Commentary*. <www.cato.org/commentary/100-years-communism-death-deprivation>.

Turnbull, Colin M. 1988 [1962]. *The Forest People*. Simon and Schuster.

Viney, Liam, and Anna Grinberg. 2014. Collaboration in Duo Piano Performance: Piano Spheres. In Margaret Barrett, ed., *Collaborative Creative Thought and Practice in Music*. Ashgate.

Vinogradova, Olga S. 2001. Hippocampus as Comparator: Role of the Two Input and Two Output Systems of the Hippocampus in Selection and Registration of Information. *Hippocampus* 11:5) <https://doi.org/10.1002/hipo.1073>.

Voegelin, Eric. 1968. *Science, Politics, and Gnosticism: Two Essays*. Regnery.

Wainwright, Rupert, director. 1999. *Stigmata*. California: Metro-Goldwyn-Mayer.

Walker, Brian B. 2011. *The I Ching or Book of Changes*. Piatkus.

Webb, James. 1988 [1974]. *The Occult Underground*. Open Court.

Wicksteed, Philip Henry. 1884. *Das Kapital*: A Criticism. *To-Day* (October). Reprinted in Wicksteed 1933, Volume II.

———. 1933 [1910]. *The Common Sense of Political Economy*. Two volumes. Routledge.

Williams, Bernard. 2002. *Truth and Truthfulness: An Essay in Genealogy*. Princeton University Press.

Williamson, Oliver E. 1983 [1975]. *Markets and Hierarchies: Analysis and Antitrust Implications*. Collier-Macmillan.

———. 1985. *The Economic Institutions of Capitalism: Firms, Markets, Relational Contracting*. Collier-Macmillan.

Woien, Sandra. 2021. Review of *Myth, Meaning, and Antifragile Individualism: On the Ideas of Jordan Peterson. Reason Papers* 42:1.

Woodford, Stephen. 2020. Jesus Smuggling: Is Jordan Peterson Guilty? *Rationality Rules*, <www.youtube.com/watch?v=on0Lziov00Y>.

Woods, Andrew. 2019. Cultural Marxism and the Cathedral: Two Alt-Right Perspectives on Critical Theory. In Christine M. Battista and Melissa R. Sande, eds., *Critical Theory and the Humanities in the Age of the Alt-Right*. Springer.

Xenophon. 1990. *Conversations of Socrates*. Penguin.

About the Authors

LUIS FELIPE BARTOLO ALEGRE AND FABIOLA VALERIA CÁRDE-NAS MALDONADO each have a Bachelor's in Social Science with a mention in Anthropology and are currently candidates for a Master's in Philosophy with a mention in Epistemology at the National University of San Marcos in Peru. Luis and Fabiola are founding members of the Peruvian Society for Epistemology and Logic, and their common interests include philosophy of science, the differences between the sexes, music, and cats (but also dogs and other cute animals). Also of interest are people who get into trouble for saying what they think, regardless of whether they agree or disagree with them.
Emails: luis.bartolo@unmsm.edu.pe; fabiola.cardenas@unmsm.edu.pe

ALEX BROCKLEHURST is an independent researcher and writer living in the United Kingdom. His preferred self-description is 'The skin of an intellectual, stretched over the flesh of a poet.' After completing his MA in Theological Understanding of Contemporary Society at University of Hull, he followed up his interest in ancient wisdom traditions by producing, as Alexander De Witte, *The Wisdom Tree and the Dormouse* (2018). These days chess and nature constitute his greatest delights.
Email: alexbrocklehurst@googlemail.com

MARC CHAMPAGNE is Chair of the Department of Philosophy at Kwantlen Polytechnic University. He is the author of *Myth, Meaning, and Antifragile Individualism: On the Ideas of Jordan Peterson* (2020) and *Consciousness and the Philosophy of Signs*

(2018). He has a PhD in Philosophy from York University, a PhD in Semiotics from the University of Quebec in Montreal, and did his post-doctoral studies at the University of Helsinki. Email: marc.champagne@kpu.ca

DAVID COTTER is an academic and musician. His current doctoral research at the University of Cambridge concerns musical creativity, and the past, present, and future of the guitar as a collaborative instrument. David is active as an educator, guitarist, and journalist. He has performed, and presented his research, in Belgium, Canada, England, Hong Kong, Lithuania, Malaysia, the Netherlands, Northern Ireland, Norway, Portugal, Russia, Scotland, Serbia, Singapore, Turkey, and the USA. Email: davidcotter101@gmail.com

RON DART has taught in the Department of Political Science, Philosophy, and Religious Studies at University of the Fraser Valley (British Columbia) since 1990. Ron has published more than forty books, the most recent being *The Gospel According to Hermes: Intimations of Christianity in Greek Myth, Poetry and Philosophy* (2021), *Myth and Meaning in Jordan Peterson: A Christian Perspective* (2020) and *Hermann Hesse: Phoenix Arising* (2019). He is on the National Executive of The Thomas Merton Society of Canada and is the Canadian contact for the Evelyn Underhill Society and Bede Griffith Sangha.

DAVID DENNEN is an assistant professor at Chihlee University of Technology in Taiwan. He received his doctorate from the University of California, Davis. His research focuses on the history and ideas of American pragmatism and behaviorism. He has previously written about Jordan Peterson for *American Studies Journal* and is currently writing a book on the pragmatist historian and critic Morse Peckham. Email: daviddennen@gmail.com

MARK GARRON is from Toronto. He is currently a doctoral candidate in philosophy of science at The University of Kent, Canterbury. His research focuses on time and temporality, specifically on whether it is possible to reconcile the scientific image of time and the manifest image of time by examining social kinds such as money. He is interested in the way social kinds demonstrate how we act out our temporal beliefs. Email: mgarron01@gmail.com

DAVID GORDON is a Senior Fellow of the Ludwig von Mises Institute in Auburn, Alabama, and Editor of *The Journal of Libertarian Studies*. He is author of *The Philosophical Origins of Austrian Economics* (2020), *An Introduction to Economic Reasoning* (2016), *The Essential Rothbard* (2007), *Resurrecting Marx: The Analytical Marxists on Exploitation, Freedom, and Justice* (1991), and *Critics of Marx* (1986). A three-volume anthology of Dr. Gordon's articles and reviews was published in 2017 as *An Austro-Libertarian View*. He is editor of *Secession, State, and Liberty* (1998) and co-editor of H.B. Acton's *Morals of Markets and Other Essays* (1993). He has contributed to *Analysis*, *Mind*, *Ethics*, and many other journals. Email: dgordon@mises.com

STEPHEN R.C. HICKS is Professor of Philosophy at Rockford University and author of *Liberalism Pro and Con* (2020), *Nietzsche and the Nazis* (2010), *Explaining Postmodernism: Skepticism and Socialism from Rousseau to Foucault* (2004), and *The Art of Reasoning: Readings for Logical Analysis* (1994). He co-edited *Entrepreneurial Living* (2016). He has published in *Business Ethics Quarterly*, *Review of Metaphysics*, and *The Wall Street Journal*. Professor Hicks has been Visiting Professor of Business Ethics at Georgetown University, Visiting Fellow at Harris Manchester College (Oxford University), and Visiting Professor at the University of Kasimir the Great (Poland). Email: Stephen@StephenHicks.org

ESTHER O'REILLY is a widely published freelance writer and social critic. Her work has appeared in *The American Conservative*, *The Spectator*, *The Critic*, *Quillette*, and *Plough*, among other outlets. She contributed to Ron Dart's anthology, *Myth and Meaning in Jordan Peterson* (2020).

PANU RAATIKAINEN is a professor of philosophy at Tampere University, Finland. He received his doctorate in philosophy from the University of Helsinki in 1998. He has been a visiting research fellow at the University of London and the City University of New York. Dr. Raatikainen is the author of numerous articles and book chapters. He has worked on logic, the philosophy of science, the philosophy of language, the philosophy of mind, and the recent history of philosophy. Email: panu.raatikainen@tuni.fi

TRISTAN J. ROGERS is Visiting Assistant Professor in the Benson Center for the Study of Western Civilization at the University of Colorado, Boulder. He is the author of *The Authority of Virtue: Institutions and Character in the Good Society* (2020). His work also appears in *The Journal of Value Inquiry*, *Journal of Social Philosophy*, and *Journal of the American Philosophical Association*. He lives in Colorado with his wife and two daughters. Email: tristanjrogers1@gmail.com

MICHAEL SHELLENBERGER is a *Time* magazine Hero of the Environment, winner of the 2008 Green Book Award from the Stevens Institute of Technology's Center for Science Writings, and an expert reviewer for the Intergovernmental Panel on Climate Change. He has written on energy and the environment for the *New York Times*, *Wall Street Journal*, *Nature Energy*, and numerous other publications. He is the author of *Apocalypse Never: Why Environmental Alarmism Hurts Us All* (2020) and *San Fransicko: Why Progressives Ruin Cities* (2021). He is founder and president of Environmental Progress, an independent, non-partisan research organization. Email: michael@environmentalprogress.org

MADELEINE SHIELD is a doctoral candidate at the University of Queensland, Meanjin, Australia. Her research to date has focused on various topics in the fields of social and political philosophy and ethics. Through postgraduate study, she is currently developing a specialized interest in the philosophy of emotions, with a particular focus on the emotions of shame and love. She lives and works on the lands of the Jagera and Turrbal people.

CATHERINE "KATIE" SKURJA runs a private counseling practice in North Plains, Oregon. She has a Master's in Marriage and Family Therapy from George Fox University as well as a Master of Spiritual Direction from George Fox Evangelical Seminary. In 2004, Katie and Jim Skurja founded Imago Dei Ministries based in North Plains, Oregon, a ministry dedicated to helping people engage in a Christ-centered healing process that transforms their relationships with God, self, and others with the aim of uncovering a person's true identity—the image of God within each of us. Email: imago@idmin.org

DAVID RAMSAY STEELE is the author of *The Mystery of Fascism: David Ramsay Steele's Greatest Hits* (2019), *Orwell Your*

Orwell: A Worldview on the Slab (2017), *Atheism Explained: From Folly to Philosophy* (2008), and *From Marx to Mises: Post-Capitalist Society and the Challenge of Economic Calculation* (1992). He is co-author, with Michael R. Edelstein, of *Three Minute Therapy: Change Your Thinking, Change Your Life* (1997; second edition 2019) and *Therapy Breakthrough: Why Some Psychotherapies Work Better than Others* (2013). Dr. Steele received the 2017 Thomas S. Szasz Award for Outstanding Contributions to the Cause of Civil Liberties.
Email: dramsaysteele@gmail.com

YING TANG is an assistant professor in the School of Economics, Shenzhen University. She got her PhD in Xiamen University, China, based partly on research in the School of Development Economics, National Institute of Development Administration, Bangkok, Thailand. In 2019 she conducted visiting research at Loyola University, New Orleans, and has published articles in China's prestigious research journals, including *Finance and Trade Economics, World Economy Study,* and *Financial Theory and Practice.*
Email: tangy@szu.edu.cn

TEEMU TAURIAINEN is a full-time PhD student in philosophy who specializes in contemporary discussions on the nature of truth. Teemu has ten years of experience as both a student and researcher in studying diverse types of truth conceptions and definitions. He is currently studying the possibility of defining truth in a way that recognizes both mind-independent and - dependent ways of being true, so that the truth of distinct types of sentences, such as physical and ethical ones, can be accounted for by a single definition.
Email: teemu.tyo@gmail.com

SANDRA WOIEN is a Senior Lecturer in the School of Historical, Philosophical, and Religious Studies at Arizona State University. Her research interests primarily comprise theoretical concepts of well-being and their practical application on pivotal life decisions such as end-of-life issues. Her work has appeared in *Reason Papers, The Conversation, American Journal of Bioethics,* and *BMC Medical Ethics.*
Email: sandra.woien@asu.edu

Index